Narrative Reading, Narrative Preaching

Narrative Reading, Narrative Preaching

*Reuniting New Testament Interpretation
and Proclamation*

Edited by
Joel B. Green and Michael Pasquarello III

Baker Academic
A Division of Baker Book House Co
Grand Rapids, Michigan 49516

Published by Baker Academic
a division of Baker Book House Company
P.O. Box 6287, Grand Rapids, MI 49516-6287
www.bakeracademic.com

Printed in the United States of America

Unless otherwise noted, Scripture quotations are taken from the New Revised Standard Version of the Bible, copyright 1989 by the Division of Christian Education of the National Council of the Churches of Christ in the USA. Used by permission.

Scripture quotations marked RSV are taken from the Revised Standard Version of the Bible, copyright 1946, 1952, 1971 by the Division of Christian Education of the National Council of the Churches of Christ in the USA. Used by permission.

Library of Congress Cataloging-in-Publication Data
Narrative reading, narrative preaching : reuniting New Testament
    interpretation and proclamation / edited by Joel B. Green and
    Michael Pasquarello.
        p.   cm.
    Includes bibliographical references and index.
    ISBN 0-8010-2721-7 (pbk.)
    1. Bible N.T.—Homiletical use. 2. Narrative preaching. I. Green,
Joel B., 1956– II. Pasquarello, Michael.
BS 2392.N37 2003
251—dc22   2003058273

Contents

List of Contributors   7
Preface   9

1. The (Re-)Turn to Narrative   11
    Joel B. Green
2. Reading the Gospels and Acts as Narrative   37
    Joel B. Green
3. Whose Story?
    Preaching the Gospels and Acts   67
    Michael Pasquarello III
4. Reading the Letters as Narrative   81
    James W. Thompson
5. Preaching the Letters as Narrative   107
    William H. Willimon
6. Revelation and Resistance:
    Narrative and Worship in John's Apocalypse   117
    Stanley P. Saunders
7. Apocalypse Now:
    Preaching Revelation as Narrative   151
    Charles L. Campbell
8. Narrative Reading, Narrative Preaching:
    Inhabiting the Story   177
    Michael Pasquarello III

Index   195

Contributors

Charles L. Campbell (Ph.D., Duke University) is associate professor of homiletics at Columbia Theological Seminary. He has written *Preaching Jesus: New Directions for Homiletics in Hans Frei's Postliberal Theology; The Word before the Powers: An Ethic of Preaching;* and, with Stanley P. Saunders, *The Word on the Street: Performing the Scriptures in the Urban Context.*

Joel B. Green (Ph.D., University of Aberdeen) is dean of academic affairs and professor of New Testament interpretation at Asbury Theological Seminary. He is the coeditor of the Two Horizons Commentary on the New Testament, a general editor of the *Dictionary of Jesus and the Gospels,* and the editor or author of more than fifteen other books, including *Introducing the New Testament* and *The Gospel of Luke* (New International Commentary on the New Testament).

Michael Pasquarello III (Ph.D., University of North Carolina–Chapel Hill) has served as a United Methodist pastor for eighteen years and is now associate professor of practical theology at Asbury Theological Seminary. He has also served as a visiting instructor at Duke University Divinity School.

Stanley P. Saunders (Ph.D., Princeton Theological Seminary) is associate professor of New Testament at Columbia Theological Seminary. He has written *Philippians and Galatians* for the Interpretation Bible Studies series and, with Charles L. Campbell, *The Word on the Street: Performing the Scriptures in the Urban Context.*

James W. Thompson (Ph.D., Vanderbilt University) is professor of New Testament and associate dean of the Graduate School of Theology at Abilene Christian University. He is the author of several books, including *Preaching Like Paul: Homiletical Wisdom for Today; Our Life Together; The Mark of a Christian; Strategy for Survival;*

7

The Church in Exile; and *Equipped for Change,* as well as commentaries on 2 Corinthians and Hebrews. He is the translator of the *Exegetical Dictionary of the New Testament.*

William H. Willimon (S.T.D., Emory University) is professor of Christian ministry at Duke Divinity School and dean of Duke University Chapel. He is the author of more than fifty books and is on the editorial board of a number of professional journals, including *Quarterly Review* and *Christian Century.* He was recently selected by a Baylor University survey as one of the "Twelve Most Effective Preachers in the English-Speaking World."

Preface

This book offers no apologetic for narrative reading and preaching of the New Testament. Rather, given the widespread and diverse deployments of this term during the past several decades, we hope this volume will extend the conversation by offering examples of narrative performance in biblical interpretation and proclamation.

Our joining of that which has been divided in the modern period, exegesis and homiletics, is intentional. Our hope is that this emphasis on a return to narrative will promote renewed conversation between two mutually informing practices that draw their life from the use of Scripture for the pastoral ministry of the church. We encourage readers, therefore, to approach these chapters from a both/and perspective. It is our intent to encourage seminarians and pastors to see themselves as exegetically informed preachers and homiletically motivated exegetes whose lives are shaped, formed, and guided by indwelling the biblical narrative as it is remembered and enacted by the church.

Our purpose, then, is to provide examples of reading and preaching that will contribute to the overcoming of such established divisions as theory and practice, text and sermon, academy and church, past and present. We hope that this volume will play some small role in assisting seminarians and pastors in theological reflection on the enactment of Christian witness.

Chapter 1 contextualizes the significance of "narrative" and focuses attention on its prospects and fecundity for the church's faith and life as it is situated within the grand narrative of Scripture, extending from Genesis to Revelation. Such reading and preaching continue the biblical narrative into the faith and witness of the church through practices that are explicitly Christian, theologically ruled, and ecclesially located.

The following six chapters constitute the book's real substance, as they explore and demonstrate how such dispositions regarding the partnership of biblical studies and homiletics are expressed in practice. These chapters are divided according to the three primary modes of discourse found in the New Testament: narrative, letter, and apocalypse. Scholars are paired and assigned the task of "reading" and "preaching" specific pericopes from these respective genres. In each case, the exegete "reads," and from this material the homiletician then generates a sample sermon. This arrangement serves to illumine the judgments and practical wisdom embodied in narrative reading and preaching.

The final chapter provides a description of preaching as a Christian practice that is created and justified by the biblical narrative itself. Insisting that preachers are called and created within and for the biblical narrative, the author of which is the Triune God, it discusses the work of Irenaeus and Augustine to display particular habits of faithful pastoral practice.

We are grateful to our colleagues who have partnered with us in contributing to this volume. May its use contribute to an increase of readers and preachers of the New Testament whose practice promotes Christian witness to the glory of God.

Joel B. Green
Michael Pasquarello III
Asbury Theological Seminary

1

The (Re-)Turn to Narrative

Joel B. Green

What makes a sermon "biblical"? This is a notoriously difficult question, and we often find ourselves retreating to the equally evasive response, "I know it when I see it!" Even more burdensome would be attempts to garner some sort of community consensus around the attribute "biblical" when used of the preaching moment. Does it have to do with following the common lectionary? With a sermon that, in the order of worship, comes after the reading of a biblical text? With a sermon whose structure is drawn from the biblical text on which it is said to be based? With one that proceeds clause by clause, verse by verse through a text, preferably peppered with references to Hebrew or Greek? With a sermon that upholds a high christology? With one that embraces the authority of Scripture without wavering? All of these definitions, and many others besides, have been championed.

To the uninitiated, these questions must and often do seem ludicrous. Whatever else they might expect, folks presume of sermons that they will hear from God, and most presume that this has something to do, directly and significantly, with God's Word, the Old and New Testaments. Indeed, the earliest "commentaries" on biblical texts among Christians took the form of homilies, a reality that speaks of the assumption that, whatever else it is, preaching is biblical interpretation that shapes the performance of Scripture in the life of the church. The immediate relation of text and sermon, long an unquestioned presupposition, can nowadays hardly be assumed, and often is flatly countered by precept or practice, or both. How this came to be, why this is unacceptable, and how it might be remedied is the focus of this chapter, which urges that the way forward is marked by the recovery of "narrative" in biblical studies and homiletics.

The Inescapable Work of (Narrative) Interpretation

In an essay entitled "It's Not What You Know, but How You Use It," Yale University's Robert J. Sternberg observes, "Traditional education, and the intellectual and academic skills it provides, furnishes little protection against evil-doing or, for that matter, plain foolishness." He hypothesizes that intelligent, well-educated people are particularly susceptible to self-deception at four points. They falsely imagine that the world revolves, or should revolve, around them; that they know all there is to know, so have no need of the counsel of others; that, on the basis of their knowledge, they are all-powerful; and that they are shielded from the machinations and retributions of others, who will never be able to figure them out.[1] Sternberg goes on to insist that our educational goals need revamping, since, however necessary academic skills may be, they are insufficient if people are to use their intelligence to seek a common good. Persons immersed in Proverbs may hear echoes of a familiar text: "The beginning of wisdom is this: Get wisdom, and whatever else you get, get insight" (Prov. 4:7).

It is a peculiar characteristic of the West that we so easily succumb to the temptation to confuse the amassing of facts with learning. Surely, our prejudices tell us, the winner of the Bible trivia contest is self-evidently the most biblical person around, just as a genuinely biblical sermon is one that most obviously weaves explicit citations of biblical texts or that takes us, verse by verse, through a Pauline letter. We should not be surprised that we are so easily fooled, even if it is appropriate that we are stunned by the deleterious effects of our folly. How could we know so much and be so ill-formed? Is it not because there is no simple line of causation from the accumulation of data to the formation of a person?

We should not be surprised because we are, after all, a people weaned on the milk of a Christian faith defined by its rational essence, distilled into its dogmatic essentials. Talk about God among

1. Robert J. Sternberg, "It's Not What You Know, but How You Use It: Teaching for Wisdom," *The Chronicle of Higher Education*, 28 June 2002, B20.

the theologically trained tends effortlessly, naturally, toward propositional statements, toward t he unequivocal, toward the objective, toward a unified witness. As John Goldingay puts it, however, scriptural reflections on God's nature have an altogether different flavor. Rather than enumerating the immutable attributes of God, the Bible has it that

> God's person emerges in a series of contexts. God is a creator, then a destroyer. God relates to a family in the concerns of its ongoing family life, such as the finding of a home, the birth of children, and the arranging of marriages; God then relates to a nation in the different demands of its life, which includes God's becoming a warmaker. Entering into a formal relationship with this people takes God into becoming a lawmaker and into becoming a deity identified with a shrine (albeit a movable one) and not merely by a relationship with a people.

That is, "the 'revelation' of God's person is inextricably tied to the events in which God becomes different things, in a way that any person does; it is thus inextricably tied to narrative."[2] This understanding of God is "storied." Its content is embodied, lived. This is the theological inheritance bequeathed to us in Scripture.

It is the peculiar inheritance of our Enlightenment past that the faith is present to us in other terms—as principles and systems that tend by their concern with their formal elements to dismiss mystery and resolve tensions left standing by Scripture (and by life!). However, our theological track record increasingly demonstrates that the formal aspects of our faith cannot be segregated or distinguished from the narrative content and context of God's revelation of himself to us. On more pragmatic grounds, this criticism is animated by observations such as those made by Robert Sternberg, who recognizes that increased intelligence and enhanced knowledge skills have not been correlated with formation in wisdom. This critique is urged already by the shape of Scripture itself. Not only is the overwhelming portion of the Bible cast as narrative, but even lists of precepts ("You shall . . .") and the formulation of truth claims ("God is . . .") appear and are rooted in the ongoing narrative of Israel's life with God. To read Genesis-to-

2. John Goldingay, "Biblical Narrative and Systematic Theology," in *Between Two Horizons: Spanning New Testament Studies and Systematic Theology*, ed. Joel B. Green and Max Turner (Grand Rapids: Eerdmans, 2000), 123–42 (here, 131).

Revelation *as Scripture* requires something more than the turning
of pages and the movement from one book to the next, Leviticus
to Numbers, Malachi to Matthew. This "something more" demands of our learning to account for the grand narrative plotted
therein, from creation to new creation. Garrett Green has argued,
elegantly and powerfully, that the narrative content of Christian
faith is essential to the logic of belief in Jesus Christ as the revelation of God in human history, and that this "content" is an un-
avoidable feature of the grammar of Christian faith.[3]

For Garrett Green, the mischief that bedevils us can be traced
back to the impulses that led G. W. F. Hegel in 1795 to reject "the
positivity of the Christian religion." By "positivity," Hegel referred
to teachings of the faith that were grounded in arbitrary appeal to
the authority of specific historical figures and occurrences; this
would become the basis for a distinction between *natural religion*
(religion accessible through reason) and *positive religion* (based on
religious authority, whether human or divine, and especially on
Scripture and the classical creeds). For Green, this represents an
indefensible accommodation to the spirit of the age, the effect of
which has been to neuter Christian theology of its power to engage the human person. "For Christians," he writes, "the chief
point of imaginative contact with God is Holy Scripture, that epic
of positivity whose narratives, poetry, and proclamation are able,
by means of their metaphoric inspiration, to render God himself
to the faithful imagination."[4]

Lest it appear that the recognition of the intimacy of narrative
and faith is merely an attempt to turn back the clock, as it were,
so as to accord privilege to "positive" over "natural" religion, it is
worth reflecting on how the natural sciences have in recent years
urged the centrality of "narrative" to what it means to be fully
human. In the early modern period, Christian theology could be
profitably explored through God's "two books,"[5] the Bible and the
natural world. If emphasis on "natural religion" came not only to

3. Garrett Green, *Theology, Hermeneutics, and Imagination: The Crisis of Interpretation at the End of Modernity* (Cambridge: Cambridge University Press,
2000).

4. Ibid., 185–86.

5. See Kenneth J. Howell, *God's Two Books: Copernican Cosmology and Biblical Interpretation in Early Modern Science* (Notre Dame, Ind.: University of
Notre Dame Press, 2002).

eclipse revealed religion, but actually to rewrite its grammar, it is ironic that science itself has come full circle now to underscore the storied quality of distinctively human existence, together with the essentially hermeneutical nature of human life. That is, we have it from God's "two books" that the proclivities championed in the Enlightenment—proclivities that were themselves expressions of an earlier science and that came to enjoy powerful ecclesial sanction—have intruded on a basic human quality: our location in a social-moral order whose meaning is neither objective nor neutral, but that is generated within and through narrative.[6]

It is increasingly clear from neurobiology that meaning-making is central to our day-to-day experience, and that we will go to great lengths to construct stories that provide a context for understanding and interpreting what we perceive to be true. My brain imposes structure on the data it receives from its sensory organs, contributing to a baseline conclusion that my sense of reality is both embodied and interpreted within the framework of my formation as a social being. Apparently, one of the distinguishing characteristics of the human family, when compared with other inhabitants of the earth, is this capacity for and drive toward making sense, storied sense, of our experienced world. My "perception" of the world is based in a network of ever-forming assumptions about my environment, and in a series of well-tested assumptions, shared by others with whom I associate, about "the way the world works." Ambiguous data may present different hypotheses, but my mind disambiguates that data according to what I have learned to expect to see. Interestingly, when taught to interpret the same data in a different way, I can do so, flipping from one interpretation to another as my perception of the input shifts.

Similarly, we typically explain our behaviors not by physical and chemical chains of cause and effect, but through the historical narratives by which we collaborate to create a sense of ourselves as persons. Memory, then, is not passive retrieval of information, but active reconstruction, through which we seek coherence. Our

6. See, e.g., Paul R. Ehrlich, *Human Natures: Genes, Cultures, and the Human Prospect* (New York: Penguin, 2000), 108–38; Ian G. Barbour, *Nature, Human Nature, and God,* Theology and the Sciences (Minneapolis: Fortress, 2002), 71–100; James B. Ashbrook and Carol Rausch Albright, *The Humanizing Brain: Where Religion and Neuroscience Meet* (Cleveland: Pilgrim, 1997).

sense of who we are is profoundly nested in our long-term memories, which, then, are the prerequisite for self-representation. "She isn't herself," we say of persons suffering significant lapses of memory, whether caused by a traumatic brain injury, for example, or by the tragedy of Alzheimer's disease.

What is more, because we are intensely social beings, the stories we tell about ourselves, through which we construct our sense of self, are woven out of the threads and into the cloth of the stories present to us in our social world and communal traditions. We can press further, observing the consequences of our interactions, our environments, on who we are and who we are becoming. Our brains, from their neural pathways right down to their synapses, are continually in the process of being shaped, sculpted, by our interactions, by our experiences, by the narratives that surround us like the air we breathe. Consequently, embodied human life performs like a cultural, neuro-hermeneutic system, locating (and, thus, interpreting) current realities in relation to our grasp of the past and expectations of the future.[7] For Christian formation, this presses the question of the character of our ecclesial lives and the importance of our ongoing reflection on Scripture to an even higher level. Accordingly, it is crucial to inquire, What stories do we tell? How do we construe the past and future, by which we make sense of the present? What stories are shaping the worlds we indwell? What stories are we embodying? In what stories are we teaching others, especially our children, to build their playgrounds, their backyards, their homes? Clearly, "truth claims," however necessary, are insufficient for vital Christian faith, since these "beliefs," these "statements," are quite capable of functioning as raw data in a narrative whose beginning, middle, and end are antithetical to the biblical story.

Of the implications that could be drawn from these ruminations, two are of particular importance for our purposes here. First, there is no escaping either the *fact* (or necessity) of interpretation, nor the *narrativity* involved in Scripture. This is not foremost a statement about method in either exegesis or homiletical theory, but rather an essential aspect of the nature of the world

7. See Daniel J. Siegel, *The Developing Mind: How Relationships and the Brain Interact to Shape Who We Are* (New York: Guilford, 1999); Stephen P. Reyna, *Connections: Brain, Mind, and Culture in a Social Anthropology* (London: Routledge, 2002).

and of human identity and comportment in it. "Reality" does not come to us "clean," but always through the filters of our perception. The world is always for us already an interpreted world. The critical question then becomes, Perceived how? Or, better, Within what narrative account will we interpret?

We can say more about this first point in relation to the second, which centers on our capacity to adopt fresh points of view from which to apprehend the world around us. Turning to philosophical hermeneutics since Gadamer,[8] we have realized that, in the never-ending work of interpretation, we cannot jump out of our skins. We bring with us always and everywhere our selves—that is, our presuppositions and histories, our stories. And these presuppositions enable our understanding, as well as disable it. We cannot escape our histories because it is in them that our identity is generated. The miracle is that the horizons of our presuppositions can be enlarged and transformed. Here is the crucial point: *The biblical narrative is present as an alternative framework within which to construe our lives, and so challenges those who would be Christian by calling for a creative transformation of the stories by which we make sense of our lives and of the world.*[9] If we all live story-formed lives, then we are confronted with the question, What stories will shape us? For Christians, the answer is nonnegotiable: *Our task is to make our lodging the Genesis-to-Revelation narrative so that our modes of interpretation are conformed to the biblical narrative, so that this story decisively shapes our lives.*

The Partings of the Ways

Our introductory claim that "narrative" needs recovery may strike some as odd. After all, "narrative" has been standard diet in homiletical circles for some time. It is at this juncture that we encounter a semantic problem of great significance. Eugene Lowry offers no less than five strategies for "narrative preaching," for example, and his is not the only relevant analysis.[10] Three observa-

8. Hans-Georg Gadamer, *Truth and Method,* 2d ed. (New York: Crossroad, 1990).

9. Dan R. Stiver, *Theology after Ricoeur: New Directions in Hermeneutical Theology* (Louisville: Westminster John Knox, 2001), 52–53 (see pp. 33–55); see also Nicholas Wolterstorff, "Living within a Text," in *Faith and Narrative,* ed. Keith E. Yandell (Oxford: Oxford University Press, 2001), 202–13.

10. Eugene Lowry, *How to Preach a Parable: Designs for Narrative Sermons* (Nashville: Abingdon, 1989); idem, *The Homiletical Plot: The Sermon as Narra-*

tions will help to point the way forward. First, by "narrative," we do not refer primarily, as in recent homiletical theory, to a particular genre of sermon, to the sermon as a particular art form, or to a certain "style" of preaching. To use the categories borrowed by Lowry from Aristotle, we are not concerned with a sermon that moves from a problem to its resolution to the consequences of that resolution. We will be concerned in part with narrative as a genre in which much of the Bible is cast, but more so with narrative as a theological category, as a way of grasping and making sense of the whole of history as this is interpretively presented in Christian Scripture. Second, the shift in homiletical theory from a pivotal concern with the performance of Scripture to a focus on sylistics and communication theory is understandable as a symptom of a more general malaise in theological studies, broadly conceived. Although not wishing to marginalize the importance of rhetoric in its classical sense of persuasive speech, I nevertheless want to observe that concern with style or form has generally come at the expense of content. And this is because, third, biblical studies and preaching have grown distant from one another as a result of the shift from an ecclesial context to a scientific framework within which to engage the biblical materials. This is due in large part to the interests of the modern period, which pressed the study of the Bible more and more in the direction of historical inquiry, opening wider and wider the chasm between "the world of the Bible" and "the world of the congregation."

It is nonetheless worth asking, as I will do momentarily, whether homiletics might not have influenced, and might not still influence, biblical studies more in the direction of its theological home in the church and in proclamation. Need homiletical theory follow in the footsteps of biblical studies, as it often has? Can it not issue a prophetic call for a needed transformation in the way the Bible is engaged as Scripture for the church?

In the seminary curriculum, or at least in the experience of many seminarians, the problem is typically felt at a deeply existential level when moving from courses in biblical studies to one's

---

tive Art Form (Atlanta: John Knox, 1980); idem, "Narrative Preaching," in *Concise Encyclopedia of Preaching,* ed. William H. Willimon and Richard Lischer (Louisville: Westminster John Knox, 1995), 342–44. See the convenient survey in Richard L. Eslinger, *Narrative Imagination: Preaching the Worlds That Shape Us* (Minneapolis: Fortress, 1995).

first course in preaching. How does what I learned in the one relate to the other? Faced with the task of preparing a sermon on a passage from Ezekiel or Galatians, the preacher faithfully walks through the "-isms" she has learned: text criticism, literary criticism, genre criticism, historical criticism, and the rest. Then she consults the major commentaries on the text. In hand are philological, structural, and historical data; exegetical issues are tackled; and the life-world of the biblical author has been thoroughly explored. What now? Without wishing to pull the rug from under a discipline of preaching informed by serious study, the reality remains that the text as imagined by the scholar is often separated by a great chasm from the world faced by the preacher. How does our preacher stand before her congregation and make use of this text, and of the pages of notes gathered from study focused on the meaning of this text back there and then, to speak of God here and now?[11] How did we come to this parting of the ways, between the way of scholarly study of the biblical materials and the way of proclamation of the Word of God?

In an important sense, the pivotal question here is one of "meaning," and especially of its *location:* What is the "address" of the text? Where can one locate what it "means"? On the broad canvas where generalizations can assist us, we can exegete the problem in terms of the relationship between biblical text and historical context. *Pre-modern perspectives* on text and history worked with the assumption that text and history were coterminous or at least that the history behind the text was not the sole or determinative factor in meaning-making. What is more, insofar as the text was not regarded as tightly bound to its history, in this perspective the voice of the text has an immediacy about it. Paul and Hosea are speaking to us. Theology and preaching do not constitute tasks separate from exegesis.[12]

The *modern perspective,* which has come to reign over the past two centuries, and is regnant still in many circles, posits a purposeful segregation of "history" and "text"—or, to put it in a slightly different way, of "history" and "textual interpretation."

11. See Richard Bauckham, "The Task of a Confessing Biblical Scholarship," *Catalyst* 23, no. 3 (1997): 1–3.
12. See Henri de Lubac, *Medieval Exegesis,* vol. 1: *The Four Senses of Scripture,* Ressourcement: Retrieval and Renewal in Catholic Thought (Grand Rapids: Eerdmans, 1998), esp. chap. 2.

Here we learn that the history to which the biblical text gives witness and the biblical text that provides such a witness are not coterminous. Since interpretive privilege is accorded to "history" in this perspective, the biblical text is to be regarded with critical suspicion, and historical inquiry is the order of the day. Biblical interpretation thus becomes a discipline of "validation" (when the biblical text is judged to represent historical events with accuracy) or of "reconstruction" (when it is not). Moreover, its history and our own are not two of a kind, but are regarded as constitutive of two worlds. Thus, if the message of that text, grasped in relation to its history, is to have significance for us, the worlds must be bridged somehow. The homiletical task thus requires of the preacher that he enter that world like a pioneer of old, subdue it, and bring back that meaning, now transformed, domesticated for his world and the world of his congregation.

Biblical interpretation according to this modern paradigm is the presumed and unquestioned norm for many preachers today, and has been deeply formative of homiletical theory. Such interpretation can be characterized as:

- *determined*—interpretation is the task of discovering the meaning of a text placed there, as it were, by the author of the text, whose intent determines what and how a text can mean;
- *atomistic*—texts are interpreted in relative isolation from each other, so that biblical books and even pericopes can be studied one at a time, and in isolation from larger canonical and theological traditions;
- *scientific*—interpreters ought to come to texts without their own presumptions or commitments, neutrally; and
- *specialized*—the work of exegesis is to be done according to accredited, learned procedures, and thus lies above all in the hands of scholars who alone possess the requisite background and skills.

The craft of shaping sermons in the image of this sort of biblical interpretation has not been an easy one. Concern with the one, true meaning of a text and pressing, negative judgments about the historical veracity of biblical narratives have left numerous preachers in the paralysis of doubt about what "truth" can be proclaimed from the pulpit. A commitment to scientific neutrality voids the biblical text of its own theological force and segregates the biblical text from the classical Christian tradition. In fact, if one takes with seriousness the call to scientific neutrality, the need for theology and creed is radically undercut in favor of a commitment to "what the Bible says." But "what the Bible says," in this paradigm, is not available to the person in the pew, nor really to the preacher in the pulpit, all of whom are dependent on those who have devoted their lives to biblical scholarship. But, even then, it has not been easy to scale the mountain of historical appraisal and linguistic opinion only to find on the other side a molehill of theological insight or ecclesial reflection.

More recently, some have migrated to forms of study for which meaning is not tied to "facts" (which are presumed to be in short supply), but to "perspectives." Accordingly, texts are sundered from the sociohistorical contexts within which they were generated, from those texts alongside which they reside within the canon of Scripture, from the traditions of interpretation that have grown up around them over these millennia, and from other interpretive constraints that might be suggested by the texts themselves. Some refer to this form of study as *late-modern*, since it continues the *modern* agenda of sundering the present from the past, while others label it *postmodern*.[13]

In any case, under the old historicism—characteristic of biblical studies over the last two centuries—textual meaning could be tied with certainty to historical reconstruction, even if the reconstruction itself was uncertain. In the historicism of the late-modern or postmodern era, this confidence is rejected in favor of endless meanings. The first saw a commitment to forms of biblical interpretation that kept at arm's length the communicative claims of scriptural texts, working with the presumption that those claims are of antiquarian interest, but neither (necessarily) compelling nor relevant. The second might also be troublesome to Christian preaching, since in this instance it could not be presumed that the interpretive enterprise could be tied to a theological tradition, or even to the canon of Scripture, so that it be-

13. See Craig Bartholomew, "Post/Late? Modernity as the Context for Christian Scholarship Today," *Themelios* 22, no. 2 (1997): 25–38.

comes difficult (impossible?) to measure a "right" reading from a "wrong" one, or a "good" reading from a "bad" one.

Again painting with broad strokes, the response to this state of affairs in the latter half of the twentieth century among persons concerned with the religious meaning of these biblical texts has taken two paths. Some have rejected the various permutations of historical criticism that have waxed and waned in nineteenth- and twentieth-century biblical studies. Others have embraced forms of historical inquiry but remained critical of the biases of historical criticism against the supernatural; they have also insisted that the theological and practical relevance of Scripture can somehow be generated on the basis of historical study.[14] Hence, the homiletical crisis of the relevance of biblical texts is posited as primarily a historical (and not theological) problem: How do we derive "what it means" from "what it meant"? The problem for the preacher is this negotiation of two historically defined worlds—captured well in the title of John Stott's classic text on preaching, *Between Two Worlds*.[15]

There have been valiant attempts to bridge the chasm between text and sermon, but these have largely been hobbled by the assumption that the homiletical task should conform itself to the presumptions and practices of biblical studies. These attempts have been unaware that the very act and challenge of preaching not only presumed but, indeed, demanded theological commitments that were undermined, neutered, or outright rejected by the historical-critical paradigm.

A Hermeneutics of Relationship

As a New Testament scholar, I am unlikely to present as a resolution to these concerns a dismissal of serious study of Scripture! I do want to sketch a way forward, however, one that moves beyond the "what it meant"/"what it means" impasse, and that concerns itself with the location of the Bible within the people of God. If the modernist perspective was a scientific hermeneutic of

14. See the early, programmatic statement in George Eldon Ladd, *The New Testament and Criticism* (Grand Rapids: Eerdmans, 1967); and its later companion, Carl E. Armerding, *The Old Testament and Criticism* (Grand Rapids: Eerdmans, 1983).

15. John R. W. Stott, *Between Two Worlds: The Challenge of Preaching Today* (Grand Rapids: Eerdmans, 1982).

neutrality, the effect of which was to objectify the biblical text in order to hold it at arm's length for examination, the alternative I want to suggest is a hermeneutics of relationship or connection, oriented in relation to a theological affirmation concerning the nature of the Bible as Scripture.

I take the claim, the Bible as Scripture, to refer to a theological stance whereby we recognize that *we* are the people of God to whom these texts are addressed. This leads us to the realization that the fundamental transformation that must take place is not the transformation of an ancient message into a contemporary meaning but rather the transformation of our lives by means of God's Word.[16] This means that reading the Bible as Scripture has less to do with what tools we bring to the task, however important these may be, and more to do with our own dispositions as we come to our engagement with Scripture. Scripture does not present us with texts to be mastered but with a Word, God's Word, intent on mastering us, on shaping our lives. Accordingly, our reading must be ecclesially located, theologically fashioned, and critically engaged.

1. *An ecclesially located reading of Scripture.* For those genuinely interested in interpreting the Bible as Scripture, the single most important practice to cultivate is involvement in reading the Bible with others who take its message seriously and who meet regularly to discern its meaning for faith and life. The best interpreters of Scripture are those actively engaged in communities of biblical interpretation. If such a group is multigenerational and multicultural, this is even better. Among the reasons for this, let me mention two. First, the books of the Bible have their genesis and formation within the community of God's people. They speak most clearly and effectively from within and to communities of believers. No interpretive tool, no advanced training can substitute for active participation in a community of Bible readers.

16. I have developed this further in Joel B. Green, "Scripture in the Church: Reconstructing the Authority of Scripture for Christian Formation and Mission," in *The Future of Methodism: Trajectories into the Third Millennium,* ed. Paul Wesley Chilcote (Nashville: Abingdon, 2002), 38–51; idem, "Scripture and Theology: Failed Experiments, Fresh Perspectives," *Interpretation* 56 (2002): 5–20; idem, "Modernity, History, and the Theological Interpretation of the Bible," *Scottish Journal of Theology* 54 (2001): 308–29; idem, "Scripture and Theology: Uniting the Two So Long Divided," in Green and Turner, *Between Two Horizons,* 23–43.

A second reason for reading the Bible with others is our proclivity toward self-deception. One of the most tragic effects of Bible reading can be that we read our lives into it in such a way that we find in its pages divine license for those of our attitudes and practices that are more base than biblical. Our experience is too often that we apply challenging messages to the lives of others, while assuming too quickly that the Bible supports our ways of thinking and acting. We read Scripture in order to be addressed by God and formed by God's Word. Other people set on the same purpose can take us to task so that we might hear more faithfully God's voice at those moments when we are tempted to substitute our word for God's.

2. *A theologically formed reading of Scripture.* As has been widely reported, the fundamental failure of scientific interpretation is the reality that no neutral ledge exists on which we might stand to engage seriously and dispassionately the biblical materials. We inevitably bring with us to the task of reading Scripture our own interests and commitments. Although a variety of interests are possible and perhaps defensible, a reading of the Bible as Christian Scripture can never be satisfied with anything less than interpretive dispositions and practices oriented toward shaping and nurturing the faith and life of God's people.

The implications of this are several, two of which require brief mention. First, it is essential that Christian study of the Old Testament interpret these writings specifically as Christian Scripture and that the New Testament be firmly situated within the grand narrative of God's purpose that is incomprehensible apart from the Old Testament. If the "main character" of the Bible is God, then it is God himself, and God's purpose, that unifies the Old and New, and we dare not imagine that we have understood or might begin to understand the significance of Jesus Christ if we have not acquainted ourselves with the God whom he addressed as "Father." Second, it is essential that we recover the mutual relationship between Scripture and the faith confessed by the church from the beginning. Sharply put, Christian appropriation of Scripture requires attention to Christian doctrine. Hence, our public concerns with biblical illiteracy in the church, and with the recovery of "biblical preaching," must be tethered to a concomitant alarm over the theological amnesia on display in pew and pulpit. Speaking of the heretics of his day, Irenaeus of Lyons notes how, when "the parables of the Lord, the sayings of the prophets, and the words of the apostles" are violently sundered from their "connections," the "oracles of God" are "adapted to useless fictions."[17] With the language of "connections," Irenaeus was drawing attention to already-developing faith statements, "rules of truth," which set parameters around the range of readings of biblical texts that might justifiably be labeled "Christian." As Luke reports of the devil, it is always possible to draw on an authoritative source, the Bible, but to do so in evil ways (Luke 4:1–13). Doctrine serves as our "rule of faith," guiding our reading of Scripture in authentically Christian ways.

3. *A critically engaged reading of Scripture.* By "critical," I refer to the need for discernment with reference to the varieties of possible readings of biblical texts, but not to the commitment to neutral scholarship characteristic of biblical studies influenced by the scientific method. Nor am I referring to a particular mode of study—even though "critical study of the Bible" for two centuries has been virtually equated with the paradigm of historical criticism. I am concerned, rather, with the question of validity in interpretation and how this might be measured.

What might this approach look like? Again, eschewing any need to construct a "technology" of biblical engagement, it is nonetheless possible to outline a series of baseline commitments. Thus, a critically engaged reading of Scripture would:

- account for the text in its final form;
- account for the text as a whole;
- welcome the "other-ness" of the biblical text and its sociocultural world as a means of expanding our own imaginative horizons (rather than assuming that all people everywhere and in all times construed their life-worlds as we do) and, possibly, decrying the attitudes and practices we have long taken for granted;
- account for the canonical address of the text, particularly with reference to the location of particular biblical witnesses within an all-encompassing story; and
- account for the witness of Scripture as seen in its effects within and among the community of God's people, not

17. Irenaeus *Against Heresies* 1.8.1.

least in the distillation of Scripture's message in the
great creeds of the church, which confess and proclaim
and worship the Triune God.

When we engage with Scripture in this way, we embody one of
Scripture's most consistently developed commitments or dispositions: hospitality, an elemental openness to the Other. It is not
without significance that it is precisely here that critical thinking
and formative spirituality have one of their most obvious points of
convergence—namely, in their joint concern to commitments
and perspective outside of one's own horizons. Critical inquiry is
not characterized by neutrality (as modernism has taught us), but
by an essential commitment to intellectual community and,
through commitments to hearing and respecting voices other
than our own, by a baseline affirmation of the essential capacity
of self-overcoming.[18] Spirituality, particularly "biblical spirituality,"
is that transformative process of personal and communal engagement with Scripture that allows the text to speak in its own voice,
to be encouraged and interrogated by this "other" voice, which
presses and empowers us toward ever greater fidelity to the vocation of Christlikeness.[19] Reading in this way locates our work with
the text among the community of the faithful—including that
crowd of witnesses to whom we have access only through the writings and practices bequeathed to us through centuries of biblical
interpretation—in ways that prod us to see what we otherwise
would not want, or even be able, to see.

A "critically engaged" reading of Scripture would take as a
point of departure the character of the text as *subject,* then, with
its own interests and voice, capable of casting its own vision of the
world. In this accounting, "meaning" would be located at the intersection of readerly interests (remembering that those interests
are ecclesially located and theologically formed) and textual interests. Such interpretation would benefit from all of the intercul-
tural sensibilities we could cultivate, countering our ego- and eth-

18. See Thomas L. Haskell, "Objectivity Is Not Neutrality: Rhetoric versus
Practice in Peter Nivock's *That Noble Dream,*" in *Objectivity Is Not Neutrality: Ex-
planatory Schemes in History* (Baltimore: Johns Hopkins University Press,
1998), 145–73.

19. See Sandra M. Schneiders, "Biblical Spirituality," *Interpretation* 56 (2002):
133–42.

nocentricities, our predispositions to domesticate the witness of Scripture for comfortable living in the places we make our homes. In this hermeneutic, historical study is valued *not* for its ability to locate the one, true meaning of the text, the one intended by the author, but especially for its capacity to expand the cultural and social-psychological horizons that have hardened among the taken-for-granted categories of the interpreter. Precisely in the juxtaposition of worlds, that of the text and our own, lies the potential for our values, commitments, and behaviors to be unmasked for what they are, *ours* (and not of necessity written by the divine hand into the fabric of the universe).

Moreover, such interpretation would recognize (and, indeed, welcome) the polysemy of this text—that is, the multiple possibilities for construing the sense of this text. Polysemy is not the consequence of an instability inherent in the text itself, nor of textual shape-shifting to meet whatever needs are brought to it. Rather, polysemy is the expected outcome where meaning is formed in the encounter of text and audience, provided the audience comes to the text in multiple iterations. Possible meanings are not infinite, of course, since they are "ruled" by grammar and syntax; by considerations of genre, culture, and literary art; and by the classical theological tradition of canon and creed whose form is demonstrated in baptism and Eucharist, and in the liturgical and other communal practices constitutive of the people of God over time.[20] In this interpretive space, at the intersection of reader and text, lies the potential for meaning as the text points us beyond ourselves and presses us to see what we could not otherwise imagine.

Reading Scripture in this key would call for dispositions of humility and expectation before the text. It would also invite an important shift of attention and energies, encouraging (again) theological conversation around biblical texts and pressing for authentic wrestling with such questions as: To what life-world is this text pointing? With what reality does it confront us? And, how might we embody this text, this Word? This having been said, it is

20. For the limits of interpretation more broadly, see Umberto Eco, *The Limits of Interpretation*, Advances in Semiotics (Bloomington: Indiana University Press, 1990). On the articulation of the concept of "canon" in terms of Eucharist, baptism, liturgy, and so on, see William J. Abraham, *Canon and Criterion in Christian Theology: From the Fathers to Feminism* (Oxford: Clarendon, 1998).

important to grasp how distant we are from such questions in our learned practices of biblical interpretation. These questions neither surface nor are they addressed in biblical interpretation as this might be characterized in the age of modernism. The way forward is marked, in part, by the recovery of "narrative."

Narrative as Rapprochement

To speak of "the narrative of Scripture" is to make a theological claim that takes us beyond the warrants of any one of the books comprising the Bible, or even what might be strictly authorized by one or another of the Bible's Testaments. It is to insist that the whole of the Bible is, in Christian engagement, more than the sum of the parts, and that we can and should account for a theological presumption behind and woven into this collection of books. The particular contribution of the concept of "narrative" is the attribution to these books of a single, coordinating and unifying, plot. These words, these books, these collections of books, read as a whole, are said to generate a coherence that might otherwise be missing, or hidden, apart from the whole.

For narrative, plot holds together and integrates into a single and complete whole what would otherwise be multiple and scattered. The result in this case is a theological schema that allows us to articulate intelligibly the significance of the whole, and that opens the door to the adventure of living in this narrative—or, perhaps better, to living out (and out of) the narrative by conforming our lives to its sense of value and time. In this final section, I explore the promise of this claim regarding the narrative of Scripture.

Early study of the character of "story" (as opposed to the more usual reading of "stories") made an important, programmatic distinction between "story" and "discourse," or "story" and "narrative." Story refers to the content, the "what" or "elements" of discourse, and has to do with the identification of a series of events and characters, the "raw materials," judged to be important. Discourse refers to the "how," or the way a medium is tasked with presenting the "what."[21] At the level of the discourse (or performance, or narrative), the elements of story are construed in relation

21. E.g., Seymour Chatman, *Story and Discourse: Narrative Structure in Fiction and Film* (Ithaca, N.Y.: Cornell University Press, 1978).

to each other, deploying any of a number of literary devices (repetition, manipulation of order, relative emphasis on character, and point of view, to mention a few). This means that a single set of story elements might be presented in diverse ways to produce differences of discourse. Consider the four Gospels of our New Testament, for example, which are obviously relating the same basic "story," and following the same skeletal time frame, but which do so in ways that produce in each case a different "discourse," a distinct "narrative."

How is all of this relevant to our interest in the promise of narrative? Let me briefly suggest five ways.

1. *Narrative as discourse.* At the most basic level, this perspective allows us to see how the various elements of the biblical story can be regarded as constitutive of a single narrative. Although different authors of the different biblical books speak and contribute to our grasp of the whole, no one of them controls the whole, since this whole is formed within the horizons of the biblical canon that was later to emerge. The canon itself, then, represents a particular "performance" of the elements of story, with the result that the canon functions as an integrating center for how the parts are to be read. Latent in these particulars is a larger plot, an encompassing narrative that creates a world of its own. This is the world of God's creation, the world whose redemption and future is conceived already in its beginning, and of the God whose creative purpose provides the frame for making sense of the totality of what is (or is perceived to be): " 'I am the Alpha and the Omega,' says the Lord God, who is and who was and who is to come, the Almighty" (Rev. 1:8).

From this perspective, someone struggling with the violence of the Old Testament's episodes of conquest or of the New Testament's account of the deaths of Ananias and Sapphira would be constrained from imagining that these accounts were determinative per se of our understanding of community life and relations, or of the eternal plan of God; theologically, these narrated events would find their meaning within the whole of the biblical narrative.

2. *Narrative elasticity.* One of the hallmarks of narrative as a particular mode of discourse is its hospitality to other forms of communication. One finds in the Acts of the Apostles, for example, sermons, letters, defense speeches, travelogues, and more. Pressing the analogy, it is unremarkable that other forms of discourse

would contribute to this narrative, the narrative of Scripture. Legal material, etiology, prophetic oracles, proverbs, wisdom literature, narrative accounts, epistles, apocalyptic literature—such discourse forms are found in Scripture, but this is only to be expected, given the nature of narrative.

This means that talk of "narrative" needs always to keep clear the distinction between different uses of the term. Narrative$_1$, let us say, refers to a particular form of writing, notoriously difficult to define, but usually regarded as the recounting of one or more real or fictitious events understood to share a causal relationship, in any of an array of forms: history writing, epics, novels, ballads, and so on.[22] Much of the Bible (1 Kings, Job, and the Gospel of John, for example) comes to us in this form, but not all.

Narrative$_2$, on the other hand, constitutes a theological claim about the coherence of the Genesis-to-Revelation story. It is the attribution to the sum of the parts of the Bible of a purposefulness that binds sometimes disparate voices into a single chorus. Episodes that seem less central to the whole of Scripture, that turn into strange paths or corridors not easily integrated into the whole, are nonetheless set within or framed by the whole, which then serves as a necessary theological context for interpretation. Using Aristotle's commentary on "narrative," both narrative$_1$ and narrative$_2$ would be characterized by having a "beginning," "middle," and "end," though in the case of narrative$_2$ these aspects would be discerned from the shape of the biblical canon read in its singularity. From this perspective, the plot of the biblical narrative would find its nonnegotiable points of reference in the purpose and action of God in creation (beginning), redemption (middle), and consummation (end). What is more, a commitment to the whole of Scripture would make necessary that we comprehend this "middle" in two primary movements: the liberating work of God in Exodus and the saving work of God in the advent of Jesus Christ (New Exodus). As a theological strategy for interpretation, this requires that these points of reference never escape our peripheral vision when reading any biblical text, even a section or book in which none of these explicitly surfaced.

To reiterate: our commitment to "narrative reading, narrative preaching" is not measured in reference to the benefits of one

22. See Gerald Prince, *A Dictionary of Narratology* (Lincoln: University of Nebraska Press, 1987), 58–60.

style of sermon craft over another, nor concerned especially with a particular genre or mode of discourse among the biblical texts. Rather, "narrative" refers first and foremost to the theological claim of the overall coherence and theological unity of the biblical materials taken as a whole, oriented narratologically in relation to creation, redemption, and consummation. Such a reading is equally apropos to a text like Obadiah or 2 Peter as it is to 1 Chronicles or the Gospel of Mark.

3. *The single aim of narrative.* Concern with narrative reading centers attention intensely on the primary "aim" being served (or not) within a narrative. Narratives classically follow predictable cycles: possibility (or probability) leads to actuality (or realization), which leads to results (or denouement); and these aspects of the narrative process concern the basic aim around which the narrative is centered. We need to know, What is this aim? Who determines this aim? Moreover, narrative drama or interest is generated through conflict revolving around attempts to frustrate that central aim, and this leads to the identification of a competing aim(s) and to the alignment of characters within the narrative in support of (helpers) or over against (opponents) this central aim. These latter categories, helper and opponent, need not be mutually exclusive, since narrative development allows for the possibility of betrayal (secret or otherwise) and other, perhaps less sinister, forms of side-swapping.

One more introductory observation: This intuitive emphasis on narrative aim and on character alignment has the effect of calling upon the narratee, the perceived reader of the narrative, to choose sides. The result is that engaging with narrative involves one in a formative and decision-making process. With what characters will I identify? Who are my heroes? How does this aim beckon me? How would I, will I, do I, respond?

Such considerations, when brought to a reading of the Christian Scriptures as narrative, press the question, Whose aim carries the narrative forward from beginning to middle to end? In our case, the answer is easy enough, as there is only one character whose voice is heard and presence felt, whether through authoritative announcement or still small voice, from Genesis to Revelation: God, enfleshed in Jesus Christ, active powerfully and formatively through Word and Spirit. That is, the Bible is not first and foremost a "human book," in the sense of "being about" the life

and times (and sorrows and happiness) of *Homo sapiens,* or even
of a particular, identifiable segment of humanity, Israel. Nor is the
Bible a christological book, in the narrow sense. Its plot is *theolog-*
ically determined. Its subject and focus is God. We can push further. From the perspective I am painting here, even a book like
the Gospel of Mark, which at least *appears* to be centered on Jesus,
must be read within a larger frame—that is, within the horizons
of the Bible's essential focus on the story of God. We read this
Gospel, therefore, not only to follow the life and times of Jesus
Messiah, but to hear what God is up to in these narrated events,
in and through this life.

As with narrative in general, so with this one, the parts are determined by and determinative of the whole. The identity of this
story's chief character, Yahweh, unfolds from beginning to end,
Genesis to Revelation, though the claim of a Christian reading of
Scripture is that the character of God is on display in an ultimate
sense in the person and work of Jesus: "Long ago God spoke to
our ancestors in many and various ways by the prophets, but in
these last days he has spoken to us by a Son, whom he appointed
heir of all things, through whom he also created the worlds"
(Heb. 1:1–2).

4. *The open-ended character of this narrative.* Tales of suspense and
mystery often move their readers to a heightened sense of anticipation by withholding *what* will happen. Even as the last chapter
is begun, readers are often able to visualize multiple paths to the
resolution of the plot. This is not the case with the narrative of
Scripture. In Scripture, what will happen in the end is not hidden.
The narrative world cast in Scripture is comprehensive in its grasp
of history, holding in one hand creation and in the other new creation. Creation, fall, the covenant with Noah, divine election of Israel, exile and promise, the advent of Jesus Christ, the outpouring
of the Spirit, the ongoing formation and mission of God's people—all of these are central features of this narrative, and all are
oriented toward the final resolution of God's purpose in the eschaton, the End. In the narrative of Scripture, we know *what* will
happen in the End ("We have read the last chapter"), but this
does not neuter this narrative of any sense of drama or suspense.
Questions remain. In particular, still being written is the narrative
of *how* God's purpose will come to fruition; the question remains,
Who will serve this purpose, and who will oppose it?

To put this somewhat differently, we find in narrative the possibility and power of participation. The narrative of Scripture projects itself beyond the pages of the New Testament, with the expectation of its continuing to be written as the ongoing history of God's people, "until kingdom come." On the one hand, this helps to locate the importance of the church, its life and mission, within the work of God, which is prior to the Scriptures but which is articulated and exhibited in its pages, and which is served among the people of God in the world beyond the apostolic period sketched in the New Testament.

The story of God is still being written. Our present is given meaning by the past work of God, and God's future casts its beacon backward so as to remind us how our present life and witness have consequences into eternity. On the other hand, this perspective presses the importance of the church's coherence with the biblical drama, its mandate to continue *this particular narrative* and *in particular ways*. It is, after all, the story of God, not our story. With so many chapters having already been written, and with the final chapter already firmly in place, the options for intervening material are limited, if we are to continue *this* story. Accordingly, our task is to align ourselves with these landmarks on the biblical terrain—or, better, to write ourselves, to inscribe ourselves, into the biblical narrative, so that our sense of past, present, and future is congruous with the story of the universe found in Scripture. Christian faith is lived at the confluence of personal, ecclesial, and biblical narrative.[23]

5. *One story, different faith communities.* The importance of indwelling the biblical narrative, of inscribing ourselves as God's people into the narrative of Scripture, brings this question to the surface: What of those communities whose rendering of the biblical story departs from ours? How does one account for the self-evident pluralism within the people of God?

This is not a new question, but was on display already in the life of Israel and the life of the early church, as communities struggled over faithful interpretation of the divine will and, then, of the Scriptures. Affirmations regarding Scripture are never enough. This truism is on display in the Gospels and Acts, where "the battle for the Bible" focuses not on *whether* the Scriptures of Israel are to

23. See Gabriel Fackre, "Narrative Theology from an Evangelical Perspective," in Yandell, *Faith and Narrative*, 188–201.

be taken seriously, but on *how* those Scriptures are to be understood within the framework of God's purpose and appropriated within the lives of God's people. Pharisees have one view, the Jewish elite residing in Jerusalem have another view, and Jesus has still another—all with regard to the same authoritative Scriptures. This is not a struggle over how best to construe biblical authority (affirmed by all, at least implicitly, in this case); rather, it is a hermeneutical quandary—and one with such high stakes that differences of viewpoint surrounding the message of the Scriptures would lead eventually to the execution of one of its interpreters, Jesus.

Even a cursory survey of the New Testament materials proposes two conclusions on this matter. On the one hand, we learn, the biblical narrative is not capable of an infinite breadth of meaning. Regularly, we are informed in the Acts of the Apostles, Paul is found in the synagogues locked in proposal and counterproposal regarding a messianic reading of the Scriptures. For him, as for Christ's followers in the New Testament more generally, it is impossible to tell the story of God in relation to God's people without showing how the path of God's eternal purpose passes through the death and exaltation of Jesus of Nazareth. To be sure, other readings of the Hebrew Bible are *possible;* the existence of other sects within first-century Judaism, for whom the Scriptures were of central importance in identity and life, is proof of this. Such readings would not be faithful to the purpose of God to which the Scriptures are to give expression, however, according to the portrait of Paul in Acts. Diversity has its limits.

On the other hand, the presence in Scripture of diverse witnesses to Jesus, of "the many faces of Jesus" in the New Testament, demonstrates that the narrative of Scripture can be plotted in different ways and still remain faithful to the one purpose of God. This is because this narrative is determined not in all of its details but only in broad outline by its key markers—that is, by its beginning, middle, and end, creation, redemption, and new creation. A telling of the story that attempts to bypass Israel cannot represent itself as Christian. A telling that attempts to bypass Jesus Christ cannot represent itself as Christian. A telling that fails to account for creation, or for the consummation of all things—such a telling could not represent itself as Christian.

Other parameters might be discussed as well. Already in the

second century, the church struggled with a diversity of readings of the Scriptures, and so constructed "rules of faith" or "rules of truth" by which to adjudicate between competing interpretations. In order to be "Christian," then, a reading had to be congruent with the narrative of Scripture as this was sketched in "rules of faith," these precursors to the classical creeds of the church. Having admitted all of this, however, it remains the case that the story of Scripture is deep and broad, capable of diverse readings, and so, at least potentially, capable of being embodied by different communities, whose faith is articulated and incarnated in diverse ways, but who nonetheless justifiably identify themselves as Christian.

At the same time that I have carved out space for diversity with and among Christian communities in the context of biblical fidelity, I have also pointed in the direction of a response to those for whom talk of "narrative" and "transformation of life-world" smacks of relativism and postmodern acculturation. Earlier, I encouraged an analysis of the commitment to objectivity in biblical interpretation as itself a fateful accommodation to a cultural climate often labeled as "modernist." Drawing on the analysis and proposal of Garrett Green, for an antidote I pointed to the need for recovery of theological sources particular to the faith, and especially to a recognition and deployment of the biblical narrative as the grammar of the faith. In concert with certain postmodern impulses, the perspective sketched here places a premium on the primacy of hermeneutics, of the incessant work of interpreting the significance of the world we perceive and experience. In tension with other postmodern impulses, though, I have located the work of interpretation within certain boundaries (grammatical, contextual, theological), bridling the potential hyperactivity of the hermeneutical enterprise.

At this juncture, it is critical to recognize that this heightened emphasis on "understanding" cuts both ways: "understanding" in the sense of "comprehending the nature and meaning of something," as well as "under-standing," or "standing under," the biblical narrative so as continually to test our view of things for its conformity to the hermeneutical paradigm provided by Scripture itself. That is, to speak of "the narrative of Scripture" is to recognize that the biblical narrative creates a world of its own that is never quite at home within the contours of our culture's reigning

assumptions *and* that God's story has interpretive priority in the
sense-making in which we perpetually engage. Given the ubiquity
of sin—which in this context comes to expression above all in
wrongly imagining "the way the world works," and especially in
the propagation of lies about who we are before God—the result
is Christian life and community engaged always in the process of
conversion as we come more fully "to understand" reality as God
has purposed, and revealed, it to be.

Looking Ahead

"Narrative reading," I have urged, is appropriate to all sorts of
biblical texts. This is because "narrative" is foremost a theological
claim regarding the nature of Scripture and, especially, regarding
its function in mapping the terrain of our lives. In this reckoning,
biblical texts—be they found in a narrative like Matthew's Gospel
or a letter like Philemon—are situated contextually within the
grand narrative of God's story. What this actually looks like in the
twin practices of reading and preaching Scripture—in biblical
studies and homiletics—is the concern of the chapters that follow.

Pairing New Testament scholar and homiletician, successive
chapters treat the Gospels and Acts, the New Testament epistles,
and the Book of Revelation (or Apocalypse). Each pair of writers
has been tasked, first, with sketching how each of these three
major divisions of the New Testament might be approached from
a narrative perspective; and, second, with demonstrating what exegesis and preaching might look like, again given this commitment to the narrative of Scripture. We trust that these ruminations and exemplars will point the way forward to a reconciliation
of homiletic and exegetical practices, and this to Christian congregations who, more and more, find their home in the grand
story of God.

2

Reading the Gospels and Acts as Narrative

Joel B. Green

It is remarkable that the Gospels and Acts, taken together, comprise almost two-thirds of the bulk of the New Testament. Here is evidence of the importance of vivid narrative in the formation of Christian faith. Of course, this interest is not focused on just any story, but more specifically on that of the ongoing work of Yahweh in the mission of Jesus and, subsequently, in the embryonic church. However one resolves the historical questions raised by the first five books of the New Testament, it is nonetheless clear that narrative memory and interpretation of what Luke calls "the events that have been fulfilled among us" (Luke 1:1) predominate.

Within the New Testament, the Gospels and Acts *appear* to be the books most susceptible to reading strategies that accord privilege to narrative. If the history of interpretation, and thus of preaching, is a reliable barometer, however, this is one of those cases in which looks can be deceiving. Despite appearances, the particular narrative quality of the Gospels and Acts has generally not been taken seriously.

Augustine concluded that the Gospel of Mark was an abridgement of Matthew (*De consensu evangelistarum* 1.2.4), effectively relegating the Second Gospel to the margins of the church. When, in the latter half of the eighteenth century, Mark was rediscovered, it was examined primarily as a source book for the historical

Jesus. In the twentieth century, the Second Evangelist moved into the limelight of critical scrutiny, but his was no enviable status. His Greek was often dismissed as barbaric, his contribution to the New Testament evaluated as a scissors-and-paste job. When interest in *narrative* did enter the study of the Gospels, it did so first with reference to the Gospel of Mark, but only in the twilight years of the last century.[1]

Although the situation with the other three Gospels is less grim, this is only marginally so. From early on, Matthew attracted special attention, with the result that the early centuries of the church saw the production of commentaries on this Gospel. Luke, however, served less as a narrative presentation of Jesus' ministry, and more as a library of episodes from which favorites might be borrowed, depending on one's interests. Luke's story of the birth of Jesus is a case in point, but one could also point to the Christian use of the parables of the Good Samaritan or the Prodigal Son—all texts typically sundered from their narrative service within the Third Gospel. The Acts of the Apostles suffered relative neglect early on, too, due in large part to its lack of formal, explicit theological affirmations. The possibility that Luke might not only be chronicling the growth of the church and extension of its mission, but doing so in a way that pressed forward a theological agenda, seems not fully to have been exploited early in the church's history. Instead, Acts provided the chronological mannequin on which to drape the clothing of Pauline biography.

If the church has traditionally expressed little concern for the Gospels *as narratives,* it may well be that this was because the narrative form of these documents has often been eclipsed by an interpretive focus on "narratives" other than the literary kind. That

1. For a brief history of interpretation of the Gospel of Mark, see William R. Telford, "Mark, Gospel of," in *A Dictionary of Biblical Interpretation,* ed. R. J. Coggins and J. L. Houlden (London: SCM; Philadelphia: Trinity, 1990), 424–28; also, idem, *The Theology of the Gospel of Mark,* New Testament Theology (Cambridge: Cambridge University Press, 1999), 214–17. The turn to narrative in study of the Gospels was signaled especially by the publication of David Rhoads and Donald Michie, *Mark as Story: An Introduction to the Narrative of a Gospel* (Philadelphia: Fortress, 1982). See now Mark Allan Powell, *What Is Narrative Criticism?* Guides to Biblical Scholarship: New Testament Series (Minneapolis: Fortress, 1990); S. Scott Bartchy, "Narrative Criticism," in *Dictionary of the Later New Testament and Its Developments,* ed. Ralph P. Martin and Peter H. Davids (Downers Grove, Ill.: InterVarsity, 1997), 787–92.

is, interest in the narrative forms of "biography" or "historiography" has fallen prey to an interest in such "narrative" patterns as would be represented in the "rule of faith," in the "life of Jesus," or in the "history of tradition." Thus, Tertullian, Irenaeus, Clement of Alexandria, and others, from the second century onward, appealed to a "rule of faith" or "rule of truth" by way of determining the soundness of particular interpretations of biblical texts and of theological formulations. In one attempt to set out the lines of scriptural faith, for example, Tertullian writes,

> Now with regard to this rule of faith . . . it is, you must know, that which prescribes the belief that there is only one God, and that he is none other than the creator of the world, who produced all things out of nothing through his own word, first of all sent forth. This word is called his son, and, under the name of God, was seen in diverse manners by the patriarchs, heard at all times in the prophets, and at last brought by the Spirit and power of the Father down into the virgin Mary. He was made flesh in her womb, and, being born of her, went forth as Jesus Christ. Thereafter, he preached the new land and the new promise of the kingdom of heaven, and he worked miracles. Having been crucified, he rose again on the third day. Having ascended into the heavens, he sat at the right hand of the Father. He sent in place of himself the power of the Holy Spirit to lead those who believe. He will come with glory to take the saints to the enjoyment of everlasting life and of the heavenly promises, and to condemn the wicked to everlasting fire. This will take place after the resurrection of both these classes, together with the restoration of their flesh. This rule . . . was taught by Christ, and raises among us no other questions than those which heresies introduce, and which make people heretics. (*De praescroptione haereticorum* 13)

As with other exemplars of the "rule of faith" form, this one possesses a narrative quality and confessional tone that addresses the church's struggle to determine its own theological commitments.

From such theological concerns, it is only a small distance to the idea of a Gospel harmony, which allows the pluriform, narrative witnesses to the significance of Jesus' life, death, and resurrection, which constitute our New Testament Gospels, to be simplified along unitary lines. A single narrative, rather than the four that comprise our Gospel collection, would be useful against the barbs of those detractors, like Celsus, who saw deceit at the root of the fourfold Gospel witness. Writing in the latter half of the second

century, he charges that "some of the faithful, as though coming
from a drinking bout, fight one another and alter the Gospel after
it had first been written down three or four times, indeed many
times, and falsify it, so that they can better reject arguments against
it" (Origen *Contra Celsum* 2.27). A single "Gospel harmony" would
also prove instrumental in the task of inducting new converts into
the church's story, and serve the church's interest in an epitome,
or synthesis, of the story of Jesus for its ongoing theological task. In
the latter half of the second century, Tatian worked material from
the Gospels of Matthew, Mark, Luke, and John, like a mosaic, into
a single narrative framework, and the result of his efforts, the *Diatessaron* (that is, "[one Gospel] from the four"), remained influen-
tial into the fifth century. Even with the ascendancy of the fourfold
Gospel, however, impulses toward harmonization have continued.
In the early eighth century, the Venerable Bede produced homilies on Gospel texts, working as though each narrative were cut
from the same cloth as the other, without attending to the particular perspective of any single Evangelist.[2] In the sixteenth century,
Calvin wrote a series of commentaries on each of the biblical
books, except the Gospels of Matthew, Mark, and Luke. He com-
mented on these last three in a synthetic way, not with regard to
the discrete witness each has to the life of Jesus, but with reference
to a composite picture of Jesus that Calvin was able to produce
from the Synoptic Gospels. Those engaged today in the quest of
the historical Jesus similarly bypass the narrative character of the
individual Gospels, preferring instead to re-create, from sometimes wildly divergent databases of material, their own accounts of
Jesus.

Further illustrations of how study of the Gospels has proceeded
without reference to the narrativity that defines their character
could be garnered from the commentaries that adorn our li-
braries. The classic work on the Third Gospel by Joseph Fitzmyer
is a good example.[3] When this two-volume set was completed in
1985, it signaled the coming of age of redaction-critical study of

2. In fact, Bede's homilies followed a "narrative" of another sort—namely,
the narrative of the church's calendar (Bede the Venerable, *Homilies on the
Gospels,* 2 vols., Cistercian Studies Series 110–11 [Kalamazoo, Mich.: Cistercian, 1991]).

3. Joseph A. Fitzmyer, *The Gospel according to Luke,* 2 vols., Anchor Bible
28–28A (Garden City, N.Y.: Doubleday, 1981, 1985).

the Gospels. Fitzmyer's work was pivotal for the newfound recognition of Luke as a theologian in his own right. But in more than 1,600 pages of erudition, Fitzmyer treats pericope after pericope of the Third Gospel, each in relative isolation, with only the rare glance to the significance of the narrative location of that pericope, and thus with only the barest of attempts to account for narrative coherence. The plotline Fitzmyer traces is the path of developing tradition—from historical events through tradition history to final inclusion in Luke's Gospel.

The astute reader will note that, thus far, I have cast a pall over Gospels-interpretation by focusing almost entirely on a singular notion of "narrative reading"—namely, the importance of "letting Matthew be Matthew," Mark be Mark, and so on. Such a reading would emphasize the finished form of the text, together with the literary, cultural, and theological unity of the text as a whole. Situating the content of the Gospels—that is, Jesus' ministry and mission—within the larger narrative of Israel's history has come more easily to readers. I want to insist, though, that this work has misconstrued the character of the Gospels and Acts as Christian Scripture when it has not accounted for the particularity of each of these documents: Matthew, Mark, Luke (together with Acts), and John. I want to insist that, if we are to read and preach these texts as Scripture, we must attend more self-consciously both to the narrativity of the Gospels and Acts, and, then, to the location of those narratives within the larger, scriptural narrative.

Hence, my agenda in this essay is to counter long-standing interpretive tendencies by insisting on hermeneutical protocols that take seriously the narrative character of the Gospels and Acts, and their location in the larger narrative of Scripture. I demonstrate, first, that the generic character of these documents has not been well-served by the harmonizing and atomistic approaches that have governed so much of their usage in the history of interpretation, and that they actually invite heightened attention to their narrativity. From there, I move on to discuss in two related ways the narratives within which these New Testament documents are embedded: the narratives of Jesus' life and ministry as these are presented by the Gospels, and of the early church as this is portrayed by Acts; and the significance of the "address" of these books in the biblical story for their interpretation as Christian Scripture. Keeping before us the particular challenge to the preacher of engaging, Sunday after Sunday, a particular text, a pericope,[4] I then suggest how particular accounts or episodes within the Gospels and Acts might be read with appropriate attention given to the larger narrative within which we access them. Finally, I sketch an exegesis of one pericope, Acts 2:42–47, in a way that exemplifies what I take to be a reading of the Gospels and Acts as narrative.

The Gospels and Acts: "History" as Narrative

"Genre criticism," the discernment of a text's genre and exploration of the implications of genre, is akin to an invitation to a dance. As familiar patterns of speech, genres promote certain effects by inviting certain readerly practices. Whether readers of the Gospels and Acts will follow the dance steps set before them—or, to shift the metaphor slightly, to perform the music emanating from these texts—is thus a question of more than passing interest. Working with these texts is not a simple task to contemporary readers, for whom Matthew or Mark may not fit familiar patterns. Even readers arrayed across a spectrum measured in degrees of competence, however, are able to attain a certain amount of satisfaction.[5] This is because, in the most simple sense, we recognize that these texts belong to the larger category of writing we know as "narrative," and narratives of all sorts call for a common set of interpretive practices.[6] By addressing more narrowly the genres of the Gospels and Acts, I will have introduced more generally im-

---

4. "Pericope," from the Greek περικοπή, refers to a passage of Scripture, of manageable size (depending on the genre, a paragraph or oracle, for example), especially for liturgical usage.

5. See Glenn W. Most, "Generating Genres: The Idea of the Tragic," in *Matrices of Genre: Authors, Canons, and Society,* ed. Mary Depew and Dirk Obbink (Cambridge: Harvard University Press, 2000), 15–35 (here, 17–18); Joseph W. Day, "Epigram and Reader: Generic Force as (Re-)Activation of Ritual," in Depew and Obbink, *Matrices of Genre,* 37–57 (here, 38–39). More generally, see James L. Bailey, "Genre Analysis," in *Hearing the New Testament: Strategies for Interpretation,* ed. Joel B. Green (Grand Rapids: Eerdmans, 1995), 197–221.

6. Despite the obvious differences separating historical from fictional narratives, their narrators face the same problems and employ the same literary conventions, and their readers employ the same interpretive protocols; see especially Wallace Martin, *Recent Theories of Narrative* (Ithaca, N.Y.: Cornell University Press, 1986), 72–75.

portant protocols for our engagement with New Testament narrative.

Within their milieu in the first-century Mediterranean world, the Gospels and Acts comprise recognizable transformations of two primary, narrative genres. The Gospels of Matthew, Mark, and John follow the familiar patterns of Greco-Roman biography, and the Gospel of Luke and Acts of the Apostles, read as a single, continuous narrative, are calibrated within the fulsome category of Greco-Roman historiography. This is not to exclude precursors within Israel's own Scriptures, of course. The historical narratives of Genesis or 1 Kings, as well as the more focused, biographical material on Elijah and Elisha or on Joseph, suggest the extent to which the Gospels and Acts may be comprehended within the biblical tradition of the Jewish people. Nor is it to draw too strict a line between biography and historiography in the Greco-Roman world, as though, say, Mark and Luke should be read in significantly different ways. Biography has as its primary focus a *bios,* a life, whereas historiography locates events on center stage, but in the Roman world of the first century biography was still the youthful offspring of the more aged tradition of writing history.[7] One can and perhaps ought to expect, then, that the production of these New Testament texts would have been characterized by intermingling of literary traditions and contamination of generic elements.

What does this say about the dance of interpretation? If, in the ancient world, we were to visit that section of the library where the Gospels of Matthew, Mark, and John would have been shelved, what would we hope to find?

We would expect a narrative that proceeded either according to a thematic outline or along chronological lines. Both sorts of biographical narratives were present in the Roman world, and both are present in the New Testament. Matthew's Gospel, for example, is more topical in its arrangement, whereas Mark's Gospel develops along more simple, chronological lines. To partner with these texts would thus be to attend to their overall structure, and to take seriously the order in which material is presented. How does our

7. See John Marincola, *Authority and Tradition in Ancient Historiography* (Cambridge: Cambridge University Press, 1997), 19–33; and, more generally, Charles William Fornara, *The Nature of History in Ancient Greece and Rome,* Eidos: Studies in Classical Kinds (Berkeley: University of California Press, 1983).

reading of John 1 shape the way we read John 2? How does John 3 fit within the larger narrative framework of John's Gospel? Here is a resounding word *against* reading passages in the Gospel on their own terms, sans reference to the whole. Here, too, is a word of warning about an atomistic use of the lectionary, as though the pericope it has chosen for the day could be grasped apart from the larger narrative.

We would expect an overarching, interpretive aim that pushed and pulled the narrative forward toward its telos, *or goal.* From Aristotle onward, narratives have been characterized as having a beginning, a middle, and an end. This speaks both simply and profoundly to how narratives progress: from *beginnings,* where an obstacle or problem or need is introduced and which requires resolution; through the *middle,* where that obstacle is complicated further, and where forces working toward resolution are joined by helpers or supporters and meet with opponents; to the *end,* where resolution is reached and the aftermath is recounted, sometimes even celebrated.

Attention to narrative development presses the question, Whose aim is at work in this narrative? For the Gospels, the answer may be so subtle as to catch us off-guard. We may want to say that the Gospels are *about* Jesus—after all, are they not biographies of him? In fact, as focused on Jesus as they may be, the narrative aim that governs their progression (and that governs Jesus' own mission) is first and foremost theocentric. The purpose at work here is God's. It is this pivotal insight which opens the way for us to speak theologically of the importance of the location of the Gospels within the canon of Scripture and, thus, within the story of God's engagement with Israel. We cannot understand the Jesus-story as this is related by Matthew, for example, without understanding the God at work in the account of Jesus' birth and childhood, the God to whom Jesus demonstrates his allegiance in the temptation account, the God to whom Jesus prays in Gethsemane and from the cross, and the God who raises Jesus from the dead. This is the God who is present to us in the Scriptures of Israel. A central if often neglected task of Gospel interpretation, then, is grappling with the nature of God and his mission as this is presented by each Evangelist.[8]

8. On this neglect, see John R. Donahue, "A Neglected Factor in the Theology of Mark," *Journal of Biblical Literature* 101 (1982): 563–94. For an exem-

We would expect a focus on a central character, whose importance rests less in individual achievement and more in his or her embodiment and lively display of community-held values. In antiquity, the famous achieved their renown not so much by astounding independent achievement, but through exemplifying the qualities valued by the community. This reality underscores our need to read the Gospels primarily as documents "addressed" to Christian communities throughout the Roman world (since Jesus' followers are those, we may presume, who would have honored Jesus' teaching and example). And, if we are to be among those who accept the Gospels' invitation to enter the interpretive dance, we would find ourselves residing in the community of those for whom Jesus' dispositions and behavior are exemplary.

If we were to move down the aisle in our ancient library, to the call numbers of books of history-writing with which Luke and Acts (or Luke–Acts)[9] would have been associated, what further shape might our interpretive expectations take? With what conventions do we operate—Luke, who wrote, and we who read this example of history-writing?

We would inquire, What choices have been made? It is the nature of all historiography that historians are faced with more data than can be integrated into a single narrative. It is in this sense that all history-writing is *partial*—that is, historiography does not tell us "what actually happened" (since this would eventuate in a narrative of such bulk and trivia as to be of little use) but "what really matters," at least from the perspective of the historian. "Partial" relates both to the inclusion of some materials, exclusion of others, and to the proclivities that direct decisions about inclusion and exclusion. At every turn, it is worth asking, Why this? How does the inclusion of this episode shape the whole?

We would inquire, What order? If the first, major contribution of

plary attempt at addressing this neglect, see Marianne Meye Thompson, *The God of the Gospel of John* (Grand Rapids: Eerdmans, 2001).

9. I am presuming the narrative unity of the Gospel of Luke and the Book of Acts, and so use the nomenclature "Luke–Acts." For this position, see Joel B. Green, *The Gospel of Luke,* New International Commentary on the New Testament (Grand Rapids: Eerdmans, 1997); more briefly, see idem, "Acts of the Apostles," in Martin and Davids, *Dictionary of the Later New Testament and Its Developments,* 7–24 (here, 12–16). For the contrary view, see Mikeal C. Parsons and Richard I. Pervo, *Rethinking the Unity of Luke and Acts* (Minneapolis: Fortress, 1993).

the historian relates to *selectivity,* the second relates to *narrativity*—
that is, the location of episodes in relation to each other in a
nexus of cause-and-effect relations. Given that earlier-related
episodes either cause or at least provide the ground for later
episodes, and that historical narrative does not necessarily pro-
ceed chronologically, readers are confronted with the interpretive
necessity of attending closely to the order in which events appear.
Notice, for example, that, in chronological terms, the sequence of
events initiated in Acts 8:4 ("now those who were scattered went
from place to place, proclaiming the word," beginning with the
mission of Philip) are, roughly speaking, contemporaneous with
that sequence begun in Acts 11:19 ("now those who were scattered because of the persecution . . . over Stephen . . . ," beginning with Antioch). Why, then, does Luke narrate the story of
Philip first? What is his narrative logic?

We would inquire, What purpose is being served? History-writing is
less about chronicling events and more about drawing out their
significance. In this meaning-making enterprise, historiography
generally serves one or more of the following aims: validation,
continuity, identity, and pedagogy.[10] In the Greco-Roman world,
history-writing was a powerful means for validating or authorizing
beliefs and practices, even peoples. By showing the antiquity of a
people, one might establish continuity with the past, give that
people a sense of identity, teach that people who they must be and
how they must live, and/or legitimate their existence and practices among outsiders. When Paul introduces the "message of salvation" to those in the synagogue at Pisidian Antioch (Acts 13:16–
41), he does so by means of a précis of Israel's history, showing
how the advent of Jesus is continuous with the work of God that
can be traced back to God's choice of Israel and the liberation of
Israel from Egypt. The good news is "nothing new," but is
grounded in the ancient purpose of God.

As narratives, then, how do the Gospels and Acts function as
Christian Scripture; and how might they be read by interpreters
intent on taking seriously their narrativity? First, we would recognize the primary interest of these narratives in drawing out the
significance of the events and persons they narrate. The first questions they invite are not about historical veracity ("Did this really

10. This is helpfully developed in David Lowenthal, *The Past Is a Foreign
Country* (Cambridge: Cambridge University Press, 1985).

happen this way?"), but about signification ("What does this mean?").
This is not to say that these narratives are lacking in historical referents. As biography and historiography, they clearly intend "history" in this more narrow sense of the term, and in electing to
work within these genres, their authors chose to work with databases of people who existed and events that happened in the real
world. It is to say that the interpretive task is not satisfied by questions of historicity, but rather by questions of meaning, aim, purpose, signification.

To push further, as Christian Scripture, these documents are
presented to us as much more than "particular perspectives" on
Jesus and the early church. They are authoritative renderings. As
Scripture, these narratives are present to us as vehicles of God's
own perspective on things. This theological claim is a reminder
that the significance of Jesus and the developing people of God is
tied to the larger story of God's promise and purpose, coming to
fruition in the world by God's own initiative.

To push still further, this means that the Gospels and Acts do
not come to us with the agenda of soliciting from us an agree-
ment that (say) Jesus did such-and-such or that Peter said so-and-
so. Their invitation, rather, is that we enter into the interpretive
dance, that we actually involve ourselves, imaginatively and bodily,
in this story. These narratives are about transforming us into ser-
vants of the divine purpose to which they provide witness.

And this, of course, means that we are not free to assign meaning to the episodes recounted in these texts willy-nilly, as though
each pericope had its own significance independent of the larger
framework within which it is found. These accounts are not like
playing cards that might be drawn from a deck and traded, so as
to produce the desired hand of cards for play. One scene leads to
another, and another, moving from beginning to middle to end,
in the service of a grand *telos* that gains its meaning from the
whole of the parts, and projects its meaning back over the parts of
the whole.

Locating the Gospels and Acts within the Narrative

The Gospels and Acts are not only narrative in form, but themselves participate in a broader narrative. With this statement, I
have moved from one sort of "narrative talk" to another, from a

literary genre to the larger story within which each of these narratives participates.

One of the problems with any narrative is the problem of a beginning: How far back does one go? Where is the suitable point to begin, a beginning capable of intending the whole of what follows?[11] New Testament narratives solve this problem in different ways, as we will see momentarily; they do so, however, by locating themselves within an ongoing story of God's engagement with his people. In no case does the advent of Jesus *start* things. His entry onto the stage of history serves instead as the midpoint in an already-developing plotline. Indeed, to use the language of "New Testament" is to press the claim that the Gospels and Acts pick up a story already in the process of telling, and that these documents reach their conclusions before that story has reached its finale. In this way, the Gospel of John (for example) helps to give shape to that story, while also leaving time and space for that story to continue—and it does so, to this very day, and will continue until history itself reaches its *telos*, its consummation according to the plan of God. What does it mean to read the Gospels in the context of these sorts of considerations?

The Narratives Presumed by the Gospels and Acts

Narratives are constructed through a reversal of cause-effect relations. Knowing how things turned out, narrators go back in time, in search of causes.[12] In the Gospels and Acts, the problem of a beginning is the quest for a point of initiation capable of supporting, even funding, the significance allocated to Jesus and the mission of his followers. This issue is raised already by the opening verse of the Gospel of Mark, ἀρχὴ τοῦ εὐαγγελίου Ἰησοῦ Χριστοῦ υἱοῦ θεοῦ, usually rendered, as in the NRSV, as a kind of title or heading: "The beginning of the good news of Jesus Christ, the Son of God." But this translation is potentially misleading, since it suggests that Mark's own narrative is this "beginning of the good news"—a reading that violates both the grammar and theology of the Second Evangelist, as recent commentators observe. Robert

11. So Edward W. Said, *Beginnings: Intention and Method* (New York: Basic, 1975), 50.

12. See Hayden White, "The Question of Narrative in Contemporary Historical Theory," in *The Content of the Form: Narrative Discourse and Historical Representation* (Baltimore: Johns Hopkins University Press, 1987), 26–57.

Guelich helpfully translates, "The beginning of the gospel concerning Jesus Messiah, Son of God, as written by the prophet Isaiah. . . ." R. T. France adopts a more traditional translation, anal-
ogous to the NRSV, but underscores nonetheless, with Guelich,
that the beginning of the good news does not lie with the advent
of Jesus, but with the prophet Isaiah.[13] The ongoing story within
which the Gospel of Mark is located, which helps to give the story
of Jesus' ministry its significance, and which is itself shaped by
Mark's presentation of Jesus, has its roots in divine promise of liberation of Israel from the bondage of exile as this is related by the
prophet Isaiah. By way of illustrating how the Gospels participate
in a larger story, which is present to their narratives as a presupposition, let me pursue Mark's "beginning" in more detail.

Throughout the Scriptures of Israel, we hear that God's people
understood that the activity of God, definitively expressed in Exodus, resides at the forefront of God's own memory and is a window into God's character. Images of Exodus are everywhere. Exodus is God's own signature: "I am the LORD your God, who
brought you out of the land of Egypt, out of the house of slavery"
(Exod. 20:2). Exodus is celebrated annually in the festival of
Passover. Exodus is the ground and warrant of Torah, and the giving of Torah at Sinai marks nothing less than the creation of a
people whose corporate vocation was to reflect God's own character. In countless texts, the Scriptures weave the story of Israel's life
with strands of yarn spun out of Exodus.[14]

Efforts at casting the hope of Israel in the well-formed patterns
of Exodus reach their zenith in Isaiah, and especially Isaiah 40–
66. Israel is now in exile on account of its drawing back from its
life as a people formed by Exodus, its having withdrawn from
covenant partnership with God. What hope remains? As God had
warred against Egypt so as to deliver Israel, so, when Israel patterned its life after oppressive Egypt, God had clashed with Israel.
Yet, God's judgment against Israel would not be the last word.

13. Robert A. Guelich, *Mark 1–8:26,* Word Biblical Commentary 34A (Dallas: Word, 1989), 3–14; R. T. France, *The Gospel of Mark,* New International
Greek Testament Commentary (Grand Rapids: Eerdmans, 2002), 49–53. See
also Joel Marcus, *Mark 1–8,* Anchor Bible 27 (New York: Doubleday, 2000),
141–49.

14. See Rikki E. Watts, "Exodus," in *New Dictionary of Biblical Theology,* ed.
T. D. Alexander and Brian S. Rosner (Downers Grove, Ill.: InterVarsity,
2000), 478–87.

And the promise of restoration is formed in the mold of Exodus. In Exodus, God delivered the Hebrew people from Egyptian subjugation, forming them into his own people, and leading them to the land of promise. In New Exodus, God would deliver his people from captivity and exile, restoring them as his people. The impression with which we are left is that the only way to characterize Israel's reformation and restoration as God's people is to evoke the story that belongs to the founding moment of Israel's life, the story of Exodus. In the hands of Isaiah, the Exodus story is transformed for its role in the service of New Exodus hope.[15] First, the pattern of Exodus has been reformulated as a future event predicated on the merciful, powerful act of God in Israel's past. Second, taking up threads already evidenced in the Song of Moses (Exodus 15), Isaiah recasts the Exodus pattern in ways that meld the restoration of Israel with the restoration of the cosmos itself. New Exodus thus merges into new creation. Third, the identity of God's people is expanded in a way that recalls the promise to Abraham, who was to be the father of many nations (Gen. 17:4–5) and not only of Israel.

Locating "the beginning of the gospel" in Isaiah 40, Mark lays bare his presupposition that the narrative he is about to develop has as its conceptual framework that larger story of Exodus, Exile, and New Exodus. Were we able to pursue Mark's narrative agenda further,[16] we would see how fully his presentation of Jesus draws on the theological and literary repertoire of New Exodus. Healings and exorcisms, feeding the thousands, mastery of the sea, the motif of journeying—in these and myriad other ways, Mark clothes Jesus in the robes of Yahweh's servant who liberates the exiles and restores the people.

Were we to turn to the other Gospels, we would see much the same. In the opening of Matthew's Gospel, the Evangelist refers to "the book of origins" (NRSV: "the genealogy"), a parallel to Gen. 2:4; 5:1, and so pointing to the consummation in Jesus' advent of the purpose of God in creation. The depths of meaning of

15. See David W. Pao, *Acts and the Isaianic New Exodus*, Wissenschaftliche Untersuchungen zum Neuen Testament 2:130 (Tübingen: Mohr/Siebeck, 2000).

16. See Rikki E. Watts, *Isaiah's New Exodus and Mark*, Wissenschaftliche Untersuchungen zum Neuen Testament 2:88 (Tübingen: Mohr/Siebeck, 1997).

the story of Jesus cannot be plumbed without engagement with
the very beginning, nor without reference to Abraham and David,
Jesus' ancestors (Matt. 1:1). The Acts of the Apostles does not suffer for lack of a "beginning," since it is manifestly the second of
the two books, Luke–Acts (Acts 1:1). What of the beginning of
Luke–Acts? Just as the story of the early church (Acts) is inscribed
into the story of Jesus (Luke), so the story of Jesus is written into
the story of Israel's Scriptures, and especially the story of Abraham. In Luke's birth narrative (Luke 1:5–2:52), echoes of the
Abraham tradition can be heard. Here in Luke's narrative, then,
is a self-conscious continuation of the redemptive story, in which
divine promises to Abraham, long latent, are shown not to have
escaped God's memory but indeed to be in the process of actualization in the present.[17] As for the Fourth Gospel, John expands
the horizons even further. For him, the story of Jesus cannot be
appreciated fully without reference to the beginning of the cosmos—indeed, to the primordial being of God: "In the beginning
was the Word, and the Word was with God, and the Word was
God" (John 1:1). Each in its own way, the Gospels and Acts self-
consciously pick up the story in midstream, and write the next
chapter of the ongoing work of God.

The Gospels and Acts and the "Canonical" Narrative

Read as a whole, from Genesis to Revelation, the Bible relates
a grand story. It is true that, within its pages, we find numerous
side stories, episodes that seem to take us along strange paths or
corridors not easily integrated into the whole. For this reason,
each reading of Scripture invites a different emphasis, since each
reading allows one or another motif to become more prominent
than it was in the previous reading. The canon of Scripture places
limits, however, on the variety of "tellings" that the Bible can support. Our interest in "narrative" has constraints. It is simply incon-
ceivable that we could plot the biblical narrative without reference to the beginning of the narrative, its middle, and its
end—that is, to the purpose and action of God in creation (beginning), redemption (middle), and consummation (end). A commitment to the whole of Scripture makes necessary that we comprehend this "middle" in two primary movements: the liberating

17. Joel B. Green, "The Problem of a Beginning: Israel's Scriptures in
Luke 1–2," *Bulletin of Biblical Research* 4 (1994): 61–86.

work of God in Exodus and the saving work of God in the advent of Jesus Christ (New Exodus).

On the one hand, this means that, if we genuinely embrace the definition given the story of God's purpose in Scripture, there is no bypassing Israel or Jesus.[18] As I have already hinted, in fact, the Gospels themselves have deep roots in the soil of Israel's liberation and identity, its failures and hopes. This form of intertextuality urges that we read the biblical story in a seamless way, refusing the facile relegation of the Old Testament to "mere background material."

On the other hand, this identification of the midpoint of the biblical story, together with our present, more narrow interests in the interpretation and performance of the Gospels and Acts, highlights for us the reciprocal relation the Gospels and Acts enjoy (or ought to enjoy) with the story's beginning and end. Situating the Gospels and Acts canonically presses the theological claim that the gospel of God comes into particular focus here, providing the pivot point for all else. If the Genesis account casts its shadow forward on all that would come after, and if Revelation casts its shadow backward on all that would precede, the Gospels and Acts ensure that those shadows intersect in the coming of Jesus and the outpouring of the Spirit to render present the saving work of God. Reading the Bible as Christian Scripture entails an affirmation that the Old and New Testaments are inseparable in their witness to God the Savior and that the coming of Christ is the point of orientation that gives all biblical books their meaning as Scripture. Even if Christians have long pushed the Old Testament to the margins, the reality is that we cannot know Jesus Christ genuinely apart from the God of Jesus Christ revealed first in the Scriptures of Israel. The Old Testament is thus the revelatory narrative of God's dealings with Israel, the story of God's saving purpose, which culminates in the advent of Jesus. The Old Testament prepares the way of the Lord and the New Testament proclaims that the Word became flesh and dwelt among us.

18. This emphasis on Israel has often been overlooked in Christian theology, but there are important signs of recovery, together with a renewal of interest in the place of the Old Testament as Christian Scripture—see, for example, R. Kendall Soulen, *The God of Israel and Christian Theology* (Minneapolis: Fortress, 1996); Ronald E. Diprose, *Israel in the Development of Christian Thought* (Rome: Instituto Biblico Evangelico Italiano, 2000); Christopher R. Seitz, *Word without End: The Old Testament as Abiding Theological Witness* (Grand Rapids: Eerdmans, 1998).

Reading Accounts within the Narrative

It is Monday morning. Some of us engaged in the preaching task are rummaging for a text for the coming Sunday. For others of us, texts have been preselected by our commitments to the common lectionary or to a series of sermons with texts already cataloged. These differences aside, we are joined in a common existential angst: how to move from point A to point B, from this text to that sermon, in six days' time. Tucked away, often completely hidden within the rough-and-tumble of sermon-craft, is the inevitability of locating this text—the text chosen, read, studied, proclaimed—within a context.

"Words have meaning in context." We all know the adage. The demand "Stop pulling my leg!" has one sense in a playful exchange, another in a wrestling match. We know what fun, and harm, can come from extracting a verse from its biblical context. Even when we are sensitive to these matters on the micro scale (how a word is used, or the location of a sentence in a paragraph), however, we may be blind to our practices of locating particular biblical stories within larger, storied contexts alien to them. In fact, it is a common practice today that, when thinking through the text-to-sermon process, we imagine first how to locate a text within our world, within the lives of our people. We want to make it relevant, after all. "Where does this text touch our lives, the lives of my congregation?" we ask. And so, often without noticing, we locate this episode or that scene within the story of our people, our lives, our culture. Guided by the best of intentions, "biblical preaching," even preaching that carefully follows the contours of the biblical account, can and often does allow the text to be spirited away to find its home in another, secular, setting.

Narrative preaching on New Testament narratives calls this rather typical process of sermon-crafting into serious question, and it does so in three ways. First, it draws back the curtain and shines needed light on the simple fact that no episode can be grasped, or preached, on its own terms. Preaching does not occur in a narrative vacuum. Biblical texts may be sundered from their contexts, but they are never free-floating; removed from one story, they are simply, inevitably, transplanted into another. Unerringly, the scene from the Gospel or Acts that comprises the center of Sunday's sermon will be located in a larger plot of some kind. The only question is, Of whose making? Will this story be the story of Scripture or some other? Competitors abound, of course, and include such life-forming, grand narratives as "the little engine that could" (if only it worked hard enough and kept pushing and kept pushing, it could conquer that mountain); the promise of "unrelenting progress" (a kind of social and religious and political Darwinism that has long been integral to our self-consciousness); or "I did it my way" or "Be all that you can be" or "We give you what you want when you want it" (a portrait of life expressed in search for selfhood that, almost invariably, leads to radical individuation, as if to say that maturation comes as we learn "to give birth to ourselves"). Relocated within such grand stories, even the most exquisite and weighty biblical account is neutered of its theological potency, and made to serve agendas not at all at home within the Bible.

Removing the horizons of Scripture from our imagination does not keep us from making sense of reality, but simply reverses the hermeneutical process. Now we imagine the Bible through the lens of alternative versions of reality. The biblical text dislocated from its storied location within Scripture is now accommodated to secular visions of reality. Because interpretation from within a narrative paradigm is inescapable, no exegetical method, no technique of sermon-craft will substitute for the cultivation of an imagination shaped by the biblical story—and, in the interpretation and performance of biblical accounts, for locating that account within the plotline of the story of God at work in the cosmos.

Second, narrative preaching from New Testament narratives presses us to account for the actual narratives from which our texts are drawn. Matthew, Mark, Luke, and John all recount the execution of Jesus, for example, but each does so in a way that sometimes overlaps with the perspective of another Gospel and that is sometimes quite distinctive. If we are genuinely committed to preaching the Scripture of the church, we will recognize that there can be no generic or objective or noncommitted perspective on the crucifixion of Jesus, since Matthew, Mark, Luke, and John—these authorized narrative accounts that we embrace as furnishing us with God's own perspective on things—have each already proclaimed the significance of the cross of Christ. Hints of this are present in the records of Jesus' last word from the cross: in Matthew and Mark, "My God, my God, why have you forsaken me?" (Matt. 27:46; Mark 15:34); in Luke, "Father, into your hands I commend my spirit" (Luke 23:46); and in John, "It is finished" (John 19:30). That Jesus can be remembered to speak his last words in these diverse ways is already a sign that the cross could fund meaning particular to each of the four Evangelists. And how these dying words "mean" can be answered only in relation to the particular Gospel narrative within which each occurs, within which each serves as climactic utterance.

Each Gospel narrative is a retelling of the same basic story, the Jesus-story. From the standpoint of the role of these narratives in the church, the question can never be, Which Gospel, or which account, is better? or Which is more accurate? All four perform as Scripture, both as they are juxtaposed in the New Testament collection and each in its own singularity. The result is that the first context within which an account of Jesus or the early church is to be interpreted is the narrative within which that account appears. Each begs to be read in light of, and for its contribution to, the fabric of the whole.[19]

Third, as we have already hinted, this perspective on narrative preaching underscores the importance of locating texts within a still larger story, the "God at work in the cosmos" story. How does this scene embody, reflect, and contribute to the grand plot of the ways of God, evident in creation, covenant, exodus and election, the promise and advent of the Messiah, the outpouring of the Spirit and restoration of God's people at Pentecost, and the consummation of all things? It is this grand narrative that invites our participation—indeed, that creates for the faithful a way to make sense of text and world.

This means that our usual quest for relevance is wrongheaded. Our presumption has often been that we need to grasp the message of a text from the distant past so that we might then prod its message imaginatively to address our own time. As a result, we work to find points of contact for this text within our world. Is this serving the Word of God, or burning incense at the altar of relevance? In fact, to claim the Bible as Christian Scripture is to claim that this "God story" is not one story among many, but is rather, already, our story. If this is true, then we would not expend energy in inviting the text into a transformation of its original meaning

19. This concern is reflected well in David J. Ourisman, *From Gospel to Sermon: Preaching Synoptic Texts* (St. Louis: Chalice, 2000).

into a new application geared toward our thought forms; rather, we would allow our thought forms to be transformed by it. We would attend to the invitation of the text, which inducts us into its world, so that this biblical story shapes our lives profoundly and decisively, personally and collectively. We would find ourselves re-made—or, rather, in the process of being remade—according to the scriptural pattern of the world as the place where God is graciously active and actively seeking and empowering faithful living. Narrative preaching places this invitation before people: to enter and to make our home in "God's story," with all that this means in the transformation of our allegiances and commitments, realizing that this transformation will manifest itself in behaviors and practices appropriate to our social worlds.[20]

A Narrative Reading of Acts 2:42–47

By way of demonstrating a reading of a narrative text funded by this hermeneutical vision, I want to focus on a key text at the close of Acts 2. This chapter of Acts will be well-known for its description of the outpouring of the Spirit at Pentecost—an event that marks for Luke the decisive proof of Jesus' status as Lord and Christ (2:36) and signals the decisive shift in history: the eschatological actualization of God's promises to his people. Additionally, Acts 2 furthers Luke's presentation of the arrangement of the believers in the form of an egalitarian community marked by unpretentiousness and the democratization of the experience of the Holy Spirit. Repeatedly, Luke emphasizes the unity of the community—both in anticipation and as a consequence of the outpouring of the Spirit—and highlights the importance of "each" person within that community. In an interesting wordplay, the "division" of tongues, like flames of fire, which alighted on each of them (v. 4), prepares for and eventuates in the "division" of the community's property and possessions according to the need of each person (v. 45).[21] In multiple ways, considerations typical in an agonistic, status-conscious world like that of the ancient Mediterranean

20. See Gabriel Fackre, "Narrative Theology from an Evangelical Perspective," in *Faith and Narrative,* ed. Keith E. Yandell (Oxford: Oxford University Press, 2001), 188–201; Nicholas Wolterstorff, "Living within a Text," in Yandell, *Faith and Narrative,* 202–13.

21. διαμερίζω appears in each case.

are excluded. No accommodation is allotted status-based (whether age-, gender-, or ethnicity-oriented, or some other) factionalism or tribalism in the economy ushered in by the outpouring of the Holy Spirit.

Our focus is Acts 2:42–47, which I have translated as follows:

> [42] They held diligently to the teaching of the apostles and to the fellowship, to the breaking of bread and to the prayers. [43] Everyone had a sense of awe, and many wonders and signs were being done through the apostles.[22] [44] Those who believed all joined in solidarity and held all things in common. [45] They would sell their property and possessions and distribute them to everyone according to each person's need. [46] Everyday, while persisting in their unity in the temple, they were breaking bread in each other's homes—sharing food joyfully and unpretentiously, [47] praising God and having goodwill toward all the people. And the Lord was adding daily to the community those who were being saved.

The first of a series of summaries that dot the landscape of the narrative of Acts,[23] this one serves the important, dual function of exhibiting the communal dimension of the consequences of the outpouring of the Spirit and demonstrating the quality of daily life characteristic of those baptized in the name of Jesus Christ. Summaries in narrative generally link scenes, present what is typical, and provide background information, and this is true in the present case.[24] In an important sense, too, Luke uses this summary as a heading for what follows in Acts 3–5, where we find particular instantia-

22. Some manuscripts add ἐν Ἰερουσαλήμ after διὰ τῶν ἀποστόλων ἐγίν-ετο, and some introduce φόβος τε ἦν μέγας ἐπὶ πάντας at the end of the verse. The text is read by B D 𝔐 et al.

23. For orientation, see Henry J. Cadbury, "The Summaries in Acts," in *The Acts of the Apostles*, vol. 5: *Additional Notes to the Commentary*, ed. F. J. Foakes Jackson and Kirsopp Lake, Beginnings of Christianity 1 (London: Macmillan, 1920), 392–402; Maria Anicia Co, "The Major Summaries in Acts: Acts 2,42–47; 4,32–35; 5,12–16, Linguistic and Literary Relationship," *Ephemerides theologicae lovanienses* 68 (1992): 49–85.

24. For theoretical discussion of the "summary," see Gérard Genette, *Narrative Discourse: An Essay in Method* (Ithaca, N.Y.: Cornell University Press, 1980), 95–99. Martin Dibelius ("Style Criticism of the Book of Acts," in *Studies in the Acts of the Apostles*, ed. Heinrich Greeven [New York: Charles Scribner's Sons, 1956], 1–25 [here, 9–10]) regards the summaries of Acts as generalizations of typical incidents; similarly, Co ("Major Summaries," 61) observes how the elements Luke catalogs in this summary prepare for the following scenes (and esp. 3:1–10).

tions of what is portrayed in broad strokes on this large canvas (e.g., focus on the apostles, life in the shadow of the temple, economic need and sharing, prayer, teaching, and wondrous works).

That Luke is here concerned with a kind of précis of the shared life of the community of the baptized is highlighted in the generalizing language he employs. The term "all" or "every" is read in verses 43, 44, 45; "to hold diligently" or "to persist" is found twice (vv. 42, 46); and two of Luke's favored terms for expressing the unity of the believers appear in verses 46–47.[25] Through the repetition of these terms, Luke weaves this summary statement into his earlier description of the believing community in 1:14–15; it is clearly important to the narrator that the twenty-five-fold increase in the *quantity* (or size) of the community not be regarded as somehow diluting the *quality* (or character) of its life together.

Perhaps more important, these generalizations allow Luke to amplify on the response urged by Peter in verse 38: "repent and be baptized. . . ."[26] In Luke 3:7–14, John the Baptist had amplified his call to repent in response to questions from the crowds gathered around him, and had done so in ways that summarized faithful response in down-to-earth, socioeconomic terms: "Whoever has two coats must share with any who has none. . . ." Luke's summary performs much the same role, defining the boundaries of the community being formed in the name of Jesus Christ with reference to its characteristic behaviors.

Particularly interesting in this regard is Luke's phrase in verse 46: "persisting in their unity in the temple." Luke's point that it was precisely while in the temple that they persisted in their unity suggests already that Jesus' followers are struggling to carve out a distinctive identity within and in conversation with Judaism. The syntax of

25. προσκαρτερέω is used ten times in the NT, six in Acts (1:14; 2:42, 46; 6:4; 8:13; 10:7); Celsas Spicq gives the translation "constant diligence" (*Theological Lexicon of the New Testament*, 3 vols. [Peabody, Mass.: Hendrickson, 1994], 3:193). ὁμοθυμαδόν appears in Acts ten times and otherwise in the NT only in Rom. 15:6. In Acts it characterizes the single-minded unity either of the company of believers (1:14; 2:46; 4:24; 5:12; 8:6; 15:25) or of those who oppose them (7:57; 12:20; 18:12; 19:29). For ἐπὶ τὸ αὐτό, see also 1:15. Cf. George Panikulam, *Koinōnia in the New Testament: A Dynamic Expression of Christian Life*, Analecta biblica 85 (Rome: Biblical Institute, 1979), 125–26.

26. See Friedrich Wilhelm Horn, *Glaube und Handeln in der Theologie des Lukas*, 2d ed., Göttinger theologische Arbeiten 26 (Göttingen: Vandenhoeck & Ruprecht, 1986), 46.

verse 46 suggests that a chief component of that identity was focused on open table fellowship in each other's homes (see below).

Within the summary, verse 42 functions as a heading, a kind of
summary of the summary, with its four items taken up and explored in verses 43–47. Thus, the teaching of the twelve apostles
is immediately correlated with the signs and wonders being done
through them. This is reminiscent of the missionary activity of
Jesus' followers in Luke 9:1–6; 10:1–12, and even more so of the
ministry of Jesus, conventionally portrayed by the Third Evangelist as teaching *and* doing (Acts 1:1!). Luke provides no window
into the content of the apostolic teaching at this juncture, though
we may gain some inkling by observing the content of their missionary preaching and intramural dialogue in subsequent chapters. By providing no enumeration of that body of teaching here
and by juxtaposing teaching with wonders and signs, Luke draws
attention away from a particular "content" and toward the central
role of the apostles in the early community. These are they whom
Jesus has placed within the community to serve as prophet-lead-
ers (see Luke 22:28–30),[27] and this is the role they now fill. The
phrase "wonders and signs" (note the atypical word order) is reminiscent of Peter's references both to Jesus in verse 22 and especially to the material from the prophet Joel in verse 19; the effect
of this echo is (1) to identify the apostles in continuity with the
ministry of Jesus and (2) to designate the apostolic ministry as
one of the referents of the prophecy from Joel concerning "the
last days." The community of believers is the locus of the divine,
eschatological work of Israel's renewal. This is highlighted again
through Luke's notation that the miraculous was performed not
"by" but "through" the apostles. Standing behind them is the
Lord. The divine presence is also the immediate cause of the
sense of awe shared by all in the community.[28]

The notion of "fellowship" (or *koinonia*) in verse 42 is amplified
in verses 44–45, especially in economic terms. This does not
mean that fellowship is simply to be *identified* with economic sharing, but rather that economic sharing is a characteristic and concrete manifestation of the unity of the believers. Interestingly,

27. For this reading of Luke 22:28–30, see Green, *Gospel of Luke,* 769–70.
28. Note that wonders and signs are not said to cause this awe. Instead, this
sense of reverence is rooted in the immediacy of the presence of the Lord
through the Spirit, of which wonders and signs constitute one expression.

those who repented and were baptized are now "those who believe," and their common faith is manifest materially in economic
solidarity. The picture Luke allows is not one of a "common
purse," however, nor of disinvestment as a prior condition of
entry into the community.[29] In fact, the focus of his presentation
does not fall on the ideal of poverty nor on the evil of material
possessions nor even on total renunciation as a prerequisite for
discipleship. Selling what one has is customary within the community that Luke depicts,[30] but such giving is voluntary and is oriented toward addressing the plight of the needy.

Those with ears tuned to the right bandwidth might hear one
or more echoes of similar practices or ideals among ancient people. (1) In the Greco-Roman world, it was proverbial that "friends
hold all things in common"; in this case, "friends" has been re-
placed in the proverb with "believers." Given Greco-Roman models of friendship, however, Luke's portrait is important for its
focus on the "ideal"—that is, on relationships that are defined by
egalitarianism and mutuality, not by webs of exchange that turn
gifts into a never-ending cycle of repayment and debt.[31] (2) There
is also evidence to suggest that the economic sharing Luke portrays draws on motifs from speculative longing for a utopian
"golden age"—a return to a paradisal Greek past. Read against
this backdrop, Luke's summary might mark an idyllic state, a new
beginning for humanity. (3) Within the patterns of Palestinian life
roughly contemporary with the early Christian community, there
are remarkable instances of property sharing, especially among
the Essenes and at Qumran.[32] Interpreted within these horizons,

29. *Contra*, e.g., Barry Gordon, *The Economic Problem in Biblical and Patristic
Thought*, Supplements to Vigiliae Christianae 9 (Leiden: E. J. Brill, 1989), 77–
81. When José Porfirio Miranda (*Communism in the Bible* [Maryknoll, N.Y.:
Orbis, 1982], 7) asserts with reference to 2:44–45; 4:32, 34–35, "If they
wanted to be Christians the condition was communism," is he engaged in
wordplay? Luke portrays disinvestment of the means of production, not re-
distribution or common ownership!

30. That is, we take ἐπίπρασκον as a customary imperfect.

31. For the weaving of economic factors with models of friendship, see,
e.g., Peter Garnsey and Richard Saller, *The Roman Empire: Economy, Society and
Culture* (Berkeley: University of California Press, 1987), 148–59.

32. For friendship, see, e.g., Aristotle *Nicomachean Ethics* 9.8.2 §1168b;
David Peter Seccombe, *Possessions and the Poor in Luke–Acts*, Studies of the
New Testament and Its World B6 (Linz, Austria: Fuchs, 1982), 200–209;
Jacques Dupont, "Community of Goods in the Early Church," in *The Salva-*

the voluntary character of the koinonia that Luke portrays would be underscored. Equally important, if not more so, would be the premium placed on concern and care for the needy, giving in the form of alms—for which there existed no material analogue in the Greco-Roman world.[33] Which of these provides *the* background for the economic koinonia portrayed here? All were within the potential ken of those in Luke's discourse situation, so it is impossible (and unnecessary) to accord privilege to one exclusively over another. More fundamental is that each punctuates in its own way the fundamental importance Luke allocates to his portrait of this community of believers as an extended kin-group. Within Luke's world, this would entail, among other things, loyalty and trust, truth-telling (see 5:1–11!), open homes and shared tables (see v. 46), care for the needy, and a sense of shared destiny.

An additional word will underscore the degree to which numerous threads of the Lukan narrative have come together in the economic sharing of the community. (1) In Acts 2, Luke demonstrates that the pentecostal outpouring of the Spirit signifies nothing less than the eschatological restoration of God's people.[34] Given that, for the narrator, the gift of the Spirit has as its imme-

---

tion of the Gentiles: Studies in the Acts of the Apostles (New York: Paulist, 1979), 85–102 (here 89–91, 102); Alan C. Mitchell, "The Social Function of Friendship in Acts 2:44–47 and 4:32–37," *Journal of Biblical Literature* 111 (1992): 255–72. For Greek utopianism, see, e.g., David Mealand, "Community of Goods and Utopian Allusions in Acts 2–4," *Journal of Theological Studies* 28 (1977): 96–99; Brian J. Capper, "Reciprocity and the Ethic of Acts," in *Witness to the Gospel: The Theology of Acts,* ed. I. Howard Marshall and David Peterson (Grand Rapids: Eerdmans, 1998), 499–518 (here, 504–12). For Palestinian life, see, e.g., Mealand, "Community of Goods"; Brian J. Capper, "The Palestinian Cultural Context of Earliest Christian Community of Goods," in *The Book of Acts in Its Palestinian Setting,* ed. Richard Bauckham, The Book of Acts in Its First Century Setting 4 (Grand Rapids: Eerdmans, 1995), 323–64; Kyoung-Jin Kim, *Stewardship and Almsgiving in Luke's Theology,* Journal for the Study of the New Testament Supplement Series 155 (Sheffield: Sheffield Academic Press, 1998), 234–52.

33. See Gildas Hamel, *Poverty and Charity in Roman Palestine, First Three Centuries C.E.,* University of California Publications: Near Eastern Studies 23 (Berkeley: University of California Press, 1990); Peter Brown, *Poverty and Leadership in the Later Roman Empire,* The Menahem Stern Jerusalem Lectures (Hanover, N.H.: University Press of New England, 2002).

34. See Max Turner, *Power from on High: The Spirit in Israel's Restoration and Witness in Luke–Acts,* Journal of Pentecostal Theology Supplement Series 9 (Sheffield: Sheffield Academic Press, 1996).

diate sequella these characteristic behaviors of the community,[35] it is clear already within this chapter of Acts that economic koinonia is an identity marker of restored Israel. (2) We could push further still, though, to observe how Luke has prepared us for this reading by means of Jesus' teaching on and practices regarding money and meals. From his inaugural address in Luke 4:16–30 to the meal on his last evening with his disciples (Luke 22:24–27), Jesus worked to show how table fellowship and economic sharing without regard to issues of status were expressions of the gospel of the kingdom of God. "Good news to the poor" is correlated with "the year of the Lord's favor" in Jesus' reading of Isaiah's promise of Israel's restoration (Luke 4:18–19), and this is now manifest concretely in the life of the community of believers. A glance forward, to the parallel summary in Acts 4:32–35, collaborates this perspective, since there Luke characterizes community practices with language from Deuteronomy 15: "[T]here was no needy person among them." This was to have been a qualification of God's people delivered from Egypt in the exodus; it is now the qualification of God's people restored in the New Exodus.

The practice of "breaking bread," mentioned in verse 42, is mirrored in verse 46, with additional qualifiers. As noted above, "breaking bread" appears in apposition to presence in the temple. What these believers were doing in the temple is unspecified, though one can imagine participation in activity typically associated with the temple, including set prayers and teaching/discussion in the temple courts. "Persisting in their unity" in this context, though, suggests the importance of delineating an identity as "believers" that would not be "typical" of common Judaism. The only clue about the shape of that identity in this immediate narrative setting is Luke's reference to "breaking bread." Within Second Temple Judaism it would not have been unusual to locate worship-related activity in the home; what is remarkable is that such activity is focused not on one's own house but in the various houses of believers. Hospitality thus moves into the fore as a cornerstone of the community of believers, with the sharing of food serving as one form of the economic koinonia noted in verses 44–45.

35. See especially Matthias Wenk, *Community-Forming Power: The Socio-Ethical Role of the Spirit in Luke–Acts,* Journal of Pentecostal Theology Supplement Series 19 (Sheffield: Sheffield Academic Press, 2000), 259–73.

The phrase "sharing of food" is shorthand for a well-developed cultural script, including the satiation of hunger (including that of the genuinely needy), of course, though signaling as well the sharing of lives—intimacy and kinship. The adverb "joyfully" situates this meal-sharing in the context of the larger experience of salvation,[36] whereas "unpretentiously" speaks to the coherence between the gospel and the practice of sharing food.[37] More specifically, just as the gospel is proffered without reference to matters of relative religious purity or social status, so meals were shared freely, without expectation of reciprocity, without concern for purity and status. The counsel Jesus had provided in Luke 14:1–24 regarding invitations to luncheons and seating arrangements—that is, his abrogation of conventions typical of meals in Roman antiquity—had found a home in the early community.

A number of interpreters have found in "the breaking of bread" a reference to the Eucharist or Lord's Supper, but this is improbable.[38] (1) Luke makes no mention in this context of the saving significance of the death of Jesus, the interpretive words associated with the Lord's Supper (cf. 1 Cor. 11:23–26), or the use of wine. (2) "Breaking bread" belongs to the normal ritual involved in beginning a meal in a Jewish household: taking the bread in one's hands, offering a prayer of thanksgiving to God, breaking the bread, and distributing it to those gathered around the table (cf. Luke 9:16). The line to be drawn, then, is not so much from "breaking bread" to "Eucharist," but from Jesus' patterns of table fellowship, on display throughout the Third Gospel, to practices of table fellowship in Acts.[39]

36. The term Luke uses, ἀγαλλίασις, is used elsewhere of joy at the advent of salvation—cf. Luke 1:44; 2:10; 10:17.

37. For the combination, ἀφελότης + καρδία, cf. *Testament of Simeon* 4:5; *Testament of Issachar* 3:8: "integrity of heart."

38. A growing number of interpreters now argue against a eucharistic interpretation of this "breaking bread"—e.g., David Peterson, "The Worship of the New Community," in *Witness to the Gospel: The Theology of Acts,* ed. I. Howard Marshall and David Peterson (Grand Rapids: Eerdmans, 1998), 373–95 (here, 392–93); Brad Blue, "The Influence of Jewish Worship on Luke's Presentation of the Early Church," in Marshall and Peterson, *Witness to the Gospel,* 473–97 (here, 488–89).

39. The importance of this connection will become clear further into the narrative, when it becomes apparent that Jesus' followers have failed to model their table practices on his (e.g., Acts 10:1–11:18; cf. Philip Francis Esler, *Community and Gospel in Luke–Acts: The Social and Political Motivations of*

"The prayers" (v. 42) finds its primary counterpart in the reference in verse 47 to "praising God," though the mention of the temple in verse 46 is also suggestive in this regard (cf. Luke 24:53). There is, however, no reason to limit prayer to the temple, especially given the explicit mention of homes as centers of activity in verse 46 (cf. 4:24–31). As these first believers are depicted by Luke as Jewish, there is also no reason to assume that "the prayers" refers to anything other than the patterns of prayer associated with Jews during this period. Unfortunately, however, we know little of the specifics of those patterns.[40] One innovation may already be recognized, though. This is that prayers will have been offered to the Lord Jesus, since his is the name on which persons are to call for salvation. At this juncture, more important than specifying the *content* of their prayer is this affirmation that the believers were devoted to prayer. For Luke, prayer is the means by which Jesus' identity is manifest, God's purpose is disclosed, and people align themselves with God's plans; prayer embodies the community's deepest convictions and essential commitments, and it is by means of prayer that the community is actually transformed so as to embrace more fully and to serve God's purpose.[41]

The outward focus of the early community is evident both in its praising God and in its gracious dispositions toward "all the people." Although almost universally translated as a reference to the popularity of the community among the people,[42] Luke's phrase has the opposite nuance: The believers are agents of God's benefaction to the larger community.[43] The effect of the outpouring of

---

Lucan Theology, Society of New Testament Studies Monograph Series 57 [Cambridge: Cambridge University Press, 1987], 71–109).

40. The data are surveyed in Daniel K. Falk, "Jewish Prayer Literature and the Jerusalem Church in Acts," in Bauckham, *Book of Acts in Its Palestinian Setting,* 267–301.

41. See Joel B. Green, "Persevering Together in Prayer: The Significance of Prayer in the Acts of the Apostles," in *Into God's Presence: Prayer in the New Testament,* ed. Richard N. Longenecker, McMaster New Testament Studies (Grand Rapids: Eerdmans, 2001), 183–202.

42. E.g., ASV, ESV, NAB, NAS, NIV, NJB, NLT, NRSV.

43. So also T. David Andersen, "The Meaning of ΕΧΟΝΤΕΣ ΧΑΡΙΝ ΠΡΟΣ in Acts 2.47," *New Testament Studies* 34 (1988): 604–10; F. P. Cheetham, "Acts ii.47: ἔχοντες χάριν πρὸς ὅλον τὸν λαόν," *Expository Times* 74 (1962–63): 214–15. For the notion of "favor from," compare the syntax of Luke 1:30; Acts 7:46.

the Spirit is realized not only in the interior life of the community of believers, but also in its ongoing missionary stance toward the larger world. Verse 47b may therefore be read in tandem with verse 47c: Grace for all people is related to the continued growth of the community. Luke's final sentence is important in several respects. (1) This last phrase is modeled after verse 41, suggesting that the faithful, everyday life of the community (that is, embodying and demonstrating the gospel in our practices) is effective for numerical growth in the same way that missionary preaching is. (Note the repetition of "daily" in verses 46–47.) (2) Luke's reference to "adding" to the community is remarkably nondescriptive. How are people added? We are left to fill in the gaps by drawing on the immediate context, in Acts 2:38: Repentance, baptism, forgiveness, and the reception of the Holy Spirit are all assumed. (3) Reference to "being saved" is reminiscent of verses 21 and 40, suggesting that the "Lord" who is adding to the community is none other than the exalted Jesus. The community's growth is the Lord's doing. Just as he poured out the Spirit, whose work gave rise to the faithful behaviors enumerated in this summary of the community's life, so the Lord adds to the membership of that community those who respond to his grace.

Epilogue

From the perspective developed here, a narrative text like Acts 2:42–47 can serve as the center of the preaching event, provided that our camera lens widens sufficiently to reveal the concentric circles within which it resides. Articulated as a series of contexts, these would include:

- its immediate context, as the climax of the pentecostal outpouring of the Spirit and as an interpretive heading for the narrative material to follow in Acts 3–5;
- the wider narrative that Luke relates, from preparations for the advent of Jesus through the ministry of Paul in Rome, as a description of the normal and expected practices of the community of Jesus' followers, endowed with the Spirit of God; and
- the still-wider narrative within which Luke–Acts itself is situated, the story of exile and New Exodus, with the

outpouring of the Spirit and its manifestation in the
community demonstrative of the eschatological work of
God to restore his people.

A focus more narrowly on Luke's summary description of the life
of the early church, concerned as it must be with the specific behaviors and dispositions it enumerates, should not mask the reality that those specific behaviors and dispositions take their meaning from the wider story within which salvation is being realized.

My analysis of this passage has undertaken especially to explore
how Acts 2:42–47 might be read within scripturally interested and
shaped horizons—that is, within the horizons of an imagination
shaped by the biblical story. It is clear that the outpouring of the
Holy Spirit and the Spirit's presence and activity in the community of believers is exhibited in a certain quality of the life of that
community. It is also clear that this community and, therefore, the
nature of both the interactions within its boundaries and the witness it broadcasts in the wider world find their identity in and are
constituted by its practices. Now the homiletical challenge rests in
crafting sermons that draw persons into this imaginative world,
initiate persons into this story, and invite them to make their
home here, with the result that their dispositions and practices
similarly exhibit the character of God's work of liberation and
restoration.

3

Whose Story?
Preaching the Gospels and Acts

Michael Pasquarello III

Old habits are not easily shed. As a product of American Protestantism, a church whose way of reading Scripture has been shaped by a gospel of "effectiveness" through stories of success or survival, my initial intuition was to approach Acts 2 to discover something that would "work" in my sermon. After reading Joel Green's chapter, "Reading the Gospels and Acts as Narrative," however, I was reminded of how much we preachers need the accountability provided by a community of interpretation. Unfortunately, I cannot remember any of my seminary professors admonishing us pastors-in-training to prepare for preaching by conversing with others engaged in reading Christian Scripture in the service of the church. We were typically left on our own to conclude that interpreting the Bible for preaching is simply a pragmatic affair, a matter of individual skill, talent, technique, creativity, and expertise applied according to personal preference or style.

Green's work on Acts 2:42–47 helps us to recognize the subtle, but powerful, cultural message that offers repeated assurance that the stories of our lives are our own. For example, during an initial reading of this text in Acts my inclinations were quickly pulled in the direction of the contemporary preoccupation with creating "community" and our frantic search for new means of evangelism to facilitate "church growth." Indeed, a quick, surface reading of Acts 2 reveals a wonderful story that possesses great homiletic po-

tential for successfully illustrating and communicating these relevant topics to contemporary listeners.

By following a mode of apologetic preaching, it would only require a few easy moves to construct a "relevant" sermon, using
Acts 2 as an illustration of the church's utility and value in providing "community" for lonely, isolated, postmodern seekers. As an
added homiletic bonus, the text also provides a strong platform for
sounding the alarm to awaken sleepy, complacent church folks,
alerting them to the urgent need to accept change and adopt new
means and methods to make declining churches grow and growing
churches larger. I suspect the initial "sermon starters" that flooded
my mind were rather typical, a familiar way of viewing Scripture
that was challenged by Green's narrative reading, which reoriented
my attention to see Acts as *God's* story rather than *our* story.

Remembering whose story it is that we are reading—God's, not
ours—is perhaps the greatest challenge in reading and preaching
Acts. Ironically, this challenge lies precisely in its appeal to our
contemporary narrative sensibilities. As preachers we are presented with a marvelous collection of engaging, exciting, surprising, dramatic, and highly personal stories. Acts is a preacher's
treasure waiting to be mined, its riches shuttled across the
homiletic bridge running from text to sermon and deposited in
the hands of our listeners for their use.

However, as Green reminds us, it is the narrative quality of the
Book of Acts rather than its theological wisdom that has typically
captured our homiletic attention. The oft-neglected theological significance of the "story of our life" was articulated by H. R. Niebuhr:

> The preaching of the early Christian church was not an argument
> for the existence of God, or an admonition to follow the dictates of
> some common human conscience, unhistorical and super-social in
> character. It was primarily a simple recital of the great events con-
> nected with the historical appearance of Jesus Christ and a confes-
> sion of what had happened to the community of disciples. . . . What
> prompted Christians in the past to confess their faith by telling the
> story of their life was more than a need for vivid illustration or for
> analogical reasoning. Their story was not a parable, which could be
> replaced by another: it was irreplaceable and untranslatable.[1]

1. H. Richard Niebuhr, "The Story of Our Life," in *Why Narrative? Readings in Narrative Theology,* ed. Stanley Hauerwas and L. Gregory Jones (Grand
Rapids: Eerdmans, 1989), 20, 22.

Interestingly, the theological significance of New Testament accounts of the church, particularly the Book of Acts, has often been overlooked despite the emergence of ecclesiology, the doctrine of the church, as a serious object of theological reflection. On the one hand, serious attention to ecclesiology was significant for refining our understanding of the church's identity and mission in the twentieth century. On the other hand, this development has encouraged a tendency to think about the church in isolation from Scripture and from the whole web of Christian faith and practice depicted in the economy of creation and redemption, or, what Green refers to as "God at work in the cosmos."

For many, unfortunately, the church has come to be perceived as a religious institution of our making, an organization that serves as little more than a sponsor for religious meetings and activities, a vendor of products and services that facilitate individual spiritual experiences and growth. Rather than participating in and being shaped by the biblical story, it has become fashionable to construe ecclesial identity in an abstract manner, thereby rendering the shape of its life vulnerable to images and identities provided by powerful stories told by democratic capitalism, civil religion, pop psychology, or something we cannot define but persist in calling "postmodernism." Stories like Acts 2 are seen as handy illustrations of topics and ideas that are foreign to and even at odds with their native habitat, the narrative world rendered by Scripture. As Green asserts, "It is this grand narrative that invites our participation—indeed, that creates for the faithful a way to make sense of text and world."

Closely related to the struggle to read Acts theologically, as God's story, and then, derivatively, as our story, is the importance of attending to the narrative in a manner appropriate to its relation to the "whole canonical story's beginning and end . . . rendering present in Jesus and the outpouring of the Spirit, the saving work of God." Honoring the place of Acts within the whole biblical narrative prevents us from excising Acts 2:42–47 and treating it as an isolated text, a static blueprint, that must be continually updated, revised, and applied, rather than a significant episode in the larger divine-human drama of salvation that graciously calls for our immersion and self-involvement.

By allowing the narrative logic of the whole Bible to guide our reading of Acts, we are positioned to become participants in the surprising enactment of God's promises to Israel and for the world through the consequences of Easter and Pentecost. Inhabiting this story, moreover, situates us to stand against the many competing stories that would claim our attention and our lives, thereby precluding a need to reinvent the church in forms accommodated to contemporary versions of reality. As members of a people whose corporate life is scripted by indwelling the world of the biblical narrative, we are thus positioned to challenge these alternative stories by asking, What god(s) do they serve; what ends, or destinies, do they promise? As Green advises, "Relocated within such grand stories, even the most exquisite and weighty biblical account is neutered of its theological potency and made to serve agendas not at all at home within the Bible."

Telling the Story

If our first task as interpreters of Acts is to remember whose narrative it is that we are reading, our task as preachers is to remember that we who tell the story are committed participants rather than detached observers. Our interest, therefore, is less in getting back into the world that produced Acts, the New Testament, and the Old Testament—the history "behind" the text— than getting ourselves into the world produced by Scripture, which, in the following sermon, is at the particular place in the drama identified as the Acts of the Apostles.

In preparing this sermon, the basic question I have asked has not been, How can I make this ancient book interesting or useful for modern listeners? but rather, What is this story doing to change our thinking, willing, and living as God's people? This way of reading is a form of listening, of obedience, which requires that we approach the biblical text with a willingness to be taught, challenged, confronted, humbled, and converted. And, if our vocation as preachers is to inhabit and speak God's story of salvation as told in Scripture, should we expect anything less to happen to us, or our people?

The first half of my sermon, then, simply tells the story of Christ and the church in a manner that situates the particular narrative of Acts 2:42–47 within Luke's account of the whole sweep of God's restorative dealings with Israel that culminated in the cross, resurrection, and ascension of Jesus, and his giving of the Spirit.

This larger narrative world is of particular importance for displaying Easter, the resurrection of the crucified Jesus, as neither a religious idea that needs to be explained or illustrated, nor as an experience limited exclusively to the past or future. Surprisingly, Easter is a present, concrete reality that embraces us. We are being incorporated into the story of the risen, exalted Lord, who, in the Spirit's power, indwells and sustains the church as a people whose destiny is the life of the Triune God.

This way of telling the story attempts to be faithful to both the theological and pastoral aims articulated by the apostolic witness through the Book of Acts. In Acts 2, the narrative recounting of Pentecost identifies the distinctive character of an eschatological (end-time) community created by the exalted Jesus through the Spirit's power. In addition, Peter's pentecostal proclamation engenders a fresh call to embodied memory and hope—through the story of Jesus and the witness of Israel's Scripture—in communal practices of resurrection. Thus, in the larger story of God's purposes and promises, the significance of Acts 2 lies not only behind us in the past, but, in a truly eschatological sense, still remains ahead of us through its authoritative rendering of God's future being made present in a people who witness to what God is doing in and for a divided, fragmented world.

Continuing the Story

Because the Word of God is communicated through Acts 2 in a particular textual form, telling its story requires that we re-narrate the lives of our listeners into its particular world and its customs, language, wisdom, and practices. If, as Green has argued, Acts 2 renders an authoritative depiction of our Christian common life, created at God's initiative, then we must confidently tell this *particular story*, since its narrative demonstrates the power of the Word, accompanied by the Spirit, as sufficient to effect what it declares. On the one hand, it is the gospel, through the apostles' witness to the God of Israel and Jesus Christ, which constitutes the church through teaching and doing; on the other hand, it is the fidelity of the church, enacted through forms of communal speech and activity inherited from Israel through the ministry of Jesus and the Spirit, that is constitutive of the gospel. It is the whole community in Acts 2 and the subsequent narrative that preaches through a distinctive way of life shared with Christ in the Spirit. As Acts 3–5 shows, it is only by continuing in this distinctive way of life that the community remains positioned to remember, receive, and respond to Christ, led by the Spirit to embody a faithful, confident witness to the reign of God in new situations and challenges

Because we preachers continually struggle to remain at home in the particular story of Acts, the sermon includes an example of seeker-oriented evangelism, which offers an alternative identity shaped by powerful stories that grip our culture: consumerism, self-importance, personal taste, economic and class distinctions. To counter this trend, I have also included an account of David, a high school senior who was converted through his participation in a youth ministry committed to ordering its life according to the pattern of Acts 2. The sermon, however, offers nothing in the way of illustrations, since the meaning of the story is only grasped through its concrete, communal enactment. There is no "higher" or "deeper" meaning that lies beyond or behind the text; there is no additional understanding waiting to be made intelligible by our superior homiletic insight or skill.

Thus the primary homiletic aim of my sermon is informed by Green's suggestion that preaching from the narrative of Acts should seek to "draw persons into this imaginative world, initiate persons into this story . . . and invite them to make their home here, with the result that their dispositions and practices similarly exhibit the character of God's work and restoration."

To accomplish this purpose, the following sermon was preached in the conviction that since the church is a creation of the ministry of Christ in the Spirit's power, we are members of the people produced by his resurrection. Just as through Christ and in the Spirit's power God's story is the story of the first Christian community, so too, through our incorporation into Christ and the church in baptism, their story is our story. By beginning with the announcement that the exalted Christ bestows our identity, which is God, given in the Spirit, the sermon calls listeners to take up the practices of resurrection with fresh commitment, thereby continuing the story of Easter people, the adventure of an alternative community that signals the appearance of God's new creation in the midst of a dying, old world.

The sermon was preached to a seminary audience during the

week following the Fourth Sunday of Easter. The liturgical context, the Great Fifty Days of Easter, informed the hymns, prayers, acts of praise, anthem, and congregational responses. The atmosphere was festive, expressing the joy evoked by God's victory over the power of sin, evil, and death through the cross and resurrection of Christ. A particular consideration in planning this service was the pervasive view that the celebration of the resurrection of Christ—Easter—is limited to one special day each year, and thus, four weeks later, might be viewed as unnecessary or redundant. Both service and sermon, however, were received and entered into with enthusiastic response.

I have preached a number of sermons from Acts 2 during twenty years of pastoral ministry. On those occasions, I have tended to place more emphasis on the particular practices described in verses 42–47, hoping to instruct and encourage lay listeners to grasp the pattern of their common life as a gift granted by the presence of the risen Christ in our midst through the Holy Spirit's work, a very practical form of "applied" ecclesiology. I have shifted the emphasis for this sermon, focusing instead on the creation of the church and its nature within the story of Israel and Christ. It was after carefully listening to the biblical narrative that I was able to discern that this approach was fitting for our seminary community. The audience was comprised of church leaders, present and future, who brought a wide range of questions, hopes, and fears related to the identity, mission, and future of the church.

⁂

Easter People—Acts 2:42–47

My name is Pasquarello. Now, I learned at a pretty early age this is not the easiest name to pronounce or spell. In fact, as a pastor, each time I moved to a new congregation I would introduce myself by teaching folks to spell my name like this: PA + SQUARE + LLO. But what is most important to me about my name is its literal meaning: "Little Lamb" or "Little Easter," since it reminds me of our Christian identity.

Have you thought about our name lately—"Christian"? It means "the ones who belong to Christ," those whose identity is given and shaped by the crucified and risen Son of God.

We are gathered in the presence of God and the world to remember and celebrate our identity as Easter people. Does this sound strange to you? Are you wondering whether I have lost all sense of time, whether I have forgotten that Easter Sunday has already come and gone for this year, having passed us by even earlier than Tax Day, April 15th? Well, I have not.

As Easter people we acknowledge that the overflowing abundance of God's reign is so extravagant that our celebration of God's victory in Christ cannot be limited to one Sunday. The new reality that burst upon the world in the resurrection of crucified Jesus is so grand, so glorious, and so far-reaching, that we devote fifty days to its celebration. Assembled by the risen Christ whom we worship, we are being incorporated into God's grand story of salvation that climaxed in the dramatic events of resurrection, ascension, and sending of the Spirit to create a new people called church.

What if Easter marks the beginning of a renewed telling of the old biblical story that began with old Abraham and Sarah? What if God, the maker of heaven and earth, is now present, alive, and loose in the world in the person of the risen Jesus and through the Spirit's power, accomplishing his good purposes? What if he is here with us this morning? Have you come expecting to meet him; have you come expecting to hear his voice calling us to imagine ourselves as inhabitants of a new creation: Easter people?

According to our story in Acts 2, resurrection is not merely about the rescue of the dead body of Jesus, as an individual person, from the grave. Peter announces that through the obedience and death of Jesus, God has appointed him Lord and Christ, and the Savior of all nations. Peter's pentecostal preaching makes this clear for us, that the resurrection and exaltation of Jesus is the action of God according to his promise to give Israel repentance and the forgiveness of sins.

And this is not just an event in the past, but a gift, which, under the sign and power of baptism, continues to draw us into its life-changing movement and force. We are the fruit of the cross and resurrection, and the Holy Spirit continues to communicate the life of the risen Christ for our participation in God's mission to the world. We are Easter people.

I have preached for my share of Easter community sunrise services. But the one I will always remember was conducted in a cemetery, which, by the way, is a wonderful place to stage a celebration of God's victory over the power of death. We were gathered on a small hill overlooking a pond. The pulpit sat at the top of the hill, where it was flanked on either side by rows of large azalea bushes. Robin, my wife, had invited Sharon, our next-door neighbor, to join us, since she had never attended an Easter sunrise service. As I got up to preach, Sharon leaned over and said, "Robin, wouldn't it be cool if someone dressed up like Jesus could come hopping out of those bushes just like the Easter Bunny."

Now, I don't know whether Sharon was serious, but her way of thinking about resurrection is not very different from that of many preachers, is it? Don't we treat resurrection as one of those strange, "irrelevant" Christian concepts that our culture no longer understands? Don't we roll it out one Sunday of the year with a whole lot of fanfare and fuss, explaining it, illustrating it, and, finally, rendering it "meaningful" in terms accommodated to our listeners' "understanding" to fit into the "comfortable" world of their experience?

And having "effectively" accomplished our goal, do we not pack up and put away the whole thing until next spring, relieved that it is over, so we can get back to the real business of running and growing the church?

Our story says that Christ, the risen Lord, can neither be packed up nor put away. The powers of this world, the religious and political rulers who thought they were in charge, that they had everything and everyone under control, even Jesus, nailed him up on a cross and shut him up in a tomb. And this act was not simply the solemn burial of a dead man; it was the ancient world's equivalent of erasing a person's identity. You know how it goes, "out of sight and out of mind." Yet listen to Peter's defiant declaration: "But God raised him from the dead, freeing him from the agony of death, because it was impossible for death to keep its hold on him."

But let's be honest. We live in a world that cannot see the One who we believe holds its destiny in his good and gracious hands. Many believe that Jesus is now dead and gone, out of sight and out of mind, nothing more than the "historical Jesus" of academia. But according to our story, the world is capable of seeing communities where the risen Christ dwells: Easter people who gather to worship him, to confess that the claims his story has made on their lives are higher and even more compelling than those made by all other names and authorities, in heaven and on earth.

Let's think about this for a minute. How often have you heard the whole story of Easter to include both the risen Christ *and* his church, the Lord *and* the people raised up with him by the Spirit of God?

Although it is true that the resurrection of Jesus gives hope for our own resurrection from death, this is neither the primary story told by the Gospels, nor the central theme of the apostolic proclamation in Acts. Moreover, the Spirit-driven preaching of the apostles not only identifies the God who raised Jesus. It also renders the promise of a new heaven and a new earth, which, under the Lordship of Christ, is already taking shape in our life as the people in whom his Spirit dwells.

And because we live in a world where the God of Israel and Jesus is busily at work making good on his promises, the future is never completely closed or fixed according to the way things are, not even to the claims of the rulers of this world. We now live by the "long view" of things as seen through the lens of the whole biblical story. Because our God has been faithful to his promises in the past, we have hope that he will be faithful to his promises again.

And so the story of Acts is our stubborn refusal to keep quiet and accept the world as unalterably given, since for Christian people the world so depicted by the biblical narrative is the one, true, real world now that Jesus has gone up to rule. And the good news is that the more we talk about, sing about, and tell stories about this God-given world, the more the world of resurrection with Jesus and in the Spirit becomes our own, identifying us as its participants, actors, and witnesses.

So let's look at the world depicted in Acts 2. It is a story both "writ large" and directed to a particular audience. It is set on the wider stage of human history, but spoken to the faithful of renewed Israel. This story takes us from the originating plan of God, through exodus and the covenant with Israel, to its center point in the life, death, resurrection, and ascension of Christ, and finally, to its chapters on the birth of the church and the coming of salvation.

This is where we assume our place in the drama. We now live in what the ancient church called the "Eighth Day of Creation."

Our parts in the story are shaped by our participation in the Spirit-filled practices given for Israel's Torah way of life and fulfilled in the ministry of Jesus. These practices are the means through which Christ graciously gives himself to us and marks us as his own, but they are also practices by which we gratefully offer and mark ourselves as belonging to him. These "means of grace" are the way we receive and respond to Christ, the Living Word who invites us to become participants in the mission he shares with the Father and the Spirit. And if we follow this script in our performance of church, it will not be just a short-term high, but a long-term commitment, a dramatic and enduring enactment of history's ultimate meaning and hope in the Triune God.

Contrary to the message of other stories that compete to shape our imagination and identity, the practices of resurrection are not optional for Easter people. Praying, attending to the apostles' teaching, welcoming strangers, loving one another, breaking bread, and caring for the needy—these all are God-given activities through which we learn and are formed to praise God and to bless the world. Acts 2 is neither a blueprint dug up from the past nor a puzzle to figure out and apply to our contemporary situation. It is our story, an authoritative depiction of the ordinary assembling of Christ's followers whose dramatic, persistent performance of this script carried the gospel from Jerusalem to Rome, and finally, to the ends of the earth. And this story continues today in our hearing and doing.

Sad to say, if you take a look around at many of our congregations, especially those with their full menus of programs and activities, one suspects that ecclesiastical busyness, warm-hearted socializing, and the latest fashions and styles are being offered in place of apostolic substance. Where is the Spirit-empowered discipleship that creates a people, shaped by following Christ in the way of the cross?

For example, a mailing sent out by a successful "seeker-oriented" church plant proudly announced, "Finding a church home doesn't take a leap of faith." It goes on to offer, in addition to coffee and doughnuts, a church home that requires just a small step to discover some of "the most meaningful connections" that can make daily life richer and more significant. Interestingly, God is nowhere mentioned.

Here is "contemporary" church shaped by an updated version

of an old story told by a culture saturated by consumerism. Here is an evangelistic strategy articulated in the language of advertising, announcing that nothing has changed in our cultural status quo of self-improvement and fulfillment.

And here is a way of identifying church read through the story of familiar social and economic arrangements, but which ignores the "strange, new world" rendered by Acts. Here is a story that identifies us as individuals in search of "connections" to improve or enrich our lives, rather than a people, lovingly sought by God, who will return his love, embodying a way of life that displays his saving purposes for the whole world.

Thank God! If we may make our home in the biblical story, we may do so with the assurance that Jesus, our crucified and risen Lord, has lavished upon us the overflowing love of the Triune God who desires to share his life with the world. And because God's love is beyond all measure, his gifts are measured neither by our seeking nor our strategies: The life of God is sheer gift, the abundance of his grace; it is simply God-given.

Perhaps God is reminding us that, when it is all said and done, only "one thing is needful." What if church is not primarily something we do or design, but something God does according to his loving design to re-create the whole cosmos for his glory? What if our part in the Easter story is a gift, received through our faithful performance of the script, following the Spirit's direction?

My friend David was in middle school when I was appointed to serve the congregation where his family attended. He did not belong to the youth group in those days, claiming he wasn't interested, that he was entirely too busy doing other things. As his mother would occasionally tell me, "David is going to try out the group one night when he is not busy running for president of the United States, or whatever he has decided to be when he grows up." She was serious. David was a gifted, talented, award-winning student, athlete, musician, and leader. As far as he was concerned, he didn't need our youth group, and he didn't give us the time of day.

After a couple of years he started to show up on Sunday nights. I am not exactly sure why, but he kept coming back for the entire school year, continuing through the summer. I will never forget a particular night when we were sitting around on the floor in our youth room, a group of about fifty to sixty kids and ten or so adults. It was an extended time of Christian fellowship, devoted to study and prayer, to confession and accountability. Finally, David spoke up. He told us that before coming to the group he had been very skeptical about the God stuff, since he thought what Christians claim as true just wasn't sufficiently reasonable nor advantageous to his career ambitions.

He went on to speak of his first year with us; of the times studying Scripture, praying, singing, and praising God; of serving on mission projects; of bearing one another's burdens and celebrating one another's joys; of sharing meals and welcoming strangers and guests like himself into our community. Finally, David confessed that he now believed himself to be Christian. Looking around the room, he addressed the whole group, "You have made a believer out of me."

As Luke tells the story,

> Everyone had a sense of awe, and many wonders and signs were being done through the apostles. Those who believed all joined in solidarity and held all things in common. They would sell their property and possessions and distribute them to everyone according to each person's need. Everyday, while persisting in their unity in the temple, they were breaking bread in each other's homes— sharing food joyfully and unpretentiously, praising God and having goodwill toward all the people. And the Lord was adding daily to the community those who were being saved.

Perhaps the best pastoral wisdom for our time is simply this: that we assemble the church around the particular story of God to perform the practices of resurrection that create our identity as Easter people in and for the world. Amen.

4

Reading the Letters as Narrative

James W. Thompson

In *Homiletic,* David Buttrick distinguishes between preaching in the mode of immediacy and preaching in the reflective mode. These two modes of preaching correspond to the genres of narrative and letter. According to Buttrick, one preaches a story in the mode of immediacy, following the plotline of the biblical narrative and adding a theological dimension to accompany the unfolding story. In the reflective mode, one conveys "a patterned field of contemporary understanding" from the text. Because the epistles are products of reflective consciousness, they lend themselves to preaching in the reflective mode.[1]

Buttrick's analysis corresponds to the recent emphasis in homiletic theory on preaching in the form of the text. As a reaction to the older homiletic that regarded all genres as receptacles for theological ideas, advocates of the new homiletic recognized that genre is a mode of revelation and that the task of the preacher is to "do what the text does." The result of this new emphasis was the sharp demarcation between narrative and reflective texts—between Gospels and epistles, for example—and the new enthusiasm for narrative preaching and narrative texts. Homileticians argued what most preachers know from their own experience: that stories sustain interest, provide anticipation, and allow listeners to identify their personal stories with that of the participants in the biblical narratives. Consequently, despite the fact that twenty-

1. David Buttrick, *Homiletic: Moves and Structures* (Philadelphia: Fortress, 1987), 367.

two of the twenty-seven books of the New Testament are letters,[2] the preaching canon has increasingly consisted of the Gospels, Acts, and the Old Testament narratives. In the popular mind, the letters belong more to the graduate seminar than to the pulpit.

One may note the reasons for the decline of letters from the preaching canon. In the first place, the letters are widely considered abstract and theological. Paul is commonly regarded as the second founder of Christianity, who turned the simple stories of Jesus into abstract theological categories. He is perceived "as the prototypical instance of a thinker for whom narrative expressions of Christian faith are in principle insignificant."[3] Although the epistles are good reference works on the great theological themes— christology, atonement, pneumatology, and ecclesiology—they are, in the estimation of many, far removed from the actual concerns of the people in the pew.

A second reason that epistles present a formidable challenge for preaching is that the historical-critical reading learned in seminary and communicated in the commentaries focuses primarily on the history behind the text: authorship, the identity of opponents, the literary integrity of the letter, and the traditions that lie behind the letter. In 2 Corinthians 5, for example, the weight of the literature has concerned the analysis of what the text reveals about Paul's opposition ("were they ecstatics?" cf. 5:13), the presence or absence of creedal material behind the passage (e.g., 2 Cor. 5:14, 19), and the historical background of Paul's theological categories.

Although one may legitimately read the letters as witnesses to the history behind the text or as documents of early Christian theology, these are not the only questions that we may ask of the text, for the believing community has its own questions. Just as few come to worship eagerly wanting to learn "what happened to the Jebusites,"[4] even less come wanting lectures on abstract theology

2. For the purposes of this discussion, I include Hebrews and Revelation as letters. Although Hebrews is generally classified as a homily and Revelation as an apocalypse, both include epistolary characteristics (Heb. 13:18–25; Revelation 1–3).

3. Richard Hays, *The Faith of Jesus Christ: The Narrative Substructure of Galatians 3:1–4:11*, 2d ed. (Grand Rapids: Eerdmans, 2002), 209.

4. Cf. Harry Emerson Fosdick, "What Is the Matter with Preaching?" *Harper's* 107, July 1928, 135.

or on the opponents of Paul in 2 Corinthians. The church assembles to hear a word that is "useful for teaching" (2 Tim. 3:16). My purpose here is to propose a reading of the letters as Scripture that moves beyond the categories that have marginalized them in the life of the church. Although the historical-critical method remains indispensable for biblical studies, the reading of the letters as Scripture requires that we hear them as sermons written to communities that faced issues that would determine the destiny of the church. I intend to demonstrate, in the first place, that epistles have a narrative dimension insofar as they propose an ongoing story. This understanding of the narrative dimension opens the way for reclaiming the epistles for the pulpit. In the second place, I illustrate this narrative dimension with an exegesis of 2 Cor. 5:11–6:2, which contains the pericope chosen by Buttrick as an illustration of preaching in the reflective mode.[5] I conclude with a reflection on the significance of this approach for appropriating the letters as Scripture.

No passage is more daunting for the preacher than 2 Cor. 5:11–6:2. Almost every line has been the subject of theological debate. For ancient writers the phrase "God was in Christ" was central to incarnational and trinitarian discussion.[6] The soteriological language of the passage has also occupied theologians for centuries. At the beginning, Paul says, "One has died for all; therefore all have died" (5:14). Near the end of the unit he speaks in words that later became a classic formulation of the atonement: "In Christ God was reconciling the world to himself, not counting their trespasses against them . . ." (5:19), then adds, "He made him to be sin who knew no sin, so that in him we might become the righteousness of God" (5:21). Bultmann found a major christological statement in the phrase κατὰ σάρκα χριστός (*kata sarka christos*, "Christ from a human point of view"; translated by Bult-

5. As I demonstrate below, Buttrick's choice of 2 Cor. 5:17–21 is problematic, inasmuch as it ignores the complete thought unit comprised of 5:11–6:2. Consequently, the logic of the movement of the text is lost when one severs 5:17–21 from the immediate context of (1) Paul's discussion of his ministry and (2) his reference to his new epistemology in 5:16. As I argue below, the *inclusio* in 5:11–13 and 5:20b–6:2 marks the boundaries of the passage.

6. See texts in R. Bieringer, "2 Korinther 5,19a und die Versöhnung der Welt," in *Studies on 2 Corinthians,* ed. R. Bieringer and J. Lambrecht (Louvain: Louvain University Press, 1994), 439; reprinted from *Ephemerides theologicae lovanienses* 63 (1987): 295–326.

mann as the "human Christ" or "Christ according to the flesh"; v. 16).[7] The reference to the "new creation" (5:17) also sets off theological sirens that call for explanation, raising questions about the nature of Pauline eschatology. One observes reflective discourse also in the pattern of logical argumentation. After Paul states his purpose in 5:12, he proceeds with the language of argumentation: γάρ (*gar*, "for"; vv. 13, 14), ὥστε (*hōste*, "so that"; vv. 16, 17), δέ (*de*, "and, but"; v. 18), and διο (*dio*, "therefore"; vv. 20, 21). Anyone who makes a sharp demarcation between reflection and narrative is likely to conclude that this passage belongs to theological reflection, not to narrative.

Reading and Preaching the Letters as Narratives

The recognition that the shape of the biblical text is significant for preaching as well as exegesis has brought us to see the importance of variety both in the biblical witness and preaching. A genre is a specific way of viewing reality, and an author chooses one genre and not another in order to visualize a certain reality.[8] As E. D. Hirsch observed, "Coming to understand the meaning of an utterance is like learning the rules of a game."[9] To play the game properly one must know what game is being played. We must acknowledge, therefore, that in the reflective-theological discourse of the epistle and the indirect speech of the narrative the authors are playing different games. Letters contain direct speech by an author to the listeners, while in the narrative the speaker generally remains off-stage without addressing the audience. Letters speak directly of the referential world, while narratives reveal this world only indirectly. Letters follow a logical and argumentative sequence, while narrative sequence is determined by manipulation of chronology and plot development. Letters have a theological density that is not characteristic of narrative. These obvious differences lie behind the contemporary insistence that the preacher neither distills theol-

7. Rudolf Bultmann, "Die Bedeutung des geschichtlichen Jesus für die Theologie des Paulus," in *Glauben und Verstehen* (Tübingen: Mohr, 1954), 208.

8. James Bailey, "Genre Analysis," in *Hearing the New Testament*, ed. Joel B. Green (Grand Rapids: Eerdmans, 1995), 201.

9. E. D. Hirsch, *Validity in Interpretation* (New Haven: Yale University Press, 1967), 70.

ogy from narrative nor reads the theological discourse of the letters as narrative.

Despite these clear distinctions between letter and narrative, recent literature has demonstrated that one cannot demarcate Paul's theological analysis from his pastoral relationship to his churches, for he writes as a pastor to his churches and addresses concrete situations in the life of the church. Nor can one assume that narrative and letters inhabit totally different worlds, for they interact with each other at a variety of levels. Both modes of communication share a common denominator of narrative and discourse. In distinguishing between the plot (*mythos*) and theme (*dianoia*) of a narrative, Aristotle indicated the reflective dimension of narrative.[10] One analyzes a story, asking not only, How does the story end? but What is the point?[11] Generations of literary critics have assumed that narrative, composed of a sequence of events, also has a message. Similarly, while one may argue that narrative and letters correspond to each other as story and reflection—*mythos* and *dianoia*—recent studies have shown that letters contain both dimensions. Letters intersect with narratives in a variety of ways, for the reflective discourse of the letters is actually reflection on a narrative. One sees this reflection at several levels.

In the first place, as the continuation of Paul's conversation with his churches, the letters inhabit a world of intersecting narratives. One may note Paul's shared narrative with his churches; he stands within a plot that includes a beginning, a middle (the occasion of the letter), and a future, which the letter is intended to effect.[12] Whereas the author of a narrative assumes that the plot has been completed, Paul writes letters in order to shape the outcome of the story.[13] As the founder of his churches, he commonly refers to the occasion when he established this community of believers and describes their ultimate destiny (1 Cor. 1:26–2:5; Gal. 4:12–20; 1 Thess. 1:5–2:13). He also projects the plot into the immediate future. He anticipates a continuing intersection of his

10. Aristotle *Poetics* 1450b. See Hays, *Faith of Jesus Christ,* 22.

11. Northrop Frye, *Anatomy of Criticism* (Princeton: Princeton University Press, 1957), 52.

12. See my book, *Preaching Like Paul* (Louisville: Westminster/John Knox, 2001), 40. See also Ben Witherington III, *Paul's Narrative Thought World: The Tapestry of Tragedy and Triumph* (Grand Rapids: Eerdmans, 1994), 340.

13. Norman Petersen, *Rediscovering Paul: Philemon and the Sociology of Paul's Narrative World* (Philadelphia: Fortress, 1985), 44.

story with that of his congregations. His letters prepare the way for the visit of emissaries (Rom. 16:1–2; 1 Cor. 16:8–10; Phil. 2:19–30) or his own reunion with his congregation (Philem. 22). In the meantime, his congregations live between their new existence and their ultimate destiny in Christ.

Closely related to the actual referential history behind the text is the "narrative world" of the text. While our knowledge of the actual events and people behind the text must always be provisional, one may trace the narrative world of the text. Here one discovers the author's perception of the sequence of events.[14] For example, the events to which Paul refers in the Corinthian correspondence have a narrative quality because they comprise a selective sequence of events between which Paul posits certain links.

One may note, in the second place, the significance of Paul's own story, which he frequently recalls and always assumes (e.g., 1 Cor. 9:1–27; Gal. 1:10–2:14; Phil. 2:12–26; 3:1–11).[15] Paul's story begins with his upbringing as a Hebrew, Israelite, and descendant of Abraham (2 Cor. 11:22; cf. Rom. 9:3), and his education as a Pharisee (Phil. 3:11; Gal. 1:13–14). It reaches its turning point with his conversion/call (Gal. 1:15; 2 Cor. 4:6), when he was "taken over" (Phil. 3:12) by Christ. Paul's story remains incomplete, for he lives in anticipation of the ultimate revelation of Christ when his shared narrative with the churches reaches its destiny at the day of Christ (cf. Phil. 2:16; 3:17–21). In the meantime, he lives in the present, making sense of his day-to-day suffering in the knowledge of the drama in which he plays a major role.[16]

Paul's letters assume, in the third place, a grand narrative of the God of Israel, who created the world and will draw it to a close (cf. Rom. 4:1–25; 5:1–12; chaps. 9–11). The narrative includes humanity's forfeiture of its idyllic original place through sin and God's initiative to reclaim humanity through Abraham and his descendants. The story continues with the exodus, the giving of the Torah, exile, and restoration. At the center of this narrative is Jesus Christ, the culmination of Israel's story. Paul frequently summarizes the story of Jesus (cf. Rom. 15:3; 2 Cor. 8:9; Phil. 2:6–11). The letters, therefore, are not merely abstract reflection, but re-

14. Ibid., 8.
15. N. T. Wright, *The New Testament and the People of God* (Philadelphia: Fortress, 1992), 404.
16. Ibid., 405.

flection on a story. Moreover, the story itself sometimes provides the narrative logic that accounts for the movement of Paul's argument.[17] Here Paul's argument is shaped, not by logical necessity, but by the pattern of the story. Therefore, Paul reflects on the narrative of the church's beginning, on the story of Jesus, and on stories from the Old Testament.[18]

To read the letters is to discover the convergence of these worlds and to recognize that the readers—ancient as well as modern—find themselves within the narrative. That letters contain a narrative dimension will not obscure the fact that letters, as discursive speech, have a logical sequence that requires the reader to follow the argument. The logical sequence of the text will, in most instances, provide the sequential movement for the sermon. Despite the limitations of historical criticism, one cannot dispense with questions about the background and logical argumentation of the text inasmuch as the letters presuppose a sequence of events prior to Paul's writing. Although the sermon is neither a lecture on the world behind the text nor an explanation of the theological categories within the epistle, careful reading requires that we recognize that this form of argumentation once had a place within a Christian assembly. The preacher's task is to grasp this argumentation in such a way that it once again shapes the continuing narrative of the believing community. In discovering these issues, we recognize our own communities within the story.

Reading 2 Corinthians as Narrative

The Story behind the Letter: Paul and the Corinthians

By the time Paul writes 2 Corinthians, he shares a narrative with this community that began with the founding of the church (1 Cor. 2:1:–5; 15:1–3, 12; 2 Cor. 11:2) and the beginning of Paul's role as a father to this congregation (cf. 1 Cor. 4:14–21; 2 Cor. 11:2; 12:14). Having begun the shared narrative with the Corinthians as father, he maintains a responsibility for the community's faithfulness until the completion of the story at the eschaton (2 Cor. 11:2). This responsibility is evident in the sequence of letters and visits that unites Paul and the Corinthians in a continu-

---

17. Hays, *Faith of Jesus Christ,* 197.
18. Witherington, *Paul's Narrative Thought World,* 2.

ing narrative. Although our depiction of the complete history behind the text and the issues raised by the opponents must remain
provisional, we discover the narrative world of the text through
the many allusions that Paul makes to the situation at Corinth.
Paul faces a triangular situation composed of himself, the readers,
and unnamed third parties (cf. "many" in 2:17; 11:18; "some" in
3:2; 10:2, 12; "they" in 11:22), who have disturbed Paul's relations
with the Corinthian church. They bring letters of recommendation (3:1), "commend themselves" (10:12), and boast "according
to human standards" (11:18). The missionaries have joined forces
with Paul's earlier opposition to question his integrity and to por-
tray him as the flatterer who cannot be trusted.[19] Specific charges
against Paul involve his refusal to accept payment for his work
(11:7–11), his fickleness in not making the visit he had promised
(1:15–23), and the criticism against his weak bodily presence and
speaking ability (10:1–2, 10–11). Much of 2 Corinthians is a narrative in which Paul places his conduct in a favorable light in
order to reestablish his relationship with the Corinthians. He
speaks with the affection of a father (11:1–6; 12:14–15) who
wishes to restore his relationship to his children. He describes
past events (1:8–11; 1:15–2:13; 7:5–16), defends his ongoing ministry in the present tense (2:14–4:15; 5:11–20), and anticipates the
future (6:1–7:2a; chaps. 8–13) in his relationship to this church.
Therefore, when Paul writes 2 Corinthians after receiving news
from Titus (7:5–16), he is in the middle of a narrative, hoping
that the letter will affect the outcome and result in his reconciliation with the Corinthians.

Making the Case: The Convergence of Narratives in Chapters 1–7

Because the Corinthians need to be reconciled to Paul (6:11–
13; 7:2–4) and to God (5:18–19), the focus of chapters 1–7 is reconciliation. Paul's statement in 7:2–4 functions as a summary of
the argument of chapters 1–7:

> Make room in your hearts for us; we have wronged no one, we have
> corrupted no one, we have taken advantage of no one. I do not say
> this to condemn you, for I said before that you are in our hearts,
> to die together and to live together. I often boast about you; I have

19. See Peter Marshall, *Enmity at Corinth*, Wissenschaftliche Untersuchungen zum Neuen Testament 2.23 (Tübingen: Mohr/Siebeck, 1987), 71–90.

great pride in you; I am filled with consolation; I am overjoyed in all our affliction.

Despite Paul's deep affection for the Corinthians, they remain unreconciled both to God and to Paul. Paul's autobiographical argument in chapters 1–7 is intended to demonstrate his integrity and devotion to this church. The argument reaches a climax in the appeals, "be reconciled to God" (5:20), "open wide your hearts" (6:13), and "make room in your hearts for us" (7:2).

This summary of Paul's asymmetrical relationship with the Corinthians allows us to see the focus of chapters 1–7 and the special role of 5:11–6:2 in the argument. In 1:3–5:10, Paul demonstrates his affection for the Corinthians and his place in the grand narrative of the world. This theological argument lays the basis for the series of appeals for reconciliation in 5:11–7:16. The turning point and center of the argument is the theological statement in 5:11–6:2, for here Paul states the theological justification (5:14–19, 21) for his conduct, hoping it will result in his reconciliation with the Corinthians.

Paul sets the tone of the argument in the opening benediction (1:3–7), speaking of the continuing reality of his ministry and implicitly referring to the opponents' charges that he is a weak, suffering figure. In his statement that "the sufferings of Christ are abundant for us" (1:5), he interprets his own experience with the claim that his present experience conforms to the past event of the suffering of Christ, introducing a dominating theme of the letter (cf. 4:10–11; 5:14–15; 13:4). Indeed, the echoes from the Psalms in Paul's description of his suffering suggest that he identifies his experience, not only with the story of Christ, but also with the experience of Israel.[20] His suffering is a continuing experience, and his readers are both the beneficiaries and the partners in a shared narrative of suffering (1:6–7). Paul suffers for the sake of others, including the Corinthians. With the repetition of the words "for your consolation" in 1:6, Paul introduces a major theme of the book: his sacrificial care for the Corinthian church. In Paul's description of recent events in Asia, when he "despaired of life itself" (1:8–11), he recalls a specific instance of his suffering and indicates that the congregation is now active in prayer on his behalf (1:11), again alluding to the narrative that he shares with the readers. This mem-

20. See Ps. 118:50, 52, 76 LXX (NRSV 119:50, 52, 76); 134:14 LXX (NRSV 135:14).

ory functions as the *narratio* of Paul's discourse, providing a case history of the issue that the remainder of the letter will address.

In the defensive tone of 1:12–14, the tensions between Paul and his readers now become evident, as Paul alludes to the story that lies behind the letter in 1:12. He moves from past conduct in 1:12 to his present outlook on his ministry in 1:13–14, anticipating an ultimate future at "the day of the Lord Jesus" (1:14). The reference to Paul's "boast" (καύχησις, *kauchēsis*) in 1:12 anticipates the argument of the entire epistle. Paul develops this theme throughout the epistle (cf. 5:12; 7:4, 14; 8:24), but he develops it with special intensity in chapters 10–13, where forms of καυχ- are used eighteen times. Closely related to Paul's personal boast is the focus on self-commendation and comparison, a theme that dominates the fool's speech in chapters 10–13. The *propositio* of the letter, therefore, is 1:12–14. As a response to the difficult situation in Corinth, Paul writes to defend his past conduct and to restore a relationship of reciprocity, according to which the Corinthians will come to know that "we are your boast even as you are our boast" (καύχημα ὑμῶν ἐσμεν καθάπερ καὶ ὑμεῖς ἡμῶν; *kauchēma hymōn esmen kathaper kai hymeis hēmōn;* 1:14) at the day of the Lord Jesus. As Paul writes, this desire is unfulfilled. Although he frequently says in chapters 1–7 that the Corinthians are his "boast" (7:4, 14; 8:24; 9:3), his listeners do not reciprocate his affections (cf. 5:12; 12:11). Because they do not reciprocate his boasting on their behalf, he writes to restore a reciprocity of boasting. Paul's statement of purpose in 1:12–14 forms an *inclusio* with the summary statement of 7:2–4 mentioned above, indicating that the intervening argument is the basis for Paul's plea for mutual boasting.

Paul's desire that the Corinthians reciprocate his boasting presupposes an unfinished narrative in his relation to the community. Together they share in a grand narrative that will come to an end only at the "day of the Lord Jesus" (1:14). Undoubtedly Paul's reference to the conclusion of the grand narrative in 1:14 presupposes the larger narrative of Israel's God, who called his people and made promises that have been fulfilled in Christ (1:20) and will ultimately bring their story to a close. The "day of the Lord" in Jewish hope has become, for Paul, "the day of the Lord Jesus." Paul assumes this narrative when he does not articulate it fully.[21]

21. See Wright, *New Testament and the People of God,* 404.

Paul moves easily from the *propositio* in 1:12–14 to argue the case for a reciprocity of boasting in 1:15–9:15, describing an unfinished narrative in which he hopes for an appropriate outcome based on his explanation of past events (1:15–2:13) and his defense of his present ministry (2:14–7:4).[22] According to 1:15, his desire for reciprocity, his love for the Corinthians (2:4), his joy in the Corinthians (1:24), and his intention to avoid shared grief (2:1–11) were the motivating factors in the change of travel plans that had occasioned the suspicions of the Corinthians. Just as he suffers for the benefit of others (1:6), the welfare of others determines his decisions.

At 2:14–7:4 he returns to the present tense,[23] describing what is "always" true (2:14; 4:10; 5:6)—the present, durative part of the story—in a grand narrative of cosmic significance, concluding this section with further confirmation that the Corinthians are "his boast" (7:4; cf. 1:14). Despite the opponents' negative estimation of his ministry, he knows that he is engaged in God's victory

22. Several factors suggest that one may approach the entirety of 2 Corinthians as a rhetorical unit and analyze the rhetorical impact of the entire work. Like other Pauline letters, it opens with a thanksgiving and concludes with Paul's future travel plans (12:14–13:4). Throughout the letter, Paul defends himself to his own community against the charges and counterclaims brought by outsiders who have disturbed his work. The topic of διακονία (*diakonia*, "ministry, service") and the διάκονος (*diakonos*, "minister, servant") is at the center of the discussion in both chapters 1–9 and chapters 10–13. This topic is associated with the issue of self-commendation, which is first introduced at 3:1 and then developed throughout the epistle (4:2; 5:12; 6:4; 7:11; 12:11, 18–19). Paul's suffering and weakness are first introduced in 1:3–11, developed in 4:7–5:10; 6:3–13, and recapitulated in 11:23–30. As in the other letters (cf. 1 Cor. 16:21; Gal. 5:1–6:10), Paul recapitulates the major themes in a rhetorically intensified form in the concluding section (chaps. 10–13). See my article, "Paul's Argument from Pathos in 2 Corinthians," in *Paul and Pathos*, ed. Thomas Olbricht and Jerry Sumney (Atlanta: Society of Biblical Literature, 2001), 127–45.

23. Paul's interruption of the narrative of past events at 2:14–7:4 and his resumption of the narrative of 1:15–2:13 at 7:5–16 does not require that we assume that 1:15–2:13 and 7:5–16 form a separate "letter of reconciliation" interrupted by the apostolic apologia (2:14–7:4). Indeed, as 1:15–2:13 (especially 1:15–23) indicates, Paul is not especially reconciled to the Corinthians in this unit. One may observe that 2:13 does not join smoothly with 7:5. Paul's transition from "my spirit did not find rest" (2:13) to "my flesh had no relief" (7:5) would be both redundant and an unusual linkage of "spirit" and "flesh."

processional, even if he is a captive on his way to death (2:14).[24]
As an aroma "among those who are being saved and among those
who are perishing" (2:15), he has a decisive role in God's grand
narrative. Indeed, his echoes from the Old Testament demonstrate that, in his ministry, he has submerged his own story within
that of Israel. After declaring the life-and-death consequences of
his work, he asks, "Who is sufficient [ἵκανος, *hikanos*] for these
things?" (2:16). His words echo the story of Moses (Exod. 4:10
LXX) and introduce an extended comparison between Paul's
ministry and that of Moses. Whereas Moses was not "competent"
(ἵκανος, *hikanos*) for his role as God's servant, Paul claims a competence from God, who "has made us competent to be ministers
of a new covenant" (3:6). To the community's request for letters
of recommendation, he replies that they are his letters, "written
on hearts . . . not with ink but with the Spirit of the living God, not
on stone tablets, but on fleshy hearts" (3:2–3; my translation)—
again contrasting his ministry with that of Moses. Paul identifies
his ministry with the new covenant of Jeremiah, suggesting that
his work is the fulfillment of the promises of God.[25] Inasmuch as
the new covenant is associated with the fulfillment of God's promises for the restoration of Israel and a New Exodus to Israel's
homeland,[26] Paul's defense is framed within Israel's story. As
Paul's letters written on "fleshy hearts," the Corinthians are now
incorporated into Israel's story, participating in God's grand narrative. Thus Paul brings together the Old Testament traditions
about the new covenant and second exodus to explain his ministry. He, as the minister of the new covenant, is engaged in the

24. Cf. W. Bauer et al., *Greek-English Lexicon of the New Testament and Other
Early Christian Literature*, 3d ed. (Chicago: University of Chicago Press, 1999),
459: "who continually leads us as captives in a triumphal procession." Recent
literature is almost unanimous that Paul is not the conqueror in the processional, but some question remains as to whether Paul is evoking the image of
the Roman triumphal procession. There is near-unanimity that the metaphor
is intended to express social shame. See the texts indicated by Victor Furnish,
II Corinthians, Anchor Bible (Garden City, N.Y.: Doubleday, 1984), 175.

25. Paul alludes to new-covenant passages from Exodus, Deuteronomy, Jeremiah, and Ezekiel. The reference to stone tablets recalls Exod. 24:12;
31:18; 32:15; 34:1; Deut. 9:10, while the reference to "tablets of human
hearts" recalls Jer. 31(38):33; Ezek. 11:19; 36:26–27.

26. William J. Webb, *Returning Home: New Covenant and Second Exodus as the
Context for 2 Corinthians 6:14–7:1,* Journal for the Study of the New Testament:
Supplement Series 85 (Sheffield: JSOT, 1993), 87.

culmination of Israel's story, leading Israel back from exile to restore its relationship to God.

As the mediator of this new covenant (cf. 3:3), Paul proclaims the word of God (2:17), knowing that his ministry is more glorious than that of Moses. As the midrash in 2 Cor. 3:7–18 indicates, Paul continues the comparison between the Sinai covenant ("the ministry of death") and the new covenant of Jeremiah ("the ministry of the Spirit"). Although he concedes that the Sinai διακονία (*diakonia,* "ministry, service") "came in glory" (3:7) when Moses descended the mountain with the shining face (Exod. 34:29–35), he argues that his διακονία (*diakonia,* "ministry, service") of the new covenant has even greater glory (3:7–11). Indeed, in describing his παρρησία (*parrēsia,* "openness, boldness," 3:12), Paul contrasts his openness with Moses' need to place the veil on his face. Like Moses, Paul confronts listeners whose hearts are "veiled" and "blinded," preventing them from seeing the glory (3:14–15; cf. 4:3–4). His ministry parallels that of the servant of Isaiah 40–66, who brings a covenant (cf. Isa. 42:6–7) of light (49:6) to those who are blind (43:8; 60:1–2). Nevertheless, Paul does not "lose heart" (2 Cor. 4:1), for he knows that he is involved in a glorious ministry that is a part of God's grand narrative. His personal narrative reached a turning point at his conversion when "light shone out of darkness" (4:6). That is, Israel's story of creation became a reality in his own life when he encountered the glory of Christ at a moment in the past. His narrative now continues in his role as minister of the new covenant as he proclaims that "Jesus Christ is Lord" (4:5). At the present time, he is engaged in a ministry of glory, and he insists that believers share his continuing narrative of glory (3:18, "we all").

As one who holds the treasure in earthen vessels, according to 4:7–15, Paul conducts this glorious ministry in the context of weakness and suffering (4:7–15). Here Paul's suffering is the manifestation of the dying of Jesus (4:10), as the past event becomes present reality. In sharing the weakness of the cross, he also participates in the power of the resurrection. As one who is "given up" (παραδιδόμεθα, *paradidometha*) to death for Jesus' sake" (4:11), he identifies with the fate of Jesus and takes up the role of the suffering servant from Israel's story (Isa. 53:12).[27] Paul associates the

27. Παραδίδωμι (*paradidōmi,* "delivered over") is used three times in Isaiah 53 for the suffering servant (53:6 [twice], 12). In 53:12, the servant "poured

language with his own ministry, placing his ministry within the story of the passion of Jesus and the larger narrative of Israel. However, in keeping with Paul's focus on reciprocity, he emphasizes his shared narrative with the Corinthians. In saying "death is at work in us, but life in you" (4:12), he appeals to the Corinthians to recognize his desire for partnership. He adds, "because we know that the one who raised the Lord Jesus will raise us . . . with you into his presence" (4:14), and, "Everything is for your sake" (4:15), indicating once more his appeal for reciprocity.

In 4:16–5:10, Paul indicates that the continuing suffering will come to an end. Again, he lives between past event and future judgment as he incorporates Israel's story, assuming the story of both the beginning and the end. Hence he now lives in anticipation. Although this is Paul's story, he occasionally hints that his readers will share in it ("we all" in 3:18; 5:10) as he moves from "we" to "we all." Thus Paul continues to invite his listeners to share his narrative. In 3:18; 5:10, they share with him in Israel's hope of future glory.

Paul's Narrative in 2 Corinthians 5:11–6:2

Paul's consistent declaration of his sacrificial existence within the grand narrative of Israel is the background for his defense in 5:11–6:2, which marks the turning point in the argument of chapters 1–7. Here his first explicit theological justification for his demeanor as a minister (5:14–19, 21) is enveloped within the discussion of the issues at Corinth, as the structure below indicates.

A   5:11–12 Paul persuades others (including the Corinthians).
B   5:13 (γάρ, *gar,* "for") A summary of Paul's selfless ministerial existence.
C   5:14–15 (γάρ, *gar,* "for") Paul's selfless ministry is based on the Christian story of Christ's sacrifice, which defines all Christian existence.

---

out his soul to death" (παρέδοθη εἰς θάνατον, *paredothē eis thanaton*). Forms of παραδίδωμι taken from Isa. 53:6, 12 are frequently applied to the suffering of Jesus in the NT (cf. Matt. 17:22; 20:18, 19; Rom. 4:25; 8:32; 1 Cor. 11:23). See Webb, *Returning Home,* 104–5.

D   5:16 (ὥστε, *hōste*, "therefore") Paul has a
new epistemology as a result of Christ's
sacrifice.

D′   5:17 (ὥστε, *hōste*, "therefore") All who
are in Christ participate in a new world.

C′   5:18–19 (δέ, *de*, "and, but") Paul's ministry is
both defined and granted by God's act of
reconciliation in the cross of Christ.

B′   5:20 A summary of Paul's ministry of persuasion.

A′   5:20b–6:2 Paul persuades the Corinthians to be reconciled to God.

Here the chiastic structure of the passage indicates that the implicit address to the Corinthians in 5:11–12 forms an inclusion
with the explicit appeal to the Corinthians in 5:20b–6:2, indicating that Paul's task of persuasion includes the Corinthians. Paul's
demeanor as a minister (5:13, 20a) has a theological basis: the
cross of Christ is an event that shapes the existence of Christians
(5:14–15, 18–19, 21). The consequence of the Christ-event—and
the structural center of the passage—is Paul's claim that his unusual ministry is defined by the standard of the new creation and
that all believers exist within the new creation.

In defense of his ministry, he describes the durative dimension
of his work within the continuing narrative. In the phrase, "Therefore, knowing the fear of the Lord, we try to persuade others," he
resumes the previous unit and begins a new one, suggesting that
the judgment (5:10)—the culmination of the grand narrative—is
the basis for Paul's "fear of the Lord" and his continuing task of
persuasion. The unusual verb "we persuade" (πείθομεν, *peithomen*),
which elsewhere has a negative association with the sophists (Gal.
1:10; 1 Cor. 2:4),[28] refers here to Paul's ministry of proclamation,
the subject of his defense (cf. 2:17; 4:2–6, 13), and to his appeal
to the Corinthians (cf. 6:1–2). Paul's life between present and future is also evident in the transition from the aorist infinitive φαν-
ερωθῆναι (*phanerōthēnai*, "to appear") in 5:10 as a reference to the

28. The phrase "to persuade the crowd" was used in Paul's time as a definition of the art of rhetoric (Plato *Gorgias* 452E). It was sometimes used by
philosophers for traveling street preachers who merely flattered and enter-
tained the crowds. See J. Louis Martyn, *Galatians,* Anchor Bible (Garden City,
N.Y.: Doubleday, 1997), 138.

future appearance before God at the judgment seat to the use of the perfect πεφανερώμεθα (*pephanerōmetha*, "well known" [to God]) and πεφανερῶσθαι (*pephanerōsthai*, "well known" [to your consciences]) in 5:11 to describe an enduring situation.[29] As in 1:13, he hopes to progress from being known by God to being known by the Corinthians in the unfolding drama, as the present tense in 5:12 indicates. This proclamation is based on Paul's narrative; he anticipates the future (5:10) and is transformed by the past (4:6).

The "I-you" relationship that resonates in 5:11–13 suggests Paul's shared continuing narrative with the Corinthians and the desire for reciprocity that is evident throughout chapters 1–7. Indeed, this unit implies an appeal to the Corinthians, which will become explicit in 5:20b–6:2. Here he reiterates the *propositio* of 1:12–14, with its emphasis on Paul's desire for the Corinthian acceptance of his ministry. Paul's statement "I hope it is well known to your consciences" (5:11; my translation) echoes the earlier statement in 1:13, "I hope you will understand until the end." To ensure that his work is "well known" to the consciences, Paul engages in self-defense. In the explanation of 5:12, Paul again echoes the letter's *propositio* (1:12–14), with its focus on the Corinthian response to Paul. His statement, "We are not commending ourselves to you again, but giving you an opportunity to boast about us, so that you may be able to answer those who boast in outward appearance and not in the heart" (5:12),[30] forms an *inclusio* with the summary statement in 7:2–4 and reiterates the cen-

29. J. Lambrecht, "'Reconcile Yourselves . . .': A Reading of 2 Corinthians 5,11–21," in Bieringer and Lambrecht, *Studies on 2 Corinthians,* 369.

30. The frequent use of "commend" (συνιστάνω, *sunistanō,* 3:1; 4:2; 6:4; 7:11; 10:12, 18; 12:11) in 2 Corinthians is a response to the opponents who engage in self-praise and bring letters of recommendation (3:1; 10:12). One may note the apparent contradiction between Paul's denial of self-commendation in 5:12 and his indication that he commends himself in 4:2; 6:4. According to John Fitzgerald (*Cracks in an Earthen Vessel,* Society of Biblical Literature Dissertation Series 99 [Atlanta: Scholars, 1988], 187), the difference in the placement of the pronoun is crucial. Every time in 2 Corinthians that Paul wishes to make a negative comment about self-commendation he places the pronoun before the verb (ἑαυτοὺς συνιστάνειν, *heautous sunistanein,* 3:1; 5:12; 10:12, 18; cf. 4:5). When he speaks positively, either of the Corinthians' self-commendation (7:11) or of his own (4:2; 6:4), he places it after the verb (συνιστάνειν ἑαυτούς, *sunistanein heautous*). Self-commendation is castigated, self-commendation is approved.

tral issue of the letter (1:12–14), alluding to Paul's unfulfilled desire for reconciliation.

Paul initiates the summary of his self-defense in verse 13, applying the Greek distinction between rationality and being "out of one's mind."[31] He reiterates the dichotomy "I-you," summarizing his numerous earlier claims that his sacrificial existence has been for the sake of the Corinthians (cf. 1:6 [twice], 7; 2:4; 4:15). The issue at Corinth is not the place of ecstatic phenomena in the argument. Paul is actually summarizing his ministerial existence as "for you," suggesting his sacrificial life for the Corinthians and his desire for their reciprocity of boasting (cf. 4:12, 15).

As γάρ (*gar,* "for") indicates in 5:14, Paul now initiates the justification for his ministerial conduct as he enters dense theological territory as part of his continuing story, indicating that the theological discussion is intended to explain Paul's selfless attitude to the Corinthians. In the present tense, Paul says, "The love of Christ urges us on," maintaining the focus on his continuing existence within the narrative. The language of compulsion (συνέχει ἡμᾶς, *sunechei hēmas,* "urges us on") suggests that Paul is not his own master. The phrase recalls his description of himself as God's captive in the victorious processional (2:14) and the recipient of a prophetic call (cf. 1 Cor. 9:15–18; Gal. 1:15). In view of Paul's identification of himself with the servant of Isaiah 40–66 in 4:10–15, Paul may once more be evoking the role of the servant in describing his destiny (cf. Isa. 49:16). The continuing reality of Paul's ministry is the power of the past event that has "taken over" his life (Phil. 3:12).

As a result of this transforming event on Paul's life, his entire ministry has been distinguished by love for others, as he consistently reminds the Corinthians. His love for them guided his travel plans (2:4). He says, "You are in our hearts, to die together and to live together" (7:3). Because of his love for this church, he refused to accept financial support from them (11:7). He is the anxious father who will exhaust himself for his children (12:14–15). The love that impels him to a life devoted to others is an expression of "the love of Christ" (ἡ ἀγάπη τοῦ χριστοῦ, *hē agapē tou*

31. Bauer et al., *Greek-English Lexicon,* 986. σωφρονεῖν (*sōphronein,* "be of sound mind, of mental health") was used in contrast to μαίνεσθαι (*mainesthai,* "to be out of one's mind, to be insane") in Plato *Phaedrus* 22, 244a; *Rep.* 331c; Ps.-Apollod. 3, 5, 1; 6.

christou), which he appears to use interchangeably with "the love of God" (cf. Rom. 5:8), the enduring reality of his life. One may compare his statement in Phil. 1:8: "I long for all of you with the compassion of Christ Jesus."

From the grand narrative of God's care for Israel, Paul knows that the saving events in Israel's story were expressions of God's love and mercy.[32] Now Paul sees in the Christ-event the ultimate expression of divine love, and he transforms this narrative understanding of God's love by associating it with the cross of Christ. Whereas Paul has earlier explained his sacrificial existence in terms of the continuing reality of the cross in his life (1:5; 4:10–15), here his existence for others is based on the death of Jesus as a past event. The introductory phrase κρίναντας τοῦτο (*krinantas touto*, "because we are convinced") points to the basis for Paul's present ministry in a decision that he has made in the past about a transforming event:[33] "that one died for all." Just as Paul speaks in Gal. 2:20 of the one "who loved me and gave himself for me," the death of Jesus here is the expression of the love of Christ. Similarly, Paul speaks of the cross as the expression of the love of God in Rom. 5:8: "God commended his love for us in that, while we were yet sinners, Christ died for us" (my translation).

Here, as elsewhere, Paul returns not only to his own story (cf. 4:6) to explain his ministry, but to the foundational story—the church's *mythos,* which is the basis for his reflection (*dianoia*). That this is the church's foundational story is evident from the numerous instances in which similar language appears in the New Testament. According to 1 Cor. 15:3, Paul summarizes the gospel that he originally preached in the words, "Christ died for our sins in accordance with the scriptures." In other instances, he recites these words with slight variation.[34] Paul's recitation of the creedal statement contains both the foundational story and his reflection on the event. Paul adapts the statement "Christ died for our sins" to create the contrast between "one" and "all." "One-all" echoes

---

32. See Deut. 7:8–9; 23:5; 33:12.

33. Linda L. Belleville, "Gospel and Kerygma in 2 Corinthians," in *Gospel in Paul: Studies on Corinthians, Galatians, and Romans for Richard N. Longenecker,* ed. Linda A. Jervis and Peter Richardson, Journal for the Study of the New Testament: Supplement Series 108 (Sheffield: JSOT, 1994), 145.

34. Note Paul's use of the ὑπέρ (*hyper,* "on behalf of") formula for the sacrificial death of Christ in Rom. 5:8; 8:32; 15:15; Gal. 1:4; 2:20; 3:13; 1 Thess. 5:10; 1 Cor. 8:10.

Paul's other contrasts between "one" and "all"—that the fate of one affects the many. By adding the "one-all" antithesis Paul must have been thinking of Christ as the new Adam (cf. Rom. 5:12–21). Christ, like Adam, is an inclusive figure.[35] Reference to the death of Christ for others also recalls the role of the servant in Isaiah 53. The consistent feature in these recitations is "die for" (ὑπέρ . . . ἀποθνήσκω, *hyper . . . apothnēskō*), a phrase that is rooted in Isaiah 53. That is, the story of Jesus' death—the foundational story—is actually Israel's story. Jesus takes Israel's fate upon himself as the one who dies for others.

By adapting the confessional statement "one died for all," Paul prepares the way for his interpretation of the foundational story in 5:14c–15. Paul's argument suggests that the "all" of 5:14 corresponds to the frequent claim that the saving event was "for us" or "for our sins" (cf. Rom. 4:25; 5:7–8; 8:32). Paul offers an initial interpretation of the story in verse 14c ("therefore all died") before repeating the creed in verse 15a and offering a second interpretation in verse 15b ("in order that they no longer live for themselves . . ." [my translation]). In the phrase "therefore all died" (5:14c), Paul speaks in the past tense to show that others are caught up in God's grand narrative. In contrast to earlier passages in which Paul has described his own experience as involving the sharing of the suffering of Christ (1:3–7; 4:10), here he extends his own experience to that of others to indicate the general principle that "all died." That is, "all"—the entire believing community—share the narrative of Christ. Their own personal stories are subordinated to the big story. The statement is a central feature of Pauline theology. In Gal. 2:19, Paul says, "I have been crucified with Christ." In Phil. 3:10, he describes his own experience as including the fellowship of the sufferings of Christ. That this fact is rooted in a moment in the past is evident in Rom. 6:1–11. In baptism, the believer takes up the story of the cross. As one who lives for others, Paul exemplifies the behavior that is shaped by the cross.

In 5:15, Paul repeats the creedal statement "he died for all" in order to offer a second interpretation: "In order that those who live may live no longer for themselves" (my translation). That is, the past events have present consequences, transforming every be-

---

35. See Lambrecht, " 'Reconcile Yourselves,' " 381.

liever. The general principle applies especially to Paul, who has consistently reminded the Corinthians that his ministry is for them. One may compare Paul's appeal to the same principle in Rom. 14:7: "No one lives to himself and no one dies to himself" (my translation). This is the principle that Paul now applies to his own life. Paul's life is "for you" (5:13) because he is caught up in God's grand narrative. We may also note the common pattern in Pauline reflection, according to which the cross is not only an event of the past, but the norm for Christian existence. In Rom. 15:3, he appeals to the readers to practice selfless conduct, motivating them with the words, "For Christ did not please himself." He expresses the same principle in 1 Cor. 8:1–11:1, when he encourages the Corinthians to abandon anti-communal behavior for the sake of others and to follow his example of selflessness (11:1). In Phil. 2:1–5, Paul encourages his listeners to consider others above themselves before he tells the story of Christ's humiliation (2:6–11). As in Phil. 2:1–11, Paul hopes that the story will create the new set of community values that he has adopted already.

Just as stories have the power to create a community with its alternative ethos, the Christian story creates a new epistemology, as Paul indicates in his continued interpretation of the narrative in 5:16–17. The twofold ὥστε (*hōste*, "so that") in verses 16–17 indicates that Paul is drawing the consequences of his statement for his own ministry, moving from his own story (v. 16) to the story of the entire Christian community (v. 17).[36] The contrast between "from now on," "once," and "no longer" reflects Paul's own narrative and the determining influence of the Christ-event on his life. Paul describes a change in epistemology—from the old existence when he knew Christ "from a human point of view" (κατὰ σάρκα, *kata sarka*) to the new existence when he knows no one "from a human point of view." Unlike his opponents who boast κατὰ σάρκα (11:18) and accuse Paul of behaving κατὰ σάρκα, he has a changed existence that conforms to the general statement in 5:17, which describes "anyone in Christ." In the reference to the "new creation," Paul recalls Israel's story, again referring to Israel's postexilic hope. According to Isa. 65:17, "For I am about to create new heavens and a new earth; the former things shall not be remembered or come to mind."

36. "We" in 5:16 does not refer to the entire Christian community, but to Paul himself. Note his distinction between "we" and "you" in 5:11–13.

Isaiah 40–66 consistently refers to the new thing that the Lord will do for Israel. In 42:9, the prophet says, "See, the former things have come to pass, and new things I now declare." In 43:18–19, he says, "Do not remember the former things, or consider the things of old. I am about to do a new thing." The former things are God's past redemptive acts—creation, exodus (43:18; 51:10–11), the giving of the covenant. When God does a new thing, Israel will return to Zion in a New Exodus (43:16–17), and God will establish a new covenant (42:6; 49:8; 54:10; 55:3; 61:8). God has acted through the servant to take away Israel's sins, to end the state of hostility, and to proclaim Israel's salvation. This narrative of Israel accounts for the logic of Paul's argumentation in his defense, for both the new covenant and the new creation are now a reality (3:1–18; 5:17); the servant has died for the people (5:14), and he is the prophetic voice who proclaims the time of salvation.

That the Christian shares in a cosmic drama is evident in the explanation of the new creation in 5:18–19. Τὰ δὲ πάντα (*ta de panta,* "now all things") in 5:18 refers to the event of the new creation with an emphasis on God's role as the initiator.[37] In 5:18–19 Paul restates the soteriological affirmation of 5:14, describing an event (or events) of the past, in parallel statements arranged in an A-B-A'-B' pattern.

A God, who reconciled us to himself through Christ,
  B and has given us the ministry of reconciliation.
A' That is, in Christ God was reconciling the world to
    himself, not counting their trespasses against them
  B' and entrusting the message of reconciliation to us.

The parallel phrases in verses 18–19, "who reconciled us to himself through Christ" and "in Christ God was reconciling the world to himself," indicate Paul's distinct emphases and clarify difficult phrases. The parallel between "through Christ" (v. 18) and "in Christ" (v. 19) suggests that the focus of the latter is not the incarnation, but an instrumental understanding of "in Christ." The parallel between "reconciled *us*" (v. 18) and "reconciled the *world*"

37. By contrast, in 5:14 Christ is the initiator. Michael Gorman (*Cruciformity: Paul's Narrative Spirituality of the Cross* [Grand Rapids: Eerdmans, 2001], 77–78) lists many passages in which Christ is the initiator in the saving event and many other passages in which God is the initiator.

(v. 19) recalls the earlier phrase "one died *for all*" (5:14) in describing the recipients of reconciliation, suggesting that the world to which Paul refers is not to be understood in cosmological terms, but with reference to humanity that has been alienated by sin (cf. Rom. 5:12). Similarly, the parallel phrases "has given us the ministry of reconciliation" and "entrusting the message of reconciliation to us," also in the aorist tense, indicate Paul's essential emphases. At the center of his concern is the emphasis on the initiative of God and the focus on the events of the past. The aorist tense describes two dimensions of the narrative that Paul recalls: God acted both in the story of Christ and in Paul's own story. The alternation between the Christian story and Paul's own ministry in 5:18–19 is consistent with the entire Pauline defense in 2 Corinthians, for here he affirms that the same God who acted in Christ to effect reconciliation has called him to be the minister of reconciliation.

The term for reconciliation is a rare soteriological term in Paul (cf. Rom. 5:11), and it is used nowhere in the Old Testament. With its imagery of the end of hostilities between God and the people, it is found only in the literature of Hellenistic Judaism (cf. 2 Macc. 1:5; 5:20), where humans are always the initiators in reconciliation. One may note, however, that Paul uses the term synonymously in Rom. 5:1, 11 with the phrase "peace with God" (Rom. 5:1), an image that is rooted in Israel's story. Paul moves naturally from the reference to "new creation" to the event of reconciliation because he follows a narrative logic based on Israel's story in Isaiah 40–66, according to which the "new creation" initiated by God will be a time of peace with God.[38] The time of exile, according to Isaiah 40–66, is an occasion for the wrath, anger, rejection, and forsakenness of Israel.[39] The return from exile is a period in which there is a cessation of anger, and "peace" is reestablished between the nation and its God. Therefore, in verses 18–21, Paul does not shift his thinking to a new, unrelated topic. He makes clear what lies beneath the surface of his allusion to Isaiah in verse 17. Christ's death for human sin (5:14–15, 21) has removed the condition of separation between God and sinful people. Paul's understanding of reconciliation is evident in the phrase "not counting their trespasses against them" (5:19). In the

38. See G. K. Beale, "Reconciliation in 2 Corinthians 5–7," *New Testament Studies* 35 (1989): 551.

39. Ibid., 556.

"new creation" and "reconciliation" in Christ, God has fulfilled Israel's hope for a new world when the nation would be restored to a peaceful relationship with Yahweh.[40] The God who acted at the cross also called Paul to service as the proclaimer of this good news.

The narrative of God's reconciling activity is incomplete, for the Corinthians remain unreconciled to God. In 5:20–6:2, Paul returns to the present role in the unfinished drama both to describe his role of persuasion (cf. 5:11) and to persuade his readers to respond to God's deed of reconciliation. As God's ambassador, he does not speak for himself; instead, he says, "God is making his appeal through us" (τοῦ θεοῦ παρακαλοῦντος δι' ἡμῶν, *tou theou parakalountos di' hēmōn*). In 5:20b and 6:1–2, Paul makes an appeal (παρακαλέω, *parakaleō*) to the Corinthians for reconciliation. That it is God who makes the appeal through Paul is reminiscent of the relationship between Yahweh and the servant in Isaiah 40–66, where God is the one who "comforts" (ὁ παρακαλῶν, *ho parakalōn*) Israel (40:1, 2, 11; 41:27; 49:10, 13; 51:3, 12, 18, 19; 54:11; 57:5, 18; 61:2, 13), and the servant is God's spokesperson. The appeal, "Be reconciled to God," the first in a series of appeals to the readers (cf. 6:1–2, 11–13; 7:4), indicates the unfinished task of reconciliation. The aorist "be reconciled" suggests a call for a conversion. In its present setting, it is both a call for the readers to make a decision, and a suggestion that their failure to be reconciled to Paul is a failure to be reconciled to God.

Paul indicates the close relationship between the story of Christ and the continuing narrative again in 5:21, as he returns to the aorist tense to tell the story of Christ. "The one who knew no sin" recalls the innocence of the servant in Isa. 53:9, and the claim that he became sin "for us (ὑπὲρ ἡμῶν, *hyper hēmōn*)," like the phrase "died for all" (ὑπὲρ πάντων, *hyper pantōn*) in 5:14, also echoes the servant's story in Isaiah 53. Indeed, the combined ideas of a sinless figure to redeem a sinful people and the granting of righteousness are uniquely traceable to Isa. 53:4–12. According to Isa. 53:11, "The righteous one . . . shall make many righteous." One may compare the similar description of a transference in Gal. 3:13–14, where Christ became a curse to those who were under a curse in order that the Gentiles might receive the blessing. Here

40. Ibid., 558.

is a narrative logic according to which the hero acts on behalf of others. The focus here is the unfinished story: "so that we might become the righteousness of God in him" (my translation). Such a transformation depends on the Corinthians' response to Paul's message.

The appeal to the Corinthians to "be reconciled to God" is parallel to the continued call for them "not to accept the grace of God in vain" in 6:1. As God's ambassador, Paul is also God's "coworker" making the appeal for a response. The grace of God is seen in his reconciling activity, which calls for humans to "receive" the message (cf. 1 Thess. 1:6; 2:13). Paul fears, however, that his labor will be "in vain" (1 Cor. 15:10, 14; Gal. 2:2; Phil. 2:16; 1 Thess. 2:1). His appeal to the Corinthians not to receive the grace of God in vain echoes the cry of the servant, "I have labored in vain" (Isa. 49:4). Like the exilic prophet, who agonizes over the community's failure to respond to his message (43:22), Paul recognizes that the Corinthians, despite their original acceptance of the gospel, may receive God's reconciling activity in vain. He supports his appeal with the words of Isa. 49:8, recalling once more the deeds of God as the basis for the church's response (cf. 5:20). For the prophet, the "right time" and the "day of salvation" when Yahweh listened and came to the aid of his people was the moment of the return from exile. For Paul, the "acceptable time" and the "day of salvation" is the "now" of his own unfinished narrative with the Corinthians. "Now" is the eschatological moment between the coming of the new creation (5:17) and the final judgment of God (5:10). To respond to the call is to "be reconciled to God" and to "receive the grace of God." Paul identifies with the servant who calls for a response.

The Convergence of Narratives: A Summary

As with all of Paul's epistolary communication, he stands within a plot that includes a beginning, a middle (the occasion of the letter), and an anticipated future. Paul attempts to overcome the suspicions about him and win the affections of the Corinthians a second time by telling his own story, describing the selfless love that has characterized his work among the Corinthians. He lives for others because he has been caught up in the larger story of the foundational narrative of the cross of Christ, the supreme expression of love. Although the Corinthians know that "Christ died for our sins" (cf. 1 Cor. 15:3), they have not recognized the power of that story to create the new community consciousness that will result in reconciliation.

The church's foundational story is nothing less than the culmination of Israel's story of the return from exile. Paul has a decisive role in announcing the good news that God has acted to end the hostilities with his people and to enable them to return from exile. Because of the death of the suffering servant who "bore the sin of many" (Isa. 53:12; cf. 53:4–5), God has reconciled Israel. The end of exile is existence in a "new creation" (cf. Isa. 65:17; 2 Cor. 5:17) when God mediates a new covenant, written on the heart (Ezek. 11:19; 36:26; Jer. 31:31–33). Although God has acted to bring Israel out of exile, the story remains unfinished. Paul is the prophetic voice who speaks for God, the new Moses who mediates the new covenant. The conclusion of the story depends upon the Corinthians' response to God's reconciling activity and Paul's selfless labor on their behalf.

The task of the preacher is not to explain this dense argument in detail, but to provide the opportunity for the congregation to enter into this ancient story of selfless love, recognizing that our community listens to many alternative stories that shape our understanding of the church's identity and mission. The sermon should reflect both the logical movement of the text and the narrative movement of a community in transition, building toward the climactic appeal, "Be reconciled to God . . . do not receive the grace of God in vain!" The chiastic structure of the passage may guide the development of the sermon. We acknowledge the reality of broken relationships and competing values that inhibit genuine community within the church (5:11–13); we hear once more the story of selfless love that creates a "new world" determined by God's reconciling activity (5:14–20a); and we invite the congregation to become caught up in this story (5:20b–6:2).

5

Preaching the Letters as Narrative

William H. Willimon

From Story to Letter to Story to Sermon

Our great challenge, as epistolary preachers, is to renarrate
Paul's letters. I assume that every Pauline letter arises from some
congregational story. The trouble is, only rarely, tantalizingly does
Paul turn from the letter at hand to grant us a glimpse of the story
behind the letter. ("I entreat Euodia and I entreat Synthyche to
agree" [Phil. 4:2 RSV] or "Be reconciled to God" [2 Cor. 5:20]). In
order to preach a letter, every preacher, even non-narrative preachers, must construct, reconstruct, and imaginatively re-create the
story and deliver it in some sort of dynamic equivalent to the biblical text in order to do what the text does. Therefore, Buttrick's
sharp distinction between the "immediacy" mode and the "reflective" mode breaks down when it comes to preaching epistles. One
reason why we preachers (some of us, at least) love the epistles as
a source for sermons is that we sense some of the tug and pull, the
stress and strain of a living, breathing congregation within these
letters. Here is theology the way it ought to be done, not as the idle
pastime of academics but as practical necessity for those trying to
be the body of Christ. In laying 2 Corinthians 5 before us, James
Thompson (chap. 4) has given us a wonderfully concrete, practical
text, a text to which I as a pastor can immediately relate—pastor
Paul slugging it out with the congregation after some troublemak-
ers have had the temerity to ask, "Who's in charge here?"

"Me, that's who, and for the following reasons," replies Paul. Then the untimely born apostle is off to the races, fighting for his pulpit with his best theological artillery. Theology arises from story and, in the reading of Paul's letter to the congregation, returns to story.

Thompson reminds me of why much of the old historical criticism is of so little use to preachers. When it comes to First Church Corinth, we do not know much of what lies "behind the text." More interesting for proclamation is the imaginative, "What lies in front of the text?"[1] That is, to whom would Paul say these things? For what purposes do we preachers apply these rhetorical strategies? What congregational squabble might give rise to such theologizing?

Here, we pastors are at an admitted advantage over New Testament professors. Even though the bishop ordained me and duly appointed me here, almost every week I must defend my pastoral/homiletical authority, if I am doing my job half right. Show me a preacher who has not, at some point during the last month, had to answer the old, "What gives you the right to say . . . ," and I will show you a prophet who has lost his teeth.

Not deterred by Thompson's caveat, "No passage is more daunting for the preacher than 2 Cor. 5:11–6:2," we like fools (2 Cor. 12:11) rush in to a sermon on 2 Cor. 5:11–6:2 because we must. Our privilege to preach the gospel and to serve the congregation is at stake here. If we fail, the jig is up and we might as well go into investment banking.

"In Christ God was reconciling the world to himself," thunders Paul (2 Cor. 5:19), "so that in him we might become the righteousness of God" (5:21). If I were forced to render the gospel in summary while standing on one foot, I could do no better than this.

Thompson reminds us that Paul "writes as a pastor . . . and addresses concrete situations in the life of the church." Right there I note a major difference between Paul and me. When my pastoral credentials are attacked, I tend to go psychological ("He is just an unhappy person right now, that's why he's attacking the pastor," or "She has never liked me. I remind her of her first hus-

1. The distinction between the world in front and the world behind the text is made clearly by David Bartlett, *Between the Bible and the Church: New Methods for Biblical Interpretation* (Nashville: Abingdon, 1999), 138–51.

band"). Paul goes dramatically, sweepingly theological. A fight over who is in charge of the gospel at Corinth becomes an occasion for Paul to pull out his biggest theological affirmations. What could be dismissed as mere church politics becomes proclamation. As Thompson says so well, Paul wants to "shape the outcome of the story." Paul wants to tell the tale in such a way that petty parochial problems become an opportunity for everyone to stand and affirm their faith in Christ. Paul wants to narrate us into the story of redemption in Christ so that we become actors in the story, so that we "become the righteousness of God" (5:21). God grant us contemporary preachers the grace to turn all our grubby congregational squabbles into high theology.

Much intrigued with Thompson's suggestion that "the logical sequence of the text will, in most instances, provide the sequential movement for the sermon," I decide to try to let the supposed setting for 2 Corinthians 5–6, as well as its striking chiastic structure, form my sermon. Can I read between the lines and re-create the story from Corinth in my church? Can I narrate Paul's letter as a letter? Can I push my pastoral political struggle toward a story, *the* story of the whole new world that has been created in Christ?

A few observations (reservations?) about my sermon:

There is a great deal of me in the sermon, much "I" and "me." Generally, I am opposed to this sort of parading of the ego. Blame it on Paul. He unashamedly goes autobiographical in chapters 1–7, all in the effort to get the Corinthians to "make room for us in your hearts" (7:2). This is the same Paul who elsewhere blurted out, "Imitate me" (Phil. 3:17). To be sure, he was *Saint* Paul and I am not. Still, this unabashed placing of himself at the center of his sermon is risky. I have had enough of these churches that are built around the personality of the preacher. (Thompson politely refers to this as Paul's "asymmetrical relationship" with the Corinthians.) Yet the gospel is meant to be embodied, incarnate. I throw caution to the wind and, blaming Paul, put myself into the sermon.

Though Paul is unimpressive in his person, his preaching, and his productivity—according to his unnamed Corinthian opponents—he is impressively confident of his place in a great victory procession (2:14). The peculiar nature of that cosmic triumph becomes the center of his argument. Everyone who is "in Christ," that is, all of us (3:18; 5:10), share in that victory. Paul writes not to indicate that he has something they do not; rather, he writes to narrate them all into a reality that only awaits acknowledgment (3:18; 5:10). His ministry is defined and defended on the basis of the new creation in Christ (5:17). His task is that of persuasion (5:20b–6:2), not so much on the basis of rational argument or display of proofs but rather on the basis of his own radically transformed life that can only be explained by reference to a radically transformed world.

At this point I realize why I am so reluctant to get personal and use myself as a sermon illustration. It is not because I am so humble and self-effacing. It is more likely because my ministry is still so much in the grip of the Old World. In so many ways *kata sarka* ("from a human point of view") is me all over. There is not yet enough of the *gar* ("for, accordingly," 5:14). Yet, in my own bumbling way, I am called to demonstrate my new citizenship and to tell others about it. Nothing less than "the love of Christ urges us on" (5:14).

As Thompson says, this story—God reconciling the world to himself, shifting the whole cosmos at the point of the cross, creating a new humanity—creates a new epistemology. It really is Isa. 65:17 fulfilled. The Lord has indeed done a "new thing" (Isa. 43:18–19); can you see it? Yet, by God's grace, none of this is done without a new people who embody and speak "the message of reconciliation" and who tell that story, God's story, in a manner that it becomes the congregation's story. This is our care and our delight as narrative preachers.

꙼

Durham, North Carolina
Fourth Sunday of Lent, 2002

Dear Church:

You know me. Church meetings are not my favorite way to spend an evening. Plodding through the business, reading reports to one another. Boredom sets in, I doze, I long to be elsewhere. Lord, deliver me from church meetings.

Except last Wednesday. Now there's a church meeting worth remembering! It's been a long time since the volume got raised that high, along with the temperature. No chairs were thrown, for which I'm grateful. I hope that the argument was productive. It took me until Friday afternoon to cool down, and when asked, "What happened at the Administrative Board meeting on Wednesday?" to answer, "Well, we had ourselves quite a fight—I mean, er, productive disagreement."

On my way home after Wednesday's meeting, when I was complaining to the Lord about some of the things some of you said to me, the Lord said, "You're the one who's always complaining about boring church meetings!"

One of your questions stuck in my mind for the rest of the week. I think it encapsulates what was on many of your minds. One of you asked, "Pastor, why are you so vehemently opposed to the war with Iraq?"

I think that was on many of your minds on Wednesday. You wanted me to account for myself—my calling a meeting last Sunday night to discuss our congregation's response to the president's call to arms, and my comments in a couple of sermons this past fall.

Church, I know what you're thinking. "He's against the war because he's an incurable sixties radical," or "He's a yellow-dog Democrat," or "He's a knee-jerk pacifist who is always against war, and this one too."

OK. I'll admit all that may have something to do with my repugnance over plans for this war. I didn't vote for George Bush even though he is my age and a sometime–United Methodist. And my memories of another war in Southeast Asia probably color my thinking.

How well you know me.

"Pastor, why are you so opposed to a war with Iraq?"

It's a question that begs for explanation. I could lay on you my quibbling about U.S. foreign policy in this case—we're being led to war by a president who has never been in war; why Iraq, when a dozen nearby regimes are as corrupt? What on earth do we do once we've won the war—occupy Iraq for the next fifty years? And so forth.

But you would say, "He's no expert on foreign policy. He's nothing but a preacher, and not a great one at that."

And you would be right.

No, I feel the way I do about the proposed war with Iraq, not, I pray, because of something I suspect about George Bush but because of something I know about Jesus. There was a day when I would have thought about these matters from the standpoint of my U.S. citizenship, that is, from an exclusively human point of view. But now I try to think about these matters from the standpoint of my citizenship in a whole new world. From God's point of view.

Let me explain. One day, on a Sunday, or maybe a Wednesday, in my eighteenth year, or maybe my twentieth, I woke up, jumped out of bed, looked out the window, and to my surprise I saw a whole new world. I was like Dorothy, when after the tornado, she regains consciousness in Oz and figures out that she is not in Kansas anymore. The world didn't look all green, or gold. Just different. No one around me seemed to notice, which at first proved to be disconcerting, as if I had landed on another planet but nobody there knew it was another planet. So I wandered the streets, stumbled along, had to learn to walk, and to count, to talk all over again, like I was born, again.

I had to learn new words, words like reconciliation, atonement, forgiveness, justification. Well-meaning friends told me to "face facts," to "get real." But they were calling to me across a great divide, attempting to lasso me back into the more conforming corral I once called home.

I had moved. It wasn't that I was being unrealistic; it was rather that I had taken up residence in new reality. I still loved "the facts," and thought it important to live in the light of those facts or else appear stupidly out of step.

In short, I had been, was being, am still being, saved. I had been "reconciled to God," as Paul might have put it. At the first, I did not know the words accurately to describe where I was, but that was me, "reconciled to God."

That God, whom I could never reach, had reached to me. That Judge, for whom I could never do enough good deeds, think enough good thoughts, feel enough good feelings, judged me good. The enemy from whom I had fled, raced to me, embraced me, revealed himself as none other than Friend. The Master to whom I owed so much, risked all, bought me in blood.

I won't bore you with the details except to say that the next day, next year, next decade, I could hardly find my way, so defamiliarized, strange, fresh, and new was the world.

I expect some of you may have had similar born-again, saved, conversion experiences. Even if you have not yet, I bet you will, and whether or not you even experience it, it doesn't change the reality of it. I've been over the mountain. I've seen the other side. It's there for sure. I know folks who've never been to France. Their lack of experience doesn't change the fact of France.

And once you've seen the whole new world, once you know for sure who rules, and who sits on the throne, and where we're all headed, and how the last chapter reads, well, it makes you walk a bit funny.

I don't mean that, as Christians, we are funny. I just mean to say that, as Christians, in the eyes of the world—the old monochrome world of conventionality, governmentally subsidized, officially sanctioned "reality"—we look to that world, well, funny. Odd.

The world still believes that, once you get up that mountain and look over the other side, there's nothing there. So we best take matters in hand and do our best to save ourselves by ourselves. The world thinks the throne is occupied by whomever we elected to sit there and act as if he is in charge. It's up to us to make history come out right, or it won't. Justice is in our hands. (George Bush's first name for his war on terror was "Operation Infinite Justice.")

That day, that week, or whatever, when I saw, I moved into a whole new world. When I got reconciled or, better, when I woke up to my reconciliation to God, it was like the painted, illusory backstage curtain descended and I saw a new world. It had always been there, long before I was given eyes to see it, been there at least since a Friday afternoon, breaking out first at Golgotha, finally broken in to me. But until then, I didn't know.

Because of that first glimpse, I've been reviewing this world ever since, and trying each Sunday, dear church, to get you to do the same. Go ahead and think of Sunday as a weekly attempt to get our vision corrected, as optometry. We gather in church, not seeking an escape from the "real world" but in order, by the grace of God, to get a gander at reality. Some Sundays, despite my bumbling homiletical efforts, you break free of the confines of convention, you journey to Bethlehem; in you, there is incarnation, in you, the cross is stamped, and you know that you have been claimed, commandeered for service to a new kingdom. On other Sundays, our eyes remain shut, no new thing is uttered or heard, and we go back to the same old world from whence we came, bored, but reassured by the routine.

We console ourselves with the slogans of an imperiled empire—can't teach an old dog new tricks, prayer is fine but sometimes you've got to face facts, this is a great struggle between good (us) and evil (them). Roll over and go back to sleep.

Oh, church, forgive me when I overstate the case for a whole new world! Forgive me, in a world at war, for too extravagantly claiming reconciliation. But put my preaching in context. I've tasted new wine that won't fit into old wineskins. I've seen a new world and now refuse to give too much honor to the old one. I've experienced the radical, world-changing power of Christ to get what he wants on the battlefield of my own soul. I'm not going back to business as usual and I don't want you to either.

And that's my answer to your question. I'm not for the war because I've been introduced to the Prince of Peace. I, who was God's great enemy, have been adopted, embraced, washed, reborn into God's family. I don't worry about who will win this battle or the next one because I already know who has won the war. I'm voting for the Prince.

Paul puts it better than I can:

> Therefore, knowing the fear of the Lord, we try to persuade others; . . . For the love of Christ urges us on, because we are convinced that one has died for all; therefore all have died. And he died for all, so that those who live might live no longer for themselves, but for him who died and was raised for them.
>
> From now on, therefore, we regard no one from a human point of view; even though we once knew Christ from a human point of view, we know him no longer in that way. So if anyone is in Christ, there is a new creation: everything old has passed away; see, everything has become new! All this is from God, who reconciled us to himself through Christ, and has given us the ministry of reconciliation; that is, in Christ God was reconciling the world to himself, not counting their trespasses against them, and entrusting the message of reconciliation to us. So we are ambassadors for Christ, since God is making his appeal through us; we entreat you on behalf of Christ, be reconciled to God. For our sake he made him to be sin who knew no sin, so that in him we might become the righteousness of God. (2 Cor. 5:11–6:2)

Presumably, before this war began, the president sent his ambassador to attempt to reason with Saddam. I hope so. When the ambassador is there, it's just like the president himself is there.

Paul says, in Christ, you've had your citizenship in the Old World exchanged for a passport to the new. Not by what you or I did, but by what Christ did, you have been brought close to God. The cross, not the Stars and Stripes, gives you your marching orders. The main difference between you and most of the people in Iraq is not that you are a citizen of a righteous, pure, good, and victorious democracy, and they are not. The difference is that you know who sits on the throne, who is in charge, and most of them don't. Tragically, too many of us act like we're still citizens of the Old World. When the United States says "jump," our only question is, "How high?" That morbid perspective, that "human point of view," is a hard habit to break.

Thanks be to God, we're citizens of a new creation. Moreover, we have our marching orders. To us has been entrusted the "ministry of reconciliation." The "message of reconciliation has been entrusted to us." Not just to me, the preacher, but also to you in your new status as "ambassadors for Christ."

It's an amazing claim to make for the church. The church is God's embassy, that place from where Christ's ambassadors are sent into the world. My job, as your pastor, is to help you see yourselves as Christ's messengers and to help you get the message.

Paul says that in you God is making his appeal. In this letter I'm making my appeal to you. In your peace making, peace praying, peace living, God is appealing to the world. You are God's letter to the world. In you, God is saying, "World wake up! Open your eyes. This is my world and I'm determined to get back what rightly belongs to me."

Though I've not been as good a pastor as you deserved, this has been my vocation while among you, whether I'm in the pulpit, or at a meeting, or beside your beds of pain—to get you to see the world as it is now that Christ has conquered. The way I figure it, if I can just get you to see, you'll figure out what to do. Pray that God will give me what I need to help you claim your ambassadorship.

Paul says in his letter what I've been fumbling to say in mine: anyone "in Christ" (that is, *us*) is a new creation, a minister of reconciliation, a messenger of the good news, an ambassador for Christ, God's letter to the world, the very righteousness of God.

So you open your eyes, dare to look at the world as God's, get real, *be* the righteousness of God!

Sincerely,
Your Pastor

6

Revelation and Resistance: Narrative and Worship in John's Apocalypse

Stanley P. Saunders

No other New Testament writing provokes such contrary reactions as the Book of Revelation, John's Apocalypse. Many readers find it both the maddest and most maddening book in the New Testament, while others are drawn irresistibly into the quest to break its code and to provide a definitive explanation. Within some circles of the church, the peculiar literary and theological character of Revelation leads readers to approach the book with grave apprehension or to dismiss it altogether, while others happily claim it as a road map of contemporary history. On the one hand, not a few readers, both professional and lay, have concluded that Revelation is the crude, inept, and badly edited product of a second-rate mind. The many images and symbols found within its pages both invite and resist translation into clear and meaningful concepts. It displays multiple structuring devices, but seems to lack a clear plot. Even the attempt to identify what this book is, to establish its genre and thus to suggest appropriate reading strategies, has proved frustrating. On the other hand, one recent interpreter describes it as "a work of immense learning, astonishingly meticulous literary artistry, remarkable creative imagination, radical political critique, and profound theology."[1]

---

1. Richard Bauckham, *The Climax of Prophecy: Studies on the Book of Revelation* (Edinburgh: T & T Clark, 1993), ix.

Amid these diverse opinions, and after nearly two millennia of struggle, we can say with certainty that the Apocalypse provokes strong reactions, invites diverse interpretations, and resists definitive closure.[2] It is, in other words, a prime example of *a narrative of resistance,* a work designed to create imaginative space for discourse and social practice that pose a sharp alternative to "empire." Revelation was created for oral performance amid the eucharistic gatherings of the early Christians.[3] In these assemblies, the Apocalypse both described and evoked worship of the Lamb who was slain as the Lord of all creation. Revelation, in fact, presents worship itself as the definitive act of Christian resistance against the idolatry and violence of Roman imperial domination. The Apocalypse as a whole also represents a particularly interesting expression of early Christian proclamation, directed apparently both to those who suffered and those who prospered under Roman imperial ideology and practice.

This chapter is devoted to locating the Apocalypse amid the narrative world of early Christianity and examining the features— orality, social location, manipulation of genre, structures and literary techniques, dialect, and critical engagement with myth and ritual—that distinguish this story as a narrative of resistance. We move toward a focus on Revelation 4–5, which describes worship in heaven and functions as a definitive scene in the development of Revelation's narrative. Along the way I appeal to the work of two students of the arts of resistance: James C. Scott, a political scientist who has focused his work on the tactics dominated peoples employ to resist their dominators, and the late French social critic, theologian, and philosopher Michel de Certeau, who also focused much of his reflections on everyday practices of resistance.[4]

2. David Barr (*Tales of the End: A Narrative Commentary on the Book of Revelation* [Santa Rosa, Calif.: Polebridge, 1998], 147–48) notes that Revelation trains its auditors to be wary of endings, thereby inviting continued reinterpretation of the meaning of the story.

3. David Barr, "The Apocalypse of John as Oral Enactment," *Interpretation* 40 (1986): 252–56; idem, *Tales of the End,* 171–72.

4. For Scott, I have drawn especially on *Domination and the Arts of Resistance: Hidden Transcripts* (New Haven and London: Yale University Press, 1990). See also his *Weapons of the Weak: Everyday Forms of Peasant Resistance* (New Haven and London: Yale University Press, 1985). For Michel de Certeau, see especially *The Practice of Everyday Life* (Berkeley: University of California Press, 1984). For brief introductions to Certeau's work with reference

John's Apocalypse as Narrative

At first glance, one might question whether the Apocalypse is really a narrative at all, especially if "narrative" implies a relatively smooth linear development, a clear sense of plot, or the kinds of character development contemporary readers expect in a good story. Despite what seems, at least superficially, a relative lack of these, Revelation is indeed a narrative.[5] In his introduction to narrative criticism of the New Testament, Mark Allan Powell defines narrative as "any work of literature that tells a story."[6] The Apocalypse, indeed, tells a story—not a simple story, however, but a story with many narrative layers intertwined.

At one level, Revelation is an account of John's visionary experiences while exiled on the island of Patmos, and especially while observing events in heaven and on earth from the exalted setting of the heavenly throne of God. The story of worship and the events that take place in the heavenly realm constitute a second distinctive, yet interrelated, level of the narrative. Revelation also tells the stories of the beast and its violent conquest of the people of God; and of Babylon, the city where Israel was both taken captive and seduced, including Babylon's commercial and military conquests and eventual destruction.[7] But even more than these, the Apocalypse tells the story of the revelation of Jesus Christ, from his appearance at the throne of God as a slaughtered Lamb who is worthy to open the scroll (Revelation 4–5) to his defeat of

to biblical studies, see Vincent J. Miller, "Certeau," in *Handbook of Postmodern Biblical Criticism*, ed. A. K. M. Adam (St. Louis: Chalice, 2000), 42–48; Mary McClintock Fulkerson, "Practices," in Adam, *Handbook of Postmodern Biblical Criticism*, 194–95. Graham Ward, ed., *The Certeau Reader* (Oxford: Blackwell, 2000), provides a useful collection of key writings by Certeau.

5. For a detailed and systematic discussion of Revelation as a narrative, including its point of view, rhetoric, literary settings, character, and plot, see James L. Resseguie, *Revelation Unsealed: A Narrative Critical Approach to John's Apocalypse*, Biblical Interpretation Series 32 (Leiden: Brill, 1998). Other works, aimed at a more popular level, that address Revelation as narrative include Barr, *Tales of the End;* Charles H. Talbert, *The Apocalypse: A Reading of the Revelation of John* (Louisville: Westminster John Knox, 1994); A. J. P. Garrow, *Revelation*, New Testament Readings (London: Routledge, 1997).

6. Mark Allan Powell, *What Is Narrative Criticism?* Guides to Biblical Scholarship: New Testament Series (Minneapolis: Fortress, 1990), 23.

7. The layers described in this paragraph correspond generally to the analysis of M. Eugene Boring, "Narrative Christology in the Apocalypse," *Catholic Biblical Quarterly* 54 (1992): 702–23.

the imperial beasts and marriage to the heavenly city, the new Jerusalem (19:11–22:7). Although Christ is not on the stage at every moment in the unified narrative of Revelation, his story is nonetheless the overarching drama within which the other layers of the narrative have their place.

The identification of Revelation as the story of Jesus Christ is basic for making sense of this work. John begins to make this identification clear at the very outset of the book. The first lines of ancient writings usually provided the cues that helped audiences identify what they were hearing and thus shaped expectations of the performance. The first line of Revelation identifies this performance as "The Unveiling of Jesus Christ" ("Apocalypse" = "revelation" = "unveiling"). As in the Gospels, Jesus is both the subject (the one doing the revealing, even if through angelic agents) and the object (the content) of the revelation. As David Barr has noted, "The Apocalypse is in its most basic sense a retelling of this story of Jesus in a new way and with new images."[8] Although this point might seem so obvious as to be banal, that Revelation has been read as a road map of the future, or as a description of the end of the world, or even as the story of what will happen in the Middle East in our lifetime,[9] makes it necessary to emphasize John's own careful, intentional identification of the nature of this work. The Apocalypse is another way of telling the story of Jesus Christ; this is its primary purpose.

This claim also provides a foundation for locating the Apocalypse within the larger narrative frame of the canon and the narrative of faith that is the Christian tradition. M. Eugene Boring has noted that the various levels of narrative within the Apocalypse all presuppose and point toward God's story, including past, present, and coming activity. In Revelation, however, the activity of God is virtually indistinguishable from Christ's activity; from Revelation 5 onward, Christ, the slain Lamb, shares God's throne, and throughout Revelation it is Christ who defines God.[10] When the Seer looks back at the past activity of God/Christ, it is primarily creation and the cross that come into focus. Like the apostle

8. Barr, *Tales of the End*, 3.

9. Arthur W. Wainwright, *Mysterious Apocalypse: Interpreting the Book of Revelation* (Nashville: Abingdon, 1993), reviews the major ways Revelation has been read.

10. Boring, "Narrative Christology," 707, 713–18.

Paul, John sees the defining apocalyptic moment not in the second coming of Jesus, but in his death and resurrection, which accomplishes God's conquest of all cosmic and historical adversaries. In the present experience of time, Christ's death and resurrection function as the definitive model of faithful discipleship, and Christ rules the whole of creation, even overpowering death itself. At the same time, Christ is also the one coming (3:11; 22:20; cf. also 1:4, 8), whose advent marks the resolution of all the levels of the narrative.

In general, these aspects of the narrative of Revelation are consistent with what one finds elsewhere in the New Testament: Jesus defines for us the nature and will of God; accomplishes reconciliation, peace, and salvation through his death and resurrection; and rules now as the Lord of all creation and of all the dimensions of time. Like much of the rest of the New Testament, and especially Paul, the Apocalypse presents the world as the locus of a cosmic battle between forces allied with and arrayed against God, with humankind functioning as both agents and victims of these cosmic forces. In its present appearance, the world is beset by violence that only God's intervention in Christ—through the power of the cross—can undo.

Like much of the rest of the New Testament, Revelation is also deeply conversant with the Scriptures of Israel, especially with Isaiah, Ezekiel, and Daniel, and presents the story of Christ and God's redemption of the world in terms that draw upon the narratives of God's dealings with Israel. The exodus story in particular provides the author with foundational images of salvation. In short, the narrative of the Apocalypse continues the story of God's judgment and salvation for God's people and the world. This is a story of the God who is full of mercy, who stands with those who suffer oppression and violence, who redeems creation through the blood of the Lamb, and who, despite appearances to the contrary within human history, rules the cosmos and is creating, even through the prayers and faithful suffering of those who follow the Lamb, a new heaven and a new earth.

In at least broad terms, then, Revelation presupposes and narrates a story that is in continuity with what we discern across the New Testament. Yet it will also become clear that the story told in Revelation is distinguished in many ways from the narratives we discern in other portions of the New Testament. The most obvious distinction is this narrative's focus on the culmination of the story of God's judgment and salvation. The Apocalypse seeks, in other words, to depict the resolution of all the stories and of the whole story of God's creation, of God's engagement with Israel and the nations, and of the struggles of God's people to remain faithful amid the violence and allures of the fallen world. For Christians, Revelation is the fitting bookend, with Genesis, of the whole canonical story.

In keeping with its focus on engendering communities that endure and resist the narratives of domination and empire, the narrative of the Apocalypse is also distinguished by its degree of focus on and engagement with Roman imperial mythology, liturgy, and politics, its graphic depiction of the violence associated with empire, and the clarity of its call to worship of the Lamb as the definitive act of resistance. Finally, although all of the New Testament documents were meant to be heard as wholes, no other work of the New Testament so clearly demands integral reading strategies in order to convey its meanings and effects. The integral character of the Apocalypse is visible first of all in its nature as a work intended for oral performance.

The Apocalypse as Oral Performance

With good reason, John's Apocalypse begins with a blessing for those who read the work aloud (1:3) and closes with a strong warning against those who would add to or take away from it (22:8–9). It is a narrative whole—one self-contained piece—meant to be performed orally as a whole. One cannot preach portions of Revelation, as we typically do when following the lectionary or when preaching by theme or pericope, without doing damage to it—that is, without turning it into something other than what it was meant to be. More than thirty years ago, Eugene Peterson noted well that no biblical book had been wrenched so far from its roots in oral media, into the foreign atmosphere of literary texts and the kinds of interpretive operations we have come to impose on the written word.[11] Merely by opening our printed Bibles to read silently, by noting the paragraph breaks, and chapters and verses (all of which are later editorial additions introduced for the sake of literate audiences), by reading the textual notes at the bottom of our Bible's

11. Eugene H. Peterson, "Apocalypse: The Medium Is the Message," *Theology Today* 26 (1969): 136.

pages, and by turning to our commentaries, we embody practices that surpass the Seer's worst nightmares. The people who first heard John's Apocalypse and the other writings of the New Testament were able to perform and make sense of complex, sophisticated, and subtle oral presentations, especially stories. These performances appealed not merely to the eyes and ears but, as the Apocalypse itself demonstrates, to the visual, tactile, olfactory, and gustatory senses. Revelation was meant to be experienced as a whole.

The shift from "aura-literacy" to textual literacy that has come in the wake of the printing press has been especially problematic for readers of a book like the Apocalypse. Allen Callahan contends that modern, critical readers (such as Bible scholars and preachers) have been taught to reformulate "classical" texts as information—that is, as lists of ideas or propositions—that conforms to critical expectations and that is thus more intelligible for modern readers. These modern hermeneutical and philosophical rubrics push toward critical, "objective" renderings of "what the text means." In contrast, the real critical task, according to Callahan, is to understand how this text affected its hearers, "how, in the parlance of technofunk musician and composer George Clinton, the text is 'doin' it to you in your earhole.'" Callahan concludes that those who first gathered to hear the Apocalypse were summoned to a transformative experience.[12]

The most important distinction between oral and text-based cultures, for our purposes, is that oral cultures conduct their thought and argument in terms of stories. Stories integrate and motivate. Stories affect emotions, and while they shape, frame, and contextualize ideas, both spatially and temporally, they also shape the nature and character of rationality itself. Elisabeth Schüssler Fiorenza rightly claims that "the language and narrative flow of Revelation elicit emotions, reactions, and convictions that cannot and should not be fully conceptualized and phrased in propositional-logical language."[13] Indeed, the discourse of Revelation can-

12. Allen Dwight Callahan, "The Language of Apocalypse," *Harvard Theological Review* 88 (1995): 459. On the cultural consequences of the increasing shift from narrative to "list," see John D. O'Banion, *Reorienting Rhetoric: The Dialectic of List and Story* (University Park: Pennsylvania State University Press, 1991).

13. Elisabeth Schüssler Fiorenza, "Revelation," in *The New Testament and Its Modern Interpreters*, ed. Eldon Jay Epp and George W. MacRae (Philadelphia: Fortress; Atlanta: Scholars, 1989), 417.

not be captured in conceptual, propositional language, for it is meant to evoke imaginative participation—a different kind of knowledge than one gains when reading, for example, the ideas on this page. For members of oral cultures, performance of John's Revelation was itself an event, "a movement in time, completely lacking the thing-like repose of the written or printed word."[14] In short, the Apocalypse is not merely an argument, but an oral performance that generates an array of experiences and reactions, thereby to transform the social space inhabited by both performer and audience. In order to remind us of its oral character, and thus of its essential strangeness to those of us who are members of text-oriented cultures, I frequently refer to John's Apocalypse in what follows as a "performance," where otherwise we might call it a text.

The orality of this narrative is an integral feature of its function as a tool of resistance. Revelation nurtures and sustains resistance by appealing to whole communities and to the whole person, by using language that integrates rationality and the senses. It accomplishes this by means of its self-conscious use of oral techniques for orally based auditors. One of the strongest threats to the operation of imperial power is the presence of strong, potentially independent communities.[15] The Christian communities in Asia Minor, gathering to worship and witness to another Lord than Caesar, posed such a threat. The performance of works like the Apocalypse was a key element in nurturing the existence of such communities, and in shaping their alternative imagination and practices.

Traditional approaches to preaching frequently have an atomizing effect on Revelation, thus preventing it from exercising its full imaginative, world-shaping, and resistance-engendering force. In a sense, by limiting the occasions when congregations can experience performances of the Apocalypse as a whole, and by turning its interpretation over to specialized elites, the church, partic-

14. Walter J. Ong, *Orality and Literacy: The Technologizing of the Word* (London: Routledge, 1988), 75.

15. Scott (*Domination and the Arts of Resistance,* 64–66) argues that systems of domination depend on the atomization and surveillance of subordinate populations. Atomization effects control by preventing potentially threatening groups from forming or by breaking apart those that do, and surveillance makes certain that when people do gather together, their discourse and actions do not become threatening.

ularly churches where conformity and social control are highly valued, engages Revelation in much the same way that empires dominate and control conquered peoples. Were we more accustomed to hearing the Apocalypse performed as a whole in our modern assemblies, as it likely was in the eucharistic assemblies of congregations in Asia Minor during the last half of the first century, we would have a more immediate and powerful sense of the ways this work alters imagination, calls forth new social bodies and practices, and evokes surprising new visions of the world.

The Social Location of the Apocalypse

As the Seer makes clear at the outset, the visions described in the performance take place while John is in exile, "because of the word of God and the testimony of Jesus," on the island of Patmos (1:9). John writes as a marginal person (a visionary), from a peripheral location (island exile), to marginal communities (Christian assemblies in the cities of Asia), with whom John may have had a peripheral relationship.[16] John's vision employs the tactics of peripheral or marginal people in order to encourage readers to "come out" (18:4)—to come away from the centers of power and honor in the Roman Empire and to embrace the peripheral existence of those who resist and give witness in the name of Jesus Christ. Small wonder, then, that John's message of resistance continues to appeal to and offer encouragement precisely to those readers in each generation who live on the margins of worldly power, wealth, and status, who practice their faith at the periphery, even of the churches.

The marginal perspective adopted by the Seer corresponds to the situation of the Christian congregations to which the Apocalypse is addressed and reflects their social experience within the social, economic, and political arrangements of the Roman Empire. The seven cities to which John addresses the individual letters in chapters 1–3 all were within the ambit of Roman imperial control and had institutional structures dedicated to the Roman imperial cult.[17] At least three of the seven cities—Pergamon,

16. Leonard L. Thompson, *Revelation* (Nashville: Abingdon, 1998), 32–34.

17. Steven J. Friesen, *Imperial Cults and the Apocalypse of John: Reading Revelation in the Ruins* (Oxford: Oxford University Press, 2001), provides a clear, carefully researched, and nuanced description of the imperial cults in Asia

Smyrna, and Ephesus—had provincial imperial cults, which focused on the maintenance and nourishment of Asia's relationship
with Rome. Epigraphic, numismatic, sculptural, and architectural
remains demonstrate that imperial cults permeated community
life in the cities to which John's Apocalypse was addressed, taking
root in the marketplaces and other settings where citizens gathered, involving at various times virtually all public spaces.

Although it is not possible to date the work with complete certainty, any of the dates usually proposed for Revelation locate it
within the context of the ancient Roman Empire, in the latter half
of the first or the beginning of the second century. Speculation
about the situation that gave rise to the Apocalypse has focused on
scenarios of persecution under the emperors Nero (i.e., ca. 68–69
C.E.) or Domitian (81–96 C.E.), but the historical evidence for such
a crisis has not proved compelling. Nor is it necessary to postulate
a crisis in order to make sense contextually of the Seer's visions.
The Christians of Asia Minor, like their non-Christian neighbors,
lived in the shadow of Roman domination. Even in periods of relative calm and prosperity, imperial practices engender situations of
conflict and tension within subordinate populations. Some might
choose to avail themselves of the resources of imperial economics,
for example, while others would adopt tactics of resistance.

To what degree could Christians participate in the politics and
economics of the empire and yet remain faithful to their calling?
Christian households would be required continually to make decisions about the ways they would engage, critically or construc-
tively, the myths and practices of the empire. One of the recurrent
terms in Revelation is ὑπομονή (*hypomonē*), frequently translated
as "patience" or "endurance." A stronger English translation may
be more appropriate, for "in standard Greek ὑπομονή refers over-
whelmingly—and positively—to independent, unyielding, defiant
perseverance in the face of aggressive misfortune, and thus to a
kind of courageousness"[18]—in short, "resistance." For Christians,
such resistance would be the product of Christian faith rather
than personal strength. Revelation offers Christian households re-

---

and their importance for the interpretation of Revelation. Friesen's work decisively shapes my reading of Revelation.

18. Walter Radl, "ὑπομονή," in *Exegetical Dictionary of the New Testament*, ed.
Horst Balz and Gerhard Schneider, 3 vols. (Grand Rapids: Eerdmans, 1993),
3:405.

sources and tools for critical discernment and practices of resistance to the mythological consciousness and practices of the imperial order. It accomplishes this primarily by creating imaginative "space" for its audiences, in particular by its manipulation of genre and structure, its use of dialect, and its critical engagement with the myths and rituals of the dominating powers.

Generic Manipulation and Structure

Genre: What Is the Apocalypse?

Although a variety of generic identifications of the Apocalypse have been set forth over the centuries, a singular, definitive identification has proven elusive.[19] Interpreters now frequently concede that Revelation is a mixed genre that includes features primarily associated with epistles and prophecy, as well as apocalyptic literature. In a perceptive discussion of the genre of Revelation, Gregory Linton has urged acceptance of the multivalent, hybrid character of the Apocalypse, and suggested ways in which this hybrid character lends itself to the task of facilitating resistance. Unlike formulaic, predictable works that clearly fit a particular generic mold, Revelation "transgresses" prior rules, offering its audience multiple generic options and interpretations from which to choose, thereby "providing more room for the reader to participate in the production of its meanings."[20] The effect is a work that repays multiple hearings, admits multiple interpretative approaches, and invites its audience to become active interpreters. Whereas works that provide cues to establish relatively simple generic identifications do not allow much creativity or participation on the part of readers, hybrid texts are more engaging, complex, and ultimately satisfying. They allow both performer and audience to become active participants in the construction of meaning: the performer is simultaneously the composer, and the audience simultaneously the writer.

19. For summaries of the discussion of the genre of Revelation see, for example, Richard Bauckham, *The Theology of the Book of Revelation,* New Testament Theology (Cambridge: Cambridge University Press, 1993), 1–22; Gregory Linton, "Reading the Apocalypse as an Apocalypse," in *Society of Biblical Literature 1991 Seminar Papers,* ed. Eugene H. Lovering Jr. (Atlanta: Scholars, 1991), 161–86.
20. Linton, "Reading the Apocalypse," 170–71.

This does not mean that the Apocalypse becomes whatever the performer or audience makes of it at the moment, nor that any interpretation is as good as any other. The point is that Revelation resists reduction to a single meaning, to one line of interpretation. Performances that suggest a singular, definitive interpretation, like many of today's popular interpretations of Revelation, are reductionistic at best. Such readings effectively suppress the literary genius of the Seer and rob the performance of its generative, resistant power. By making room for different lines of interpretation, the Apocalypse reveals a world that is more complex and fundamentally different than the mythic story line of empire, which would admit no alternatives. Rather than merely replace the imperial myth with yet another singular, imperialistic narrative, and rather than rendering readers passive in the face of yet another monolithic worldview, Revelation invites and supplies resources for active, critical interpretive engagement not only with itself, but with the world of empire.

Structure and Itinerary in Revelation

One of the reasons many preachers find preaching from Revelation difficult is its complex, nonlinear structure. Adela Yarbro Collins has noted that, though the letters to the seven churches (1:9–3:22) lend themselves readily to the move from text to sermon, problems of sequence and repetition make the rest of the book, chapters 4–22, less accessible.[21] Contrary to what Collins's argument might suggest, however, it is not the text of Revelation that is the problem so much as the ways we typically approach biblical texts for preaching. The "problems of sequence and repetition" are only problematic when we attempt to violate the Seer's directions for how to use this work. Again, the Apocalypse poses a distinctive challenge to preachers because it was meant to be *performed as a whole,* not taken apart and preached piece by piece.

Revelation begins with a clear prologue (1:1–8) that corresponds to an epilogue (22:6–21), both of which draw on epistolary convention (1:4–6; 22:21), contain prophetic oracles (e.g., 1:7 [cf. Dan. 7:13; Zech. 12:10, 12 LXX]; 22:16b [cf. Isa. 11:10; 60:3]),[22] and echo one another verbally (1:1–3//22:6–7; 1:8//

21. Adela Yarbro Collins, " 'What the Spirit Says to the Churches': Preaching the Apocalypse," *Quarterly Review* 71 (1984): 69–84.
22. See Bauckham, *Climax of Prophecy,* 318–26.

22:13). Everything between the epilogue and prologue is presented as a single vision, although that vision has several distinct, yet interrelated, elements. The first and most clearly distinguishable of these three movements (1:9–3:22) tells what happens to the Seer on Patmos, "in the Spirit on the Lord's Day" (1:10), when a majestic human being appears and calls upon the Seer to write letters to the angels of the churches in seven cities of Asia Minor. Then a door opens in heaven (4:1) and John is called up to witness a divine court scene in which the Lamb who was slaughtered opens (chaps. 4–5) and reveals the contents of a scroll, which depicts the judgment of the world and the vindication of the righteous (chaps. 6–22). But the Seer's careful interlacing of the material in chapters 4–22 resists any single organizational scheme—or, rather, permits diverse outlines. The effect is a performance that resists fragmentation, whether by ancient or modern audiences, and that presents an integrated, unified alternative to the mythic patterns of the empire. This in turn alters the way audiences engage the work.

Michel de Certeau's explanation of the distinction between "maps," on the one hand, and "tours" or "itineraries," on the other, provides a helpful analogy.[23] Maps are (purportedly) objective and abstract representations of relations in space, in which space itself is divided into grids of homogeneous units, and items are located beside one another, with no two items occupying the same space. Maps arise as the tools of empires and nation-states, of hierarchical social institutions interested in surveying and controlling spaces and movements. Itineraries, on the other hand, mark space in terms of experienced relations: "We walked around the lake to where the old oak tree stands, then turned up the hill, stopping for a moment by the rocks to catch our breath." When we approach Revelation as modern readers of texts, we are quickly tempted to look for a road map, which freezes our perspective on the performance from some supposedly objective point of view. The itinerary of the Apocalypse, with its many stops and starts, it repetitions, its shifting referents— and its inexorable journey toward the wedding of the Lamb— provides yet another indication of its character as a narrative of resistance.

23. Certeau, *Practice of Everyday Life,* 115–30.

The Dialect of Resistance

James Scott's study of the ways dominated people create social space through the use of "hidden transcripts" helps us make sense of the peculiar dialect with which the Seer speaks. Dialect is often a reflection of social-class solidarity—an expression of resistance to the cultured, standardized speech of the dominant class. Scott lists the use of dialect among the tactics by which dominated groups resist the atomization and surveillance associated with domination, while preserving a sense of group identity.[24]

The language of the Apocalypse has long been the object of critical disdain on the part of Greek grammarians.[25] Most of John's "solecisms" (blunders of speech, or breaches of decorum or etiquette) involve disagreements in case, number, gender, or person, the mixing of verb tenses or moods for no apparent reason, or expressions that seem to mimic Hebrew or Aramaic (e.g., 4:9–10). Sometimes John's expressions simply create spatial disorientation, as in 5:6a, where the Seer locates the Lamb in the throne scene, but in such a way that it is never quite clear where or with whom he is standing ("between the throne and the four living creatures, and among the elders"). In light of John's peculiar use of language, some have held the author to be linguistically incompetent or careless, someone writing in Greek while thinking in Hebrew.[26] Yet another version of this position sees in Revelation the expression of Greek as it was spoken in Diaspora Jewish communities in Roman provinces such as Asia—Greek spoken in the accent of the Jewish quarter—a language that itself embodies the accommodations of subordinate peoples to the dominant elites.[27] This position offers a broad analogy to the way dialect functions to distinguish subordinate groups in Scott's research, but misses the element of resistance to which he points.

24. Scott, *Domination and the Arts of Resistance*, 129.

25. See the summary in Stanley Porter, "The Language of the Apocalypse in Recent Discussion," *New Testament Studies* 35 (1989): 582–603; also G. K. Beale, *The Book of Revelation*, New International Greek Testament Commentary (Grand Rapids: Eerdmans, 1999), 100–107.

26. R. H. Charles, *The Revelation of St. John*, 2 vols., International Critical Commentary (New York: Scribner's, 1920), 1:cxliv.

27. Steven Thompson, *The Apocalypse and Semitic Syntax*, Society of New Testament Studies Monograph Series (Cambridge: Cambridge University Press, 1985), 108.

Allen Dwight Callahan's analysis of the Seer's language, however, picks up precisely on the element of resistance. Callahan contends that John is intentionally speaking an "idiolect," an artifice that employs grammatical transgressions as part of an attempt to alter the collective consciousness of its audience. Building on Schüssler Fiorenza's claim that Revelation should be read as an evocative performance, rather than propositionally or representationally, Callahan claims that John intentionally adopts and decolonizes the (Greek) language of the (Roman) colonizer.[28] John must use the Greek in order to be understood, but he adapts it to his own agenda, rendering it a discourse of resistance. John accomplishes this not only by introducing grammatical and syntactical miscues, or by mimicking the cadences of the Greek version of the Old Testament, but by "relexicalizing" imperial speech. The juxtaposition of messianic images with a slaughtered lamb in Rev. 5:5–6, for example, effectively undermines both Jewish and Roman notions of power. In similar ways, John brings new associations to imperial terms for victory and conquest, faith, and eternity. The Seer reassociates victory with "the blood of the Lamb" (12:11; 5:6; 7:14; 17:14) and with faithful resistance/endurance (2:10–11; 3:4–5, 10–12). The Seer also uses Jesus to establish a normative model for faith, expressed both in his witness to God in his crucifixion and in his faithfulness to his followers, who also are called in turn to manifest their faithfulness unto death (e.g., 2:10, 13; 7:14–17; 20:4–6). Finally, eternity is discerned not in Roman imperial dominion, but in the presence of God and the reign of the Lamb. The effect of John's peculiar dialect, in short, is to tell the story of Jesus in the language people heard every day, but to speak this language with an alien inflection and alternative meanings.[29]

Cultivating Critical Mythic Consciousness

Societies and cultures embody stories. The foundational stories that express and shape the self-understanding of communities

28. Callahan, "Language of Apocalypse," 464–65; see the similar argument in Jean-Pierre Ruiz, *Ezekiel in the Apocalypse: The Transformation of Prophetic Language in Revelation 16,17–19,10,* European University Studies 23/376 (Frankfurt: Peter Lang, 1989), 220.
29. Callahan, "Language of Apocalypse," 466–70.

and cultures are *myth*, a term related to the same Proto-Indo-European root from which come such words as "ma-ma," "mother," "muttering," and "mystery."[30] Myth is the organization of "mystery" and "muttering" in the form of primary stories—myth and narrative are integrally related—by which we communicate with one another, make sense of life, and form our social contracts. They function most powerfully when they become "second-nature," when they are so pervasive, powerful, and "true" as to seem "natural" or to represent the divine order. Myth is still very much alive and powerful in modern societies.

As the author of Revelation and the other writers of the New Testament recognized, affirming the Christian faith entailed cultivating a "critical mythic consciousness"—that is, the capacity to discern, critically engage, and fashion alternatives to the mythic consciousness that passes for "the way the world is." Thus, the Apocalypse tells the story of Jesus Christ in mythical terms, as a world- and imagination-shaping story. In order to gain a clearer sense of the ways John cultivates critical mythic consciousness, I examine aspects of the Roman imperial cult as well as additional tactics John employs in order to subvert and replace Roman myth.

The Embodiment of Myth in the Roman Imperial Cult

John directly engages expressions of Roman imperial myth while telling the story of Jesus Christ, precisely in order to be able to offer a compelling alternative to the foundational stories that govern life in the Roman Empire. The most prominent mythic pattern developed in the Apocalypse is the combat myth, which is found in different forms throughout the cultures of the ancient Near East, as well as in the Old Testament.[31] Elements of this mythic story stand at the heart both of Roman imperial cult and ideology and John's vision of the conflict between the Lamb and

30. William G. Doty, *Mythography: The Study of Myths and Rituals*, 2d ed. (Tuscaloosa: University of Alabama Press, 2000), 6.

31. See Adela Yarbro Collins, *The Combat Myth and the Book of Revelation* (Missoula, Mont.: Scholars, 1976). Barr summarizes the typical elements of this mythic pattern: appearance of one or more dragons, chaos and disorder, attack, the appearance and apparent defeat of a champion, the dragon's reign, renewed battle and victory of the champion, fertility of the restored order, procession and victory shout, a temple built for the warrior god, a banquet, and manifestation of the champion's universal reign (*Tales of the End*, 122).

the beast/Babylon. Because John used a mythic pattern known broadly to people throughout the Mediterranean world and also appealed particularly to the Israelite versions of it, John's story would have characteristics that were recognizable and appealing even to a mixed audience of Jewish and Gentile Christians. John's peculiar, innovative use of the combat myth and other mythic images provides audiences with a powerful cornerstone of resistance.

The imperial cults were but one element of a larger complex of traditions within the polytheistic context of the Greco-Roman world. The imperial cults did not seek to overthrow or displace prevailing stories about the mythic origins of the world, but to incorporate imperial mythology into existing myths. For example, the imperial family found its place within the Olympian branch of the pantheon, thereby establishing a connection between imperial order and the prevailing story about the origin of the world. This story was filled with violence and conflict embracing both human and divine realms. The hierarchical and violent order of this world mirrored that of the divine world. Yet the whole cosmos yearned for a different reality, for a time of peace and stability. In response to this yearning, the imperial dynasty also represented itself as founding a "new world order," begun at the birth of Augustus, and represented pervasively throughout the empire both spatially and temporally. In 9 C.E., for example, the cities of the province of Asia—to which the Seer writes the Apocalypse—decided to reorder their reckoning of time to the birth of Caesar Augustus in 63 B.C.E., around September 23 or 24, which became the beginning of the new year.

Caesar's birth was celebrated as the realization of divine will and providence; the world would have come to an end if he had not been born. Caesar ends war and brings freedom. He is the "savior" whose benefactions surpass all others, whether past or future. The birth of this god was the beginning of the "good news" for the cosmos.[32] The Roman poet Virgil celebrated the reign of Augustus (and his successors) as a "dominion without end"—an age of peace, faith, and sustained righteousness (or justice).[33]

---

32. Hubert Cancik, "The End of the World, of History, and of the Individual in Greek and Roman Antiquity," in *The Encyclopedia of Apocalypticism*, vol. 1: *The Origins of Apocalypticism in Judaism and Christianity*, ed. John J. Collins (New York: Continuum, 1998), 99.

33. Virgil *The Aeneid* 1.268: "To them (the Romans, the city Rome) no bounds of empire I assign, Nor term of years to their immortal line" (1.268).

This new order presented Roman rule as both the culmination of ancient origins and the realization of divine will, purpose, and order within history.

Imperial mythology also shaped the social structures and spatial patterns of everyday life (i.e., cosmology). Rome itself was the center of the world. Even within the cities of a Roman province such as Asia, space was defined by the presence of temple structures dedicated to the emperor and members of the imperial family, and other civic institutions such as gymnasia and theaters added spaces dedicated to imperial-cult activity. Even domestic architecture included elements that recalled aspects of Roman mythology. In short, imperial cults shaped topography, public spaces, and human interactions on both a large and small scale, thereby organizing relationships and reminding the population constantly of the reality of Roman beneficence and domination, justifying and even idealizing the oppression, conflict, exploitation, and violence of the imperial order.

Cultivating Critical Mythic Consciousness: Public and Hidden Transcripts

Public acceptance of the Roman imperial myth, demonstrated by participation in and cooperation with the cult, provided people living in the province of Asia with a way to avoid conflict with Rome and perhaps even to advance their lot within the imperial system. On the part of the dominated, the goal of most public interactions would have been to maintain at least the appearance of conformity. In his work on domination and resistance, James Scott calls apparent conformity with the myths, rituals, and social patterns of systems of domination "the performance of the public transcript." The public transcript is active when subordinates conform their speech and behavior to the ways the dominant would wish to have things appear. But public conformity may also mask other realities, including the existence of alternative mythic convictions and communities of resistance. Of necessity, "relations of domination are, at the same time, relations of resistance."[34]

Much of the language associated with Christianity in modern, popular imagination—for example, gospel, peace, faith, righteousness, savior, Son of God—was already "in the air," associated with the Roman imperial cult, before the New Testament documents were written.

34. Scott, *Domination and the Arts of Resistance*, 45.

In order to nurture such resistance, however, it is necessary to cultivate social spaces and discourses in which such alternatives can be articulated, developed, and embodied. According to Scott, when subordinates gather apart from the direct observation of the power holders, they are likely to nurture imagination and actions that counter the public transcript, adopting what Scott calls "the hidden transcript." The hidden transcript consists of those speeches, gestures, and practices that contradict or inflect what appears in the public transcript.[35] If the dissemination and preservation of the public transcript is one of the chief tools of the dominant, the nurture and use of the hidden transcript is one of the most powerful, and perhaps the foundational, means of resistance. John's Apocalypse is both a means to nurture the hidden transcript of first-century Christians in Asia Minor and a representation of the "hidden transcript" itself. The hidden transcript is not only a tool used to cloak and defend the subordinate, but a tactic of constructive resistance, which entails the creation of imaginative space. How does John's Apocalypse create space for its audience? As we have already seen, *discursive tactics* such as the strategic manipulation of genre and structure and the use of dialect are among the steps toward the creation of such imaginative space.

Another tactic of resistance is *dislocation*. Revelation's visionary movement carries the audience back and forth between the heavenly and earthly realms, blurring both temporal and spatial orientations in the process.[36] The process of dislocation from the everyday existence of the world begins already in the prologue and salutation, and continues in the introductory description of the Seer's vision (1:12–16), but comes to full expression in 4:1, when the door in heaven is opened for John, and with him the auditors of Revelation, to come up. Amid the shifts and the dislocations that follow throughout the book, the narrative reconstructs the audience's perspectives on reality (1) by reorienting the audience to a different defining center of identity and power; (2) by affirming that human perception of time and space is partial and lim-

35. Ibid., 4–5.
36. Wes Howard-Brook and Anthony Gwyther describe this dislocation in terms of the "bifurcation" of time and space—that is, the creation of a sense that the world's constructions of reality in fact hide the true reality (*Unveiling Empire: Reading Revelation Then and Now* [Maryknoll, N.Y.: Orbis, 1999], 121).

ited; (3) by redefining the notions of space and time that tell the audience how to see and act; (4) by offering an alternative vision of power; and (5) by articulating a new vision of where the creation is headed.

In Revelation 4, John first describes the heavenly realm, where reality is defined by the ceaseless, timeless worship of God and the Lamb. The throne of God is the center of this space, around which a variety of creatures, including the martyrs who await vindication, are gathered. The throne of God thus displaces all other contenders as the defining center of human perception of reality and identity construction. As the narrative of John's Apocalypse continues to unfold, the two cities around which John's first-century audiences would have defined their religious, social, economic, and political identities—Rome (cf. Revelation 18) and earthly Jerusalem (cf. 11:8)—are both stripped of their claims to contain divine presence and to define or express divine power. Recentering the audience's imagination on the heavenly throne thus entails dislocation from whatever alternative center holds them in thrall.

Time is also undone and reimagined. The worship that takes place around the throne transcends the human conception of time, whether these conceptions are oriented around ancient agrarian calendars, reckoned from the birth of Caesar, or oriented toward the clock as in modern, Western notions of time. In contrast to the timelessness of heavenly reality, the earthly realm is governed by time, the end of which is announced by the angelic figure (who transcends ordinary spatial boundaries, 10:1–2, 5–7) introduced in 10:6. Similarly, when God appears on the white throne to judge the living and dead, earth and sky flee from God's presence (20:11). These passages point to the contingent and transitory nature of the earthly realm.

The Seer offers the audience new categories for making sense of time. Friesen claims that Revelation develops five different kinds of time: worship time, vision time, present time (reinterpreted), vindication time, and new-creation time.[37] Worship time provides the defining orientation for other notions of time in Revelation because worship spans the two realms between heaven and earth and provides the critical temporal (and spatial) locus

37. Friesen, *Imperial Cults*, 157–61.

through which all of the rest of reality is perceived. "Vision time" describes the movement of the Seer and audience alike through the unfolding, dislocating, ever-new experiences of space and time within this narrative. "Present time" was defined by the imperial cults as the time of Caesar and Roman eschatological dominion, but for John present time is the period just before the destruction of the imperial power. John designates this present time as "three and a half years" ("time and times and half a time," 12:14; or "forty-two months," 11:2, 13:5; or "1,260 days," 11:3, 12:6), drawing on Dan. 9:24–27 and 11:29–12:13.[38] John associates this present time with imperial attacks on God's people (e.g., 13:5–7), and with the faithful resistance and prophetic witness of God's people (e.g., 11:3–10). It is thus also a time characterized by the call to repentance. After the violence of the present time (i.e., forty-two months) comes "vindication time," which John designates as "the first resurrection" (20:5–6) and "thousand years" (20:5), a time when Satan is bound and the martyrs and those who refused to worship the imperial beast are raised from the dead (20:1–4). Finally, Revelation presents its auditors with a category of time—and a corresponding spatial image—that transcends all the other categories presented in this narrative. Friesen designates this "new time."[39] At the culmination of John's visions, God's glory eclipses the sun and moon (21:23), by which the passing of time is ordinarily marked. Death itself, which distinguishes this life from whatever follows, also passes away (21:4). John witnesses a new heaven and a new earth, and a new Jerusalem, also described as the Lamb's bride (21:9), coming down out of heaven, a space and time characterized by God dwelling among mortals (21:1–3). The imagery John draws upon in Revelation 21 to describe this vision stretches the imagination beyond the breaking point. This space and time is even marked by the absence of a temple or worship, because in the pure presence of God nothing of this prior world survives, not even its primary religious referents and practices. In the "new time" of "new Jerusalem," where a "new heaven and earth" come into being, even John's own mythic discourse runs against its limits.

How does this perspective on new time and new space in God's

38. Beale identifies a range of experiences in Jewish tradition that would have been associated with three and a half years (*Revelation*, 565–68).

39. Friesen, *Imperial Cults*, 161.

presence challenge the prevailing notions of the world? Whereas imperial cosmology and eschatology sought to blur the boundaries between the divine and human realms so that Caesar might be hailed as God, the Seer refuses to locate God or the goal of creation in conjunction with any contingent reality, be it Rome, Jerusalem, the Temple, an empire, or even the realm of human symbolization. God and the new creation ultimately exist beyond any human significations, even John's own.[40]

John's Mythic Alternative to Violence

John's apocalyptic performance presents the audience with a paradoxical reality: a living-slaughtered Lamb as the divine warrior who vanquishes Satan and the imperial beast by means of the witness of suffering. Although this image draws upon the myth of the cosmic warrior, it also undoes it by replacing the conventional notions of power and victory with signs normally associated with weakness and defeat. The mythic description of the victorious Christ as the slaughtered Lamb thus seeks not merely to replace the imperial myth of Caesar as divine with a more powerful alternative, but to disrupt the foundational script within which these characters function. Among the foundational scripts undone by the Apocalypse is the myth of redemptive violence.[41]

In the Seer's version of the combat myth, imperial power is not the agent of peace and order, but a force of violence and seduction. In 13:1–8, for example, John uses imagery from Daniel 7 to depict empire as a beast with ten horns and seven heads, whom the whole earth worships (13:3–4) and that makes war against the saints and exercises authority over all the earth (13:7–8). John depicts empire alternately as a dragon, the beast from the sea, a harlot, and as Babylon, the city of Israel's captivity—all images of violence and thrall. The imperial beast is worshiped because it defeats all challengers: "Who is like the beast, and who can fight against it?" (13:4).

But the beast meets its end at the hands of the Lamb, and the whore/Babylon is reduced to smoke. The one truly worthy of worship is the Lamb who suffers violence and apparent defeat. With

40. Ibid., 165–66.
41. Walter Wink, *Engaging the Powers: Discernment and Resistance in a World of Domination* (Minneapolis: Fortress, 1992), 13–31.

the vindication of the Lamb comes the end of violence itself. Throughout Revelation, the followers of the Lamb never take up arms themselves. Even when the image of the Lamb transforms into a warrior on a white horse in 19:11–21, his weapons are his own blood and "the sword of his mouth." It is not more and greater violence that brings the empire to its end, but the power of the victim, the Word that names the reality of God's new creation.

But Word alone does not suffice to establish spaces of resistance. In order to complete the performance, the narrative must be embodied; it must be performed again within the corporate life of the community. Thus, John turns repeatedly to liturgy, to worship, as the primary locus and activity of resistance.

Worship as Resistance

Just as the imperial cult operated not only at the level of ideas, but through social, economic, liturgical, and physical structures, so, too, John's critical engagement with structures of empire is not merely a contest of ideas, but takes on bodily form in the repeated images of worship throughout the book. The images of a triumphant Lamb and a warrior whose weapons are his own blood and the sword of his mouth have particular affinity with the ritual of the Lord's Supper, where the Lamb's story is embodied and creates a new world.

Commentators have long noted that the narrative of Revelation alternates between scenes of heavenly worship (4:2–11; 5:8–14; 7:9–17; 11:15–18; 13:1–15; 14:1–5; 15:2–4; 19:1–8) and descriptions of events unfolding in heaven and on earth. In order to develop the liturgical aspects of this narrative, John draws on the resources and models of both his cultural setting and the traditions of the Old Testament, including Isaiah and Daniel, just as he did in his treatment of myth. The primary sources for the Seer's ritual images, however, are Psalms 95–100, which celebrate the victory and enthronement of the divine warrior.[42] Thus, John innovatively employs models of ritual and liturgy that would have been familiar to his audience.

Leonard Thompson has rightly argued that the language of

---

42. Howard-Brook and Gwyther, *Unveiling Empire*, 198.

worship plays a key role in unifying the Apocalypse.[43] The performance not only is set within the worshiping assembly on the Lord's Day, but is itself riddled with scenes and discourse of worship. Worship is the defining activity to which the community is called, providing both the ritual space in which the community is formed and the primary tool in and expression of its resistance to the imperial ordering of reality. Worship is the means by which the assembly gains perspective on its world and strength to endure. Worship is both a foretaste of life in the new Jerusalem and the realization of heavenly reality within the time and space of this creation. It is worship that "creates and recreates the community."[44] With the centrality of worship as the Seer's primary tool of resistance in mind, we now turn to a more detailed examination of the first worship scene in the Apocalypse, chapters 4–5.

"Who Is Worthy to Open the Scroll?": Worship and Resistance in Revelation 5

The Role of Revelation 4–5 in the Performance

The first explicit description of worship in the heavenly realm takes place in chapters 4 and 5, just after the door to heaven is opened and John is lifted up in the spirit (4:1–2). Many scholars regard these chapters as the heart of the book; to be sure, they are the hinge between the letters of chapters 1–3 and the visions of chaos and destruction that comprise the bulk of the performance. The account in chapter 5 of the Lamb opening the scroll provides the narrative foundation for all that follows in this book, for it is this seven-sealed scroll that contains the visions of salvation and judgment that comprise chapters 6–20. The visions of God as Creator and Redeemer (chaps. 4–5) who is making a new heaven and a new earth (21:1–22:5; see esp. 21:1–5) form an interpretive frame around chapters 6–20, where the images of judgment and destruction are dominant. This structural frame prevents the audience from hearing the visions of chapters 6–20 merely as descriptions of destruction and chaos or as a cry for vengeance on the part of the saints.

43. Leonard L. Thompson, *The Book of Revelation: Apocalypse and Empire* (Oxford: Oxford University Press, 1997), 53–73.
44. Elochukwu E. Uzukwu, *Worship as Body Language: Introduction to Christian Worship—An African Orientation* (Collegeville, Minn.: Liturgical, 1997), 70.

The visions of chapters 4–5 make clear that the power of God displayed throughout the book is the power of the Lamb who was slain, whose death redeems his followers to serve as priests, and whose worship unifies the whole creation (cf. 5:11–14). God's power, in other words, is not coercive or violent,[45] even if the Lamb's rule brings judgment and a chaotic end to the powers and dominions of this world. God's good and merciful will, accomplished through the victory of the Lamb, is the complete redemption of heaven and earth. The interpretive lens supplied by the visions of heavenly worship in chapters 4–5 is thus indispensable for interpretation of the whole performance.

The audience has already been prepared for what is to come in these chapters by the concluding statement in the last of the letters to the seven churches: "To the one who conquers I will give a place with me on my throne, just as I myself conquered and sat down with my Father on his throne" (3:21). This statement affirms that Christ has already "conquered" (cf. 5:5) and is already reigning in heaven, sharing the throne of God. The aorist tense of νικάω (*nikaō,* "to conquer") used in both 3:21 and 5:5 suggests the once-for-all character of Christ's victory. Moreover, 3:21 holds forth the promise that all those who likewise conquer will also share that throne. The idea that God shares the throne of heaven with Christ, and ultimately with all those who conquer, already begins to suggest the ways power will be redefined—as relational and shared rather than unilateral and exclusive—in chapters 4–5. The visions of worship in chapters 4 and 5 tell the story of how this shocking reality came to be, especially how Christ was found worthy to share the throne of God.

In these chapters one can also discern many of the features that distinguish the Seer's narrative of resistance, especially the spatial and temporal dislocations that move the audience toward a different imagination of space and time, and the striking ways John reinvents the dialect of power. If, as many have argued, Revelation is fundamentally about the clash between the powers of this world and God's power, it is in these chapters that John not only affirms the reality of God's power but lays the foundation for a new understanding of the nature of true power. In these two

45. So Ron Farmer, "Divine Power in the Apocalypse to John: Revelation 4–5 in Process Hermeneutic," in *Society of Biblical Literature 1993 Seminar Papers,* ed. Eugene H. Lovering (Atlanta: Scholars, 1993), 96.

chapters we learn that John's God is the one, the only one, who creates and sustains all of life in heaven and earth, and that God is moving creation toward a final conquest of evil through the death and resurrection of Jesus, the Lamb who is slain. With God, the Lamb alone is worthy of worship and honor and faithful obedience. The worship of the Lamb is already taking place in heaven and in ever-greater concentric circles that ultimately include every creature in heaven and on earth. In implicit contrast to the claims of the Roman imperial cult, all power and honor resides with the Lamb and with God, in all spaces and times. The vision of worship in these chapters is thus the first major step in John's dislocation and reorientation of the auditors.

The Movement of the Narrative in Revelation 4–5

On the face of it, the scene John describes in these chapters has a static quality. Especially in chapter 4, the Seer focuses on a description of the throne and the beings who surround it. Although the action is constant and dramatic, it is limited to emanations of power from the throne (lightning and thunder, and flames; 4:5) and to the singing and prostration of the heavenly worshipers. Even when the Lamb is introduced in 5:6, he does not move into the scene so much as he is suddenly depicted as present, "standing" in the midst of both the throne and the four living creatures and in the midst of the elders, as if he were present all along without being recognized. John's depiction of heavenly worship thus contributes to the Seer's program of affirming the stability, certainty, and timelessness of the God who is the focus of this narrative.

Subtly, John conveys a sense of progression and dramatic movement that is also important to the overall narrative. As the story moves through chapters 4 and 5, the focus of the narrative shifts from worship of God as a solitary figure on the throne (4:2), to worship of Christ the Lamb in the midst of the throne and the four living creatures (5:6–12), to worship of God and the Lamb (5:13).[46] The sense of progression is also conveyed within chapter 5 itself, in the movement from the search for one who is worthy to open the scroll (5:2–5), to recognition of the Lamb as the one who is worthy (5:6–7), and finally to worship of the Lamb and

---

46. Frederick J. Murphy, *Fallen Is Babylon: The Revelation to John* (Harrisburg, Pa.: Trinity, 1998), 188–89.

God together. The identity of the singers also progresses in ever greater circumference, from the four creatures and the twenty-four elders (5:8–10), to the angels who surround the throne, the four creatures, and the elders (5:11), and finally to every creature in heaven, on earth, and under the earth (5:13). The narrative movement in these chapters thus describes the recognition of the Lamb's worthiness to open the scroll and to take his place with God, and to receive the worship not only of heavenly beings but of all creation.

This movement is foundational for the Apocalypse as a whole, as well as for the underlying narrative to which the Seer's story of Jesus points. The drama that John unfolds is about identifying God who has brought this world into being, the recognition of the Lamb who was slain as the One who alone is worthy to rule with God, and the inexorable movement of the whole of creation toward worship of God and the Lamb. This story stands in contrast to the emperor's claims to define and embody divine power in the world and the assertion that Roman dominion is without end.

God on the Throne (Revelation 4)

Revelation 4 sets forth the Seer's foundational vision of God as creator of this world and as the one who is worthy to be worshiped. The images in this throne scene both draw upon and disrupt the associations people might have had with imperial worship. John's descriptions of heavenly worship and the One seated on the throne nurture an imagination of God's transcendence of human ways of seeing and acting, thus challenging Roman notions of power and divinity, and making space for the shocking images of divinity associated with the Lamb.

The throne scene described in 4:2–11 recalls elements of the throne vision of Ezek. 1:4–28, but may also have suggested images of the emperor hearing cases while surrounded by members of imperial administration, senators, and others.[47] Unlike the image of a very human emperor, and unlike Ezekiel's reference to God as "something that seemed like a human form" (1:26), the Seer refuses to offer anything more than the most allusive description of the One seated on the throne, whom John experiences as the

47. See especially David Aune, "The Influence of Roman Imperial Court Ceremonial on the Revelation of John," *Biblical Research* 28 (1983): 5–26.

image of "jasper and carnelian" (cf. Exod. 28:17)—that is, as colors. Jasper especially is an opaque stone that is usually red, but is also found in yellow, green, and grayish blue; it thus defies singular description. Jasper, moreover, will later be used to describe the image of the new Jerusalem, where it provides the material for the walls and the first of the city's twelve foundations (21:18–19). The rainbow of green (emerald) that surrounds the throne alludes to Ezek. 1:27–28, but here in Revelation it may be a full circle of light, which would signify perfection.[48] Unlike the divine imagery of the imperial cults, the image of the divine in Revelation defies description in all but elusive, impressionistic characteristics.

Likewise, the images of the twenty-four elders (4:4, 10), who are present in six of the seven worship scenes in the Apocalypse,[49] of the seven torches that are the seven spirits of God (4:5), and of the four living creatures with four faces and four wings (4:6–9), all defy simple or singular interpretations. John's depictions of these figures are apparently meant to be multivalent, allusive, and elusive. The description of the four living beings near the throne of God is a conflated vision drawn from the throne scenes in Ezek. 1:4–21 and Isaiah 6. Like Ezekiel, John has four creatures, but rather than each having four faces (a human, a lion, an ox, and an eagle), each creature now has its own discrete identity (lion, ox, human, or eagle). Like the seraphim in Isaiah 6, the four living creatures of Revelation have six wings. Their chant also echoes Isa. 6:3, but now they also name God as the One whose being comprehends past, present, and future. At least some elements of parody may be present in these descriptions: the golden crowns of the elders, which are cast in subordination before the throne in 4:10, might recall to a first-century audience the gold crowns worn by imperial-cult priests in Asia, and the seven torches/spirits might parody the torchbearers of the imperial cult, whose flames symbolized the perpetuity of the emperor's power. In short, the rich, multivalent imagery by which John describes the throne and the participants in heavenly worship has the effect of making the worship witnessed in imperial-cult settings seem puny by comparison.

The images of praise and thanksgiving offered by the elders and the living creatures are drawn primarily from, but do not pre-

48. Howard-Brook and Gwyther, *Unveiling Empire*, 203.
49. Revelation 15:2–4 is the exception.

cisely replicate, Isa. 6:3. The ceaselessness of the worship, the naming of God as almighty, as the One who transcends time and space ("who was, who is, who is to come," 4:8), as the One who created all things and by whose will all things exist (4:11), and as the one who is worthy (4:11), all lend themselves to a sense of the divine that overshadows what would have been named in the imperial cult. Because God has created and maintains all that exists, the imperial claim to establish or maintain the created order is rendered blasphemous. The God who was, who is, and who is to come stands in contrast to the "beast" who "was and is not" (17:8, 11). Because the worship of God stands in contrast to the worship of the emperor through the imperial cult, worship in Revelation is inescapably a political act, by which participants discern and name who and what they confess to be true about their God, the world, and themselves. This worship raises two primary and integrally related questions at stake in worship: Who is named as worthy of such honor? and, What kind of power do they manifest in the world? The next scene and each subsequent worship scene in the larger performance further develop John's answers to these two questions, while continuing to unfold the central story line of the whole book: the discovery that the Lamb who was slain alone is worthy of worship.

"Worthy is the Lamb that was slaughtered!" (Revelation 5)

The second worship scene (5:8–14) in the Apocalypse follows quickly after the first. Between them, however, the Seer recounts the drama of the quest for one who is worthy to open the scroll that is held in the right hand of the One seated upon the throne (5:1–7). No one in heaven, on earth, or under earth—including anyone associated with the imperial cult—is found who is worthy to open the scroll and look into it. The attempt to identify the contents of the scroll has proved to be another of the matters in Revelation that resist definitive interpretation.[50] As with other images in these chapters, John draws primarily from Ezekiel (2:9–10) for the image of the scroll, although Dan. 7:10 may also be in view.[51] In the Bible and in apocalyptic literature, such heavenly

50. See Beale, *Revelation,* 339–48; David E. Aune, *Revelation 1–5,* Word Biblical Commentary (Dallas: Word, 1997), 341–46.
51. A strong proponent of the primary role of Daniel 7 in these chapters is Beale (*Revelation,* 314–16, 337–38; idem, "The Influence of Daniel upon

scrolls often contain the names of those who will be among the re-
deemed, as in the books mentioned in Exod. 32:32–33; Ps. 69:28;
or Isa. 4:3, or the book mentioned by the Seer himself in 3:5.
Psalm 139:16 speaks of a book that contains "all the days that were
formed for me, when none of them as yet existed," which suggests
the capacity of such books to foretell the future, a sense that is
commonly associated with heavenly books in apocalyptic literature. Some scholars argue that the contents of the scroll in chapter 5 are the same as the scroll that is described as already opened
in chapter 10, which the Seer eventually eats and experiences as
sweet to the taste but bitter to the stomach.[52] Because the unseal-
ing of the scroll of chapter 5 leads to the events described in the
subsequent chapters, it is safe to presume that the contents of this
scroll are at least generally commensurate with the narrative of
God's purposes for the creation and God's judgment and redemption of the world. The most important thing we can know
with certainty about the scroll in Revelation 5, however, is just
what the Seer tells us: It is perfectly sealed with seven seals. That
is, the contents of the scroll are closed and secret, awaiting perfor-
mative disclosure by the one who is worthy.

The first sense of a dramatic crisis in the narrative of these two
chapters comes as the Seer begins to weep bitterly because no one
is found who is worthy to open the scroll (5:4). The Seer's tears
suggest the despair of humankind in the face of the oppression
and violence of this world's systems of domination. With the scroll
still sealed, John and his audiences would be left without hope in
the world, knowing neither the definitive manifestation of God's
power and true character nor the ultimate resolution of their own
stories. John does not dwell on the crisis, however, for it has already been resolved. Just as the Seer begins to lament, an elder
comforts him with the announcement that the Lion of the tribe
of Judah, the Root of David, has conquered and can open the
scroll and its seven seals (5:5).

The two designations in 5:5 of the one who is worthy to open
the scroll carry clear messianic associations. "The Lion of Judah"

---

the Structure and Theology of John's Apocalypse," *Journal of the Evangelical
Theology Society* 27 [1984]: 413–23).

52. The consumption of the scroll clearly draws upon the imagery of
Ezek. 2:9–10; 3:1–3. For the argument identifying the scroll in chapter 5 with
the opened scroll of chapter 10, see Bauckham, *Climax of Prophecy*, 244–57.

is derived from Genesis 49, where Jacob blesses his twelve sons and names Judah as the "Lion" who will rule (49:8–13). Genesis 49:10 carries a promise that fed messianic hopes: "The scepter shall not depart from Judah, nor the ruler's staff from between his feet, until tribute comes to him, and the obedience of the peoples is his." The "Root of David" expresses Israelite hopes for a king from the Davidic line who would restore the nation and rule in justice (Isaiah 11). Both images suggest traditional notions of power: Judah will put his hand on the neck of his enemies and his brothers will bow before him (Gen. 49:8); like a lioness, no one dares disturb him (49:9). The David of Jewish tradition, of course, is a mighty warrior and king who establishes the nation and makes Jerusalem the center of the Israelite world. With these designations, the audience is primed for the revelation of a warrior king.

But in a surprise that articulates the defining paradox of the Apocalypse, the one John sees between the throne and the four living creatures and among the elders is a Lamb, standing as one having been slaughtered.[53] Whatever else we might say about this vision, it is at least stunning—an audacious parody of both Israelite messianic hopes and Roman imperial conceptions of power.

With the introduction of the Lamb, John establishes the primary christological image for the whole work; the Seer refers to Jesus as the Lamb twenty-eight times in the performance. But scholars disagree over the primary field of reference of the lamb image: Does it draw primarily upon the associations between the lamb and Passover sacrifice, or is it an image of servant leadership and rule, as expressed most clearly in the "Servant Song" of Isa. 52:13–53:12 (cf. especially 53:7)?[54] The alternatives need not be seen as exclusive, however, for in either case, the Lamb's suffering accomplishes redemption and the victory of God's people. As with many of the Seer's images that we have already examined, the image of the Lamb invites more than one meaning, thereby opening up imaginative space for the interpreting community.

But the scene does not affect its audience primarily by the array

53. Farmer ("Divine Power in the Apocalypse," 93) rightly notes that the paragraph break between verses 5 and 6 in most Greek editions and many English translations, including the NRSV, can cause readers to miss the impact of the two contrasting images.

54. See the discussion in Aune, *Revelation 1–5*, 367–73.

of meanings one might associate with the image of a lamb so much as through the juxtaposition of messianic images of powerful warriors with the picture of a slaughtered Lamb, which achieves a provocative burlesque of human notions of power. Warriors and lions conquer by inflicting death on others; the Lamb has conquered over all others by himself enduring death.[55] As M. Eugene Boring has noted, the only act of the historical Jesus that is mentioned in Revelation is his death, which the Seer understands as the expression of God's power and love.[56] The slaughter of the Lamb, the death of Christ, is not the story of the power of humans to control and dominate by means of violence, as the world might think, but the very means by which God's conquest of the powers of this world and the creation of a new heaven and earth are accomplished.

The Seer's juxtaposition of messianic notions (the Lion of Judah, the Root of David) with sacrifice and servanthood (the Lamb) redefines "conquest" or "victory" (5:5) in association with weakness, vulnerability, and sacrifice—not military power. If the Lamb has triumphed over death itself, the military victories of the emperors over the living as well as their use of the threat of death in order to impose power and maintain control are both rendered insignificant. Moreover, the living-slaughtered Lamb manifests as hollow the claims of divinity made for the emperors, who themselves suffer death. The juxtaposition of messianic identifications with the image of the Lamb also undermines any Jewish or Christian hopes for messianic conquest by violent military means, as well as any "narrowly nationalistic expectations of Jewish triumph over the Gentile nations."[57] In short, the juxtaposition manifests how Jesus accomplishes the most important conquest, the victory of God over evil. Both God's victory and the Lamb's worthiness are established through Jesus' death.

As if the juxtaposition of messianic images with the Lamb were not enough, the Seer goes on to describe the Lamb in ways that further unsettle the audience's notions of reality and expand its imagination of God's world. The Lamb has "seven horns and

55. Craig R. Koester, *Revelation and the End of All Things* (Grand Rapids: Eerdmans, 2001), 78.

56. M. Eugene Boring, "The Theology of Revelation: 'The Lord Our God the Almighty Reigns,'" *Interpretation* 40 (1986): 265.

57. Bauckham, *Climax of Prophecy*, 215.

seven eyes, which are the seven spirits of God sent out into all the earth" (5:6). Horns are symbols of power (cf. Ps. 132:17; Dan. 7:7–8:4; *1 Enoch* 90:6–12, 37). The seven horns of the Lamb convey a sense of fullness: The Lamb's power is complete and perfect. In Daniel 7, the beast with seven horns defeats the saints of God, but now the Lamb with seven horns conquers on behalf of the saints.[58] The seven eyes (cf. Zech. 4:10) suggest God's omniscience, wisdom, and sovereignty, here associated with the Lamb. The eyes are also the seven spirits of God (cf. Isa. 11:2), which had heretofore been confined to the throne room (Rev. 1:4; 3:1; 4:5), but now, when the Lamb conquers, are released into the world.

When the Lamb takes the scroll, the second worship scene in heaven begins. Now the four living creatures and the twenty-four elders fall before the Lamb, just as they had before the One seated on the throne in the first scene. Whereas God was worshiped as Creator and Sustainer in the first scene, now the Lamb is worshiped as Redeemer, as the one who has "ransomed for God holy ones from every tribe and language and people and nation" (5:9). The elders now hold harps, an instrument used in the imperial cults as well as in Israelite worship. The elders "sing a new song," a liturgical act associated in Jewish tradition with divine acts of liberation (e.g., Pss. 40:2–4; 96; 98; 144:9–11; 149; Isa. 42:9–10). The release of the holy ones from their bondage climaxes in the claim that "you have made them an empire and priests for our God, and they will reign on earth" (5:10; author's translation). The Lamb thus brings into being a new empire, an empire for God made up of priests for God, and an empire founded on the defeat rather than the threat of death.

This second scene of worship extends the praise directed toward the One on the throne in the first scene. Suddenly the voices of countless angels are added to those of the living creatures and elders (5:11). Whereas the first scene named God as "worthy . . . to receive glory and honor and power" (4:11), the Lamb is worthy to receive "power and wealth and wisdom and might and honor

58. In Revelation 13 the audience will hear of the beast with ten horns and seven heads, one of which has received a mortal wound. This beast is worshiped in fear: "Who is like the beast, and who can fight against it?" (cf. 13:1–4). Soon after this, yet another beast is introduced, who serves the first and who resembles a lamb with two horns (13:11–18). These beasts mimic the power of the Lamb for the sake of deceiving the people of the earth.

and glory and blessing" (5:12). Then, in a vision that seems to transcend the temporal and spatial perspective of the scene to this point, John hears "every creature in heaven and on earth and under the earth and in the sea, and all that is in them," singing praise both to the One seated on the throne and the Lamb: "blessing and honor and glory and might forever and ever" (5:13). The living creatures say "Amen" and the elders once again fall down and now worship both the One on the throne and the Lamb.

The second worship scene thus tells the story of the recognition, first by those gathered around the throne and then by all creation, that the living-slaughtered Lamb embodies the redemptive and liberating power of God, just as the One seated on the throne is the Creator and Sustainer. Who is worthy of worship? Only these two: God and the Lamb. What kind of power do they manifest? The power to create and sustain, to redeem and liberate, and to create a new empire of priests who serve God. What story do they embody? The story of the creation of a new empire by means of sacrifice, the conquest of death, and the liberation of the holy ones from empires of death. As the answer to each of these questions takes form in the Seer's opening descriptions of worship in heaven, a new people comes into being, made up of those who join their praise with the holy ones and with the heavenly liturgists. In this way John uses worship to reveal the emptiness of imperial worship and imperial constructions of reality, to create space for a new empire formed around the worship of God and the Lamb, and to engender both imagination and practice—worship itself—that offers resistance in a world of domination and death.

7

Apocalypse Now:
Preaching Revelation as Narrative

Charles L. Campbell

As Stanley Saunders has argued, Revelation is resistance literature. From exile in Patmos, John the Seer seeks to unveil the
myths of empire that pass for common sense, to envision God's in-
breaking reign, and to build up a community of resistance in the
midst of the "powers that be." When performed orally in the worshiping community, the testimony of Revelation enables the participants, through story and ritual, to experience and begin living
into the new creation that invades the world in Jesus Christ.
Through such performance John's testimony becomes "one of
the church's most powerful tools for inculcating and sustaining
countercultural discipleship."[1]

Preaching from Revelation today will likewise be a practice of
resistance to the "powers that be." Indeed, such resistance will be
the fundamental characteristic of preaching shaped by the testimony of John. This character of preaching as resistance not only
grows out of the nature of Revelation as resistance literature, but
is also internal to the understanding of proclamation within the
Apocalypse.

As Saunders notes, the fundamental practice of resistance in
Revelation is worship. The empire and its minions primarily de-

---

1. Wes Howard-Brook and Anthony Gwyther, *Unveiling Empire: Reading
Revelation Then and Now* (Maryknoll, N.Y.: Orbis, 1999), 2.

mand human worship; their goal is idolatry. The beast and the
dragon seek the worship of the entire earth (13:4). In the face of
empire's idolatrous demands, the church's most radical act of resistance involves worshiping Jesus, the slaughtered Lamb, as Lord.
In the face of the "powers that be," who wish to be recognized as
the divine regents of the world, worship becomes a radical political act that resists such idolatry. As an integral component of such
worship, preaching itself becomes a practice of resistance in the
liturgical assembly.

Throughout Revelation, preaching is presented as central to
Christian resistance to empire. That the words "martyr" and "testimony" come from the same Greek word suggests the intimate
connection between preaching and resistance. Moreover, in Revelation the "sword" that issues from Jesus' mouth serves as the primary means of overcoming the "powers that be" (see 1:16; 2:12,
16; 19:15, 21), reminding the reader of the "sword of the Spirit,
which is the word of God," which Paul understands to be the primary means of resisting the principalities and powers of the world
(Eph. 6:17). Further, the Christ-figure himself, who resists the imperial powers of death, is referred to in Revelation as the Word of
God (19:13), suggesting that preaching this Word must itself be
an act of resistance. Finally, the blood of the Lamb and the *word
of testimony* ultimately overcome Satan (12:11).[2]

In all of these ways, Revelation highlights the role of the Word
in resistance, naming internally the role that the oral performance of Revelation itself actually serves in the worshiping community. Throughout Revelation, preaching the Word or bearing testimony to Jesus is a critical means for engaging the powers and
resisting the empire. When preaching from Revelation, contemporary preachers continue this practice of resistance to the "powers that be" through the oral performance of the sermon in the
context of the church's ritual resistance.

This understanding of Revelation as literature of resistance
that calls for preaching as a practice of resistance provides a helpful hermeneutical framework for contemporary preachers who
stand in the pulpits of privileged congregations. Often, such
preachers wonder what Revelation has to say to their congrega-

2. It is not surprising that the Word plays such an important role, for the
beast blasphemes God and deceives human beings in part through the use
of language (13:5–6, 11–15).

tions, as the Apocalypse has often been understood as addressed solely to marginalized, persecuted Christians in the first century. The hermeneutical move to privileged, contemporary congregations often seems unmanageable. When understood through the lens of resistance, however, Revelation becomes more accessible to such preachers. For marginalized, persecuted groups, the Apocalypse may indeed fashion resistance to oppression and help people endure in the midst of suffering. For privileged groups, the call to resistance may be just as strong, though in this context congregations will be challenged to "come out" of the empire that has seduced us by its values (18:4) and to resist accommodation to the ways of the "powers that be." Indeed, recent scholarship on the Book of Revelation has suggested that John addressed his testimony both to marginalized churches that were persecuted and to churches that had comfortably and perhaps unconsciously accommodated themselves to the ways of empire.[3] The hermeneutical lens of resistance thus provides a means for Revelation once again to serve in various contexts as a powerful tool for nurturing and sustaining communities of resistance in our time.

In what follows, I examine several specific characteristics of preaching from Revelation that emerge within this framework of resistance. I then explore the relationship between preaching from Revelation and narrative preaching. The concluding sermon will, I hope, demonstrate a kind of preaching from Revelation that is possible within a privileged, mainline congregation.

Some Guidelines for Preaching from Revelation

With the turn of the millennium, preaching from Revelation has received renewed attention. Several important books have been published that take significant steps toward restoring Revelation (and apocalyptic literature in general) to a significant place in the mainline Christian pulpit.[4] Seeking to wrest this difficult, apoc-

3. See Howard-Brook and Gwyther, *Unveiling Empire.*
4. See, for example, Cornish R. Rogers and Joseph R. Jeter Jr., eds., *Preaching through the Apocalypse: Sermons from Revelation* (St. Louis: Chalice, 1992); Larry Paul Jones and Jerry L. Sumney, *Preaching Apocalyptic Texts* (St. Louis: Chalice, 1999); and David Schnasa Jacobsen, *Preaching in the New Creation: The Promise of New Testament Apocalyptic Texts* (Louisville: Westminster/John Knox, 1999).

alyptic text from "wild-eyed fanatics" who would turn John's testimony into literal predictions of contemporary events, these recent works lament the silence of Revelation in much contemporary Christian preaching, acknowledge the unique challenges of preaching from this text, and offer concrete suggestions for appropriating Revelation in Christian preaching. Although this chapter does not allow for an exhaustive discussion of these matters, several key characteristics of preaching from Revelation, considered as a work of resistance, may be highlighted.

Principalities and Powers

Revelation paints on a large canvas. John's testimony deals with the enormous material and spiritual forces that aggressively seek to shape human lives. The conflict depicted in John's vision is a conflict between Jesus and the "principalities and powers."[5] These powers, with the empire being the dominant one, are superhuman forces that seek to have dominion in the world and, to that end, require human devotion and service. Having both material and spiritual dimensions, the powers are embodied in institutions, ideologies, nations, economic systems, and a legion of other entities. Pretending to be the divine regents of the world, these powers, though created by God, live in rebellion against God's purposes and are in fact the purveyors of death, rather than life. Represented most often by the beast in its chaotic, oppressive multiplicity, and by Satan, the spirit or driving force of the beast, the powers wreak havoc on the world and threaten the followers of Jesus with death. Embodied also in the figure of the Seducer,

5. Space does not permit a thorough discussion of the principalities and powers. For a fuller treatment, see the important works of Walter Wink: *Naming the Powers: The Language of Power in the New Testament* (Philadelphia: Fortress, 1984); idem, *Unmasking the Powers: The Invisible Forces That Determine Human Existence* (Philadelphia: Fortress, 1986); idem, *Engaging the Powers: Discernment and Resistance in a World of Domination* (Minneapolis: Fortress, 1992); and idem, *The Powers That Be: Theology for a New Millennium* (New York: Doubleday, 1998). For an account of the powers that draws directly on the Book of Revelation, see William Stringfellow, *An Ethic for Christians and Other Aliens in a Strange Land,* 3d ed. (Waco, Tex.: Word, 1979). For an account of preaching in the context of the powers, which contains more extensive reflection on many of the topics in this chapter, see Charles L. Campbell, *The Word before the Powers: An Ethic of Preaching* (Louisville: Westminster/John Knox, 2002).

these powers lure human beings into accommodating to their ways, often capturing the spirit of people without having to resort to the threat of persecution or physical death.[6] This confrontation with the principalities and powers of death in all their multiplicity provides the context of Revelation's resistance.

Such powers are not foreign to contemporary congregations. People are aware of these enormous forces that impinge on their lives, capture their spirits, and often make resistance and change seem hopeless. Indeed, each Sunday morning I attend a church that provides concrete physical reminders of these forces and the apocalyptic context in which churches exist even today. Within the sanctuary of the church, one might not sense any apocalyptic context. The church is a Presbyterian one, consisting primarily of privileged, powerful people—hardly the marginalized, persecuted folks one normally associates with apocalyptic literature. In this congregation, Revelation is rarely the text for the sermon, and there are no fanatics declaring the imminent end of the world.

When one steps out of the sanctuary, however, the principalities and powers become immediately evident. Casting its shadow on the church from across the street, the State Capitol of Georgia, with its gleaming gold dome, directly confronts the church. The two buildings face each other in an unending standoff—the enormous Capitol building and the significantly smaller church. And if one looks closely, one notices on the lawn of the Capitol building a number of cannons, public reminders of the "myth of redemptive violence" on which states of all kinds ground their power.[7] And these cannons are pointed directly at the church. Although no longer operational, the cannons provide symbolic reminders that the church always lives in the "shadow of empire" and under the threat of the "powers that be."[8] Under the influence of these powers, in fact, Christianity in the United

6. The image in Revelation is that of the "whore" (chap. 18; 19:2). Because this image is degrading to women, I will speak of the Seducer.

7. According to the myth of redemptive violence, the way to bring order out of chaos is through violence. See Wink, *Engaging the Powers*, 13–31. I deal with this myth in more detail in the sermon.

8. See Walter Brueggemann, "Always in the Shadow of Empire," in *The Church as Counterculture*, ed. Michael L. Budde and Robert W. Brimlow (New York: State University of New York Press, 2000), 39–59.

States has often withdrawn into the private and personal realm and neglected the radical, public implications of the Christian faith.[9]

But that is not the end of the powers' presence around the church. Across the street in another direction lies the Coca-Cola museum: "The World of Coca-Cola." Here one is reminded of the power of global capitalism, embodied in enormous corporations that seek dominion over the world, not primarily through physical threats, but through the seduction of our spirits through advertising and consumerism.[10] Such seduction shapes the lives of countless people today, including those in our churches, who consume and consume and consume, even though we know it is killing us and we know it is killing others who work in sweatshops around the world. Yet we often seem powerless to resist; we almost seem to be possessed. Such is the seductive lure of the principalities and powers. And when they succeed in seducing us, they no longer need to use threats.

John, the Seer of Patmos, stood precisely in the midst of these kinds of powers, highlighting their conflict with the way of Jesus and seeking to resist them through the Word. He was not concerned primarily with individual sins, but with these enormous forces that threaten and seduce the people of God into the ways of death, overwhelming us by their power and numbing our spirits to the way of life. The drama of John's visions is shaped by the enormous powers the church is called to resist in the name of Jesus.

Over against these powers, John proclaims the story of Jesus— "the crucified, resurrected, and enthroned" one.[11] John proclaims the victory of the slaughtered Lamb, who has overcome the powers of death with the way of life and who seeks to build up the church as a community of resistance. Here, too, the focus of John's testimony is not on individuals, but on the *community* of

9. See Stanley Hauerwas, "The Politics of Freedom: Why Freedom of Religion Is a Subtle Temptation," in *After Christendom? How the Church Is to Behave if Freedom, Justice, and a Christian Nation Are Bad Ideas* (Nashville: Abingdon, 1991), 69–92.

10. According to Howard-Brook and Gwyther, global capitalism is the contemporary form of the beast depicted in Revelation (*Unveiling Empire,* 236–77). See also Revelation 18, which emphasizes the economic lure of Babylon.

11. Jones and Sumney, *Preaching Apocalyptic Texts,* 34.

faith. John's "letter" is addressed to *churches*—indeed, to the "seven" churches, which symbolically represent the church as a whole. His purpose is not to address individual pastoral or therapeutic issues that persons in the congregation may be facing. Rather, he seeks to build up the church as a community with the resources of faith and hope required to resist the threats and seductions of the principalities and powers. In the face of the powers, a concrete community of resistance is essential, for isolated individuals rarely have the resources required for enduring resistance. John thus seeks to set the church free from its captivity to the powers, whether that captivity results from the fear and suffering of oppression or the spiritual numbness of seduction and accommodation. He seeks to build up a church that embodies the reign of God—the new creation—that is breaking into the world.

John thus paints on a big canvas, rather than focusing on individual problems and needs. The story John tells is shaped by three primary actors: the principalities and powers that live in rebellion against the ways of God and seek to enslave humanity; the God who has been revealed in the redemptive work of the "crucified, resurrected, and enthroned Jesus," who, as the slaughtered Lamb, has overcome the powers of death with the way of life; and the church, which John seeks to build up into a community of resistance that lives into the redemption accomplished in Jesus. Revelation is not a book for therapeutic preachers who wish simply to address the needs and problems of individual congregation members. It is a book that invites preachers into the public, political arena of capitols and cannons and Coke. That fact, even more than the bizarre imagery and obscure metaphors, may present the greatest challenge to Christian preachers today, pushing us to come to terms with our own captivity to the principalities and powers.

Unveiling Empire

In resisting the principalities and powers and seeking to build up a community of resistance, John takes a particular path. He does not engage in detailed ethical analysis of particular social issues, but instead seeks to engage the imagination of the church. He seeks to enable the people to "see" the world in new ways.[12]

12. I use the words "see" and "vision" metaphorically. I am not referring to physical sight, but to a way of "inhabiting" the world. Consequently, I often use "imagination" as a synonym for "vision," and I refrain from using "blind-

Like the ethicists Iris Murdoch and Stanley Hauerwas, John understands that "we can only live in a world we can see."[13] So, not
surprisingly, "vision" becomes central to the method of Revelation. Through dramatic, visual imagery and metaphor, John seeks
to rouse the church from fear and numbness and to enable the
church to see and live in the world in new ways in light of the story
of Jesus.

John's efforts to help the church "re-imagine" the world take
two basic forms. On the one hand, he seeks to *unveil* the deadly,
rebellious ways of the powers; he exposes them not as the divine
regents of the world and the givers of life, but as the purveyors of
domination, violence, and death.[14] On the other hand, John *envisions* an alternative to the world of the powers: the new creation
that is breaking into the world in Jesus Christ. He "pulls back the
curtain" on the heavenly realm to help the church glimpse God's
alternative to the idolatrous claims of the powers of death, an alternative that John affirms is becoming a reality in the new creation. Through this twofold movement of unveiling the powers of
death and envisioning the new creation, John of Patmos seeks to
break the church's "spell of delusion" in order to build them up
for the way of resistance.[15]

Although there are numerous ways to "unveil" the deadly ways
of the powers, John primarily uses large, dramatic metaphors and
images to do this work, giving helpful guidance to preachers who
would similarly expose the ways of the principalities and powers.
Over against the myths through which the powers claim to be the
divine, life-giving regents of the world, John provides a counter-
imagery that reveals them for what they are: rebellious and violent
powers of domination and death. Such "big pictures" are critical,

---

ness" as an alternative to "vision" (though I do not alter the quotation from
Flannery O'Connor, below). The opposite of Christian vision is numbness or
lack of imagination or deathly vision.

13. See Iris Murdoch, "Vision and Choice in Morality," in *Christian Ethics
and Contemporary Philosophy*, ed. Ian T. Ramsey (London: SCM, 1966), 203;
idem, *The Sovereignty of Good* (London: Routledge and Kegan Paul, 1970;
reprint, London: Ark Paperbacks, 1986), 37; and Stanley Hauerwas, *The
Peaceable Kingdom: A Primer in Christian Ethics* (Notre Dame, Ind.: University
of Notre Dame Press, 1983), 29.

14. I have taken the language of "unveiling" from Howard-Brooks and
Gwyther, *Unveiling Empire.*

15. Wink, *Engaging the Powers,* 103–4.

particularly for people who have grown numb to the ways of the powers or who have been seduced by their claims. When the deadly ways of empire have become "common sense," such dramatic metaphors may be essential to stir the church from its numbness. As Flannery O'Connor, the Christian short-story writer with a decidedly apocalyptic bent, wrote about her bizarre and disturbing stories, "You have to make your vision apparent by shock—to the hard of hearing you shout, and for the almost-blind you draw large and startling pictures."[16]

In the face of the all-encompassing claims and demands of the empire, John uses such "large and startling pictures" to unveil the empire as a beast that violently destroys people and as a Seducer who lures people to trust in its deadly ways. It is difficult to imagine a more dramatic unveiling of the divine claims and deadly ways of empire than one finds in the metaphorical visions of Revelation:

> And I saw a beast rising out of the sea, having ten horns and seven heads; and on its horns were ten diadems, and on its heads were blasphemous names. And the beast that I saw was like a leopard, its feet were like a bear's, and its mouth was like a lion's mouth. And the dragon gave it his power and his throne and great authority. One of its heads seemed to have received a death-blow, but its mortal wound had been healed. In amazement the whole earth followed the beast. They worshiped the dragon, for he had given his authority to the beast, and they worshiped the beast, saying, "Who is like the beast, and who can fight against it?" (13:1–4)

John pulls back the veil of empire and exposes it for what it is: a deadly, idolatrous, blasphemous beast. In so doing, John seeks to set the church free from empire's deceptive claims, whether the church is suffering oppression at the hands of empire or has simply grown complacent and accommodating to its ways.

Such "big pictures" can be equally powerful today. In his important book, *One World, Ready or Not: The Manic Logic of Global Capitalism,* William Greider opens with an apocalyptic-type metaphor that unveils the seductive and destructive power of global capitalism:

> Imagine a wondrous new machine, strong and supple, a machine that reaps as it destroys. It is huge and mobile, something like the

16. Flannery O'Connor, *Mystery and Manners: Occasional Prose,* ed. Sally Fitzgerald and Robert Fitzgerald (New York: Farrar, Straus & Giroux, 1961), 34.

machines of modern agriculture but vastly more complicated and powerful. Think of this awesome machine running over open terrain and ignoring familiar boundaries. It plows across fields and fencerows with a fierce momentum that is exhilarating to behold and also frightening. As it goes, the machine throws off enormous mows of wealth and bounty while it leaves behind great furrows of wreckage.

Now imagine that there are skillful hands on board, but no one is at the wheel. In fact, this machine has no wheel nor any internal governor to control the speed and direction. It is sustained by its own forward motion, guided mainly by its own appetites. And it is accelerating.[17]

Greider here depicts global capitalism, not as a humanly managed or humanely concerned system, but as an impersonal machine driven and devouring by its own "manic logic." The "big picture" is both shocking and eye-opening, unveiling global capitalism as a principality and helping us to see the world in a new way. Like John of Patmos, Greider demonstrates that "big pictures" and shocking metaphors continue to be one way of unveiling the powers of death and empowering people for resistance. Contemporary sermons from Revelation will also explore ways to employ "big pictures" to unveil the powers of death in the world and to set the church free from captivity to them.

In a similar way, the dramatic and often violent images of God's judgment in Revelation serve as "big pictures" that shock the reader or hearer into an awareness of God's opposition to the ways of the powers. These graphic accounts of God's judgment should not be taken as literal predictions of the way in which God will inaugurate the new creation. Interpreted in this way, these violent accounts contradict the way of the slaughtered Lamb, who is the only one who opens the scroll and reveals the meaning of history (Revelation 5). As Saunders notes, while these accounts of judgment make use of the myth of the cosmic warrior, they intentionally subvert themselves by holding out the slaughtered Lamb as the ultimately victorious one. Even when the image of the Lamb becomes a warrior on a white horse, the "warrior" is victorious only through his own blood and the "sword of his mouth"—the Word of God (19:11–21).

17. William Greider, *One World, Ready or Not: The Manic Logic of Global Capitalism* (New York: Simon and Schuster, 1997), 11.

In this way, Revelation burlesques the empire's myths of violence and domination, undercutting them even as they are used to depict the empire's own defeat. As Saunders writes, "The primal word, the myth that triumphs, is not the word of violence and domination, but the word of the victim, the story of the Lamb." The image of the slaughtered Lamb thus actually subverts the violent images of judgment that run through the Book of Revelation. Consequently, these metaphors of judgment should be read as shocking, "big pictures" that depict God's opposition to the ways of the powers and reveal the end of the powers to be not life, but death. These graphic metaphors unveil the ways and ends of the powers even as they depict the powers' defeat. Indeed, the metaphors often painfully unveil the desire for violent domination that lies in each of us, and even in the church itself. At the very moment we are tempted to relish God's violent victory over the enemy, the rug is pulled out from under us, and we are reminded that the slaughtered Lamb is the one who overcomes. The metaphors thus not only unveil the ways and ends of the powers, but also expose the ways in which our own spirits can get caught up in the violent myths of empire.

Envisioning the New Creation

The writer of Revelation, however, does not simply unveil the ways of the powers as the ways of death. John also envisions the alternative of God's ultimate, peaceable reign in the world. Here too, John employs dramatic, audacious "big pictures" that engage the congregation's imagination, give people hope, and empower the community to begin living now in God's new creation. The writer of Revelation employs what Stephen Webb calls "hyperbolic imagination."[18] Such imagination has a disjunctive character to it; it audaciously holds before the congregation a vision of the new creation that is coming, even when there is no evidence for it in the present.[19] As Webb notes, this kind of imaginative speech invites a "rhetoric of excess"—the poetics of the impossible rather than the prose of the probable.[20] Such an imagination "sees the

18. See Stephen H. Webb, "A Hyperbolic Imagination: Theology and the Rhetoric of Excess," *Theology Today* 50 (1993): 56–67.
19. See also James F. Kay, "Preaching in Advent," *Journal for Preachers* 13 (Advent 1989): 11–16.
20. Webb, "Hyperbolic Imagination," 67.

world as it really is, but, in addition, sees it as it most certainly is not—that is, as what it can become and, therefore, was meant to be."[21]

Such hyperbolic envisioning, with its imaginative rhetoric of excess, characterizes much of the Book of Revelation. Chapter 5, for example, provides an audacious vision of the worship of God and the Lamb. In the midst of a tiny, marginalized Christian community, John holds out a vision of all creation worshiping God and the Lamb, with the implication that the small community's worship itself participates in this audacious liturgical vision:

> Then I looked, and I heard the voice of many angels surrounding the throne and the living creatures and the elders; they numbered myriads of myriads and thousands of thousands, singing with full voice,
>
>> "Worthy is the Lamb that was slaughtered
>> to receive power and wealth and wisdom and might
>> and honor and glory and blessing!"
>
> Then I heard every creature in heaven and on earth and under the earth and in the sea, and all that is in them, singing,
>
>> "To the one seated on the throne and to the Lamb be blessing and honor and glory and might forever and ever!" (5:11–13)

In the midst of empire, there is certainly no concrete evidence of such universal worship of God and the slaughtered Lamb, worship that includes not just human beings, but all of creation. Against all odds, however, John envisions the heavenly worship as a means of empowering the community with the hope that is necessary to sustain faithful resistance in the face of the powers. When one remembers that worship represents the primary practice of resistance in the Book of Revelation, it is not surprising that this central "hyperbolic vision" is a liturgical one.

Equally unsurprising, the Apocalypse ends with one of the grandest and most audacious visions in the Bible—the vision of God's new creation:

> Then I saw a new heaven and a new earth; for the first heaven and the first earth had passed away, and the sea was no more. And I saw the holy city, the new Jerusalem, coming down out of heaven from

21. Ibid., 64.

God, prepared as a bride adorned for her husband. And I heard a loud voice from the throne saying,

> "See, the home of God is among mortals.
> God will dwell with them as their God;
> they will be God's people,
> and God will be with them;
> God will wipe every tear from their eyes.
> Death will be no more;
> mourning and crying and pain will be no more,
> for the first things have passed away." (21:1–4; my translation)

Through this use of hyperbolic imagination, John of Patmos takes up the poetic, visionary work of the prophet, who does not simply speak words of judgment, but inspires hope by envisioning God's reign. As Walter Brueggemann has written, "The poet/prophet is a voice that shatters settled reality and evokes new possibility in the listening assembly. Preaching continues that dangerous, indispensable habit of speech. The poetic speech of text and of sermon is a prophetic construal of a world beyond the one taken for granted."[22] Preachers who would proclaim the Word that comes to us in the Apocalypse will not only seek to expose the powers of death at work in the world, but will also engage in audacious, hyperbolic imagining of God's new creation.

As the verses from Revelation 21 suggest, however, such hyperbolic imagination does not exist in a vacuum. The writer of Revelation draws upon the larger canonical story to envision the new creation. The visions are deeply rooted in the storied memories of God's people, which give shape to the radical hope proclaimed in Revelation. Through implicit and explicit allusions to the larger biblical story, the Apocalypse ultimately serves to draw that story together and bring it to fulfillment.

Revelation 21:1–4 represents an extraordinary, though not isolated, example of the connection between Revelation and the larger canonical story. In these few verses John envisions the fulfillment of God's purposes as a culmination of the ongoing story of God and God's people recounted throughout Scripture. In doing so, the writer pulls together an extraordinary number of strands from that story through multiple allusions and figures.

22. Walter Brueggemann, *Finally Comes the Poet: Daring Speech for Proclamation* (Minneapolis: Fortress, 1989), 4. See also Walter Brueggemann, "Preaching as Reimagination," *Theology Today* 52 (1995): 313–29.

The vision of the new heaven and new earth, including the disappearance of the waters of chaos, not only takes the reader back to the original creation in Genesis 1, but brings to fulfillment specific prophecies from Isaiah (65:17; 66:22). The new Jerusalem, which provides a central figure for describing the new creation, transforms and brings to fulfillment the long story of that city, which provides a central thread for the story of God's people. Revelation does not envision a return to the Garden of Eden, but rather the fulfillment of the work God began with Israel, expressed through the figure of Jerusalem, which represents both the faithfulness and rebellion of God's people. The glorious City of David, which also killed the prophets and crucified the Lamb of God, has now been transformed into the holy city, the new Jerusalem.[23]

Similarly, in taking up the language of covenant—God will dwell with them as their God, and they will be God's people (v. 3)—the vision in Revelation 21 draws upon the larger story of God's faithfulness and brings it to completion. From the covenant with Abraham to the covenant with Moses to the new covenant in Jesus and the covenant with the church, that promise echoes: "I will be your God and you shall be my people." Indeed, that promise and that relationship give shape to the ongoing story told in Scripture. And in John's vision of the new creation, the restoration of the covenant brings the story to fulfillment. Through these and countless other allusions, the vision of John the Seer both grounds itself in the story of God's people and brings that story to its dramatic completion. Although, as I discuss below, Revelation fundamentally tells the story of Jesus, preachers who seek to unveil the powers of death and envision the new creation will remember this larger story of which the story of Jesus is the center.

Narrative Preaching and Revelation

Although, as Stanley Saunders argues, it is impossible to confine Revelation within a single genre, there are unquestionably narrative elements in the book, both in specific texts and in the

23. For an extraordinary account of the biblical story seen through the figure of the city, and particularly the city of Jerusalem, see Jacques Ellul, *The Meaning of the City* (Grand Rapids: Eerdmans, 1970). For a more general discussion of the use of figures—and figural imagination—as a means of unifying the biblical story, see Charles L. Campbell, *Preaching Jesus: New Directions*

movement of the book as a whole. As Saunders also makes clear, however, the primary story of Revelation is the story of Jesus. This particular story of the crucified, resurrected, and enthroned Lamb shapes the Apocalypse and provides the "counterstory" that subverts and challenges the myths of empire. Although told with images and metaphors that are quite different from the Gospel stories, the story of Jesus nevertheless remains primary. As David Barr notes, "The Apocalypse is in its most basic sense a retelling of this story of Jesus in a new way with new images."

Narrative preaching from the Book of Revelation will thus be shaped by this particular story of Jesus. Like other New Testament books, Revelation is not interested in narrative for narrative's sake, but rather employs story as the necessary vehicle for proclaiming the person and work of Jesus.[24] "Narrative preaching" thus is fundamentally preaching that grounds itself upon and functions within the story of Jesus; its concern is not narrative in general, but the particular story of Jesus. In this sense, narrative preaching from Revelation is not primarily concerned with narrative *forms,* which have tended to shape the way in which narrative preaching has been understood in contemporary homiletics.[25] Narrative preaching from Revelation, for example, will not necessarily involve storytelling, though one may use stories along the way if they contribute to proclaiming the story of Jesus. Nor will narrative preaching necessarily involve following a general movement of plot, though elements of disequilibrium and reversal will certainly be involved in any preaching from the Book of Revelation (and other apocalyptic literature). Rather, narrative preaching from the Book of Revelation will proclaim the particular story of Jesus as the counterstory to the myths of empire in order to empower the community's resistance to the powers of death.

Narrative preaching in this sense involves, in Richard Hays's

for Homiletics in Hans Frei's Postliberal Theology (Grand Rapids: Eerdmans, 1997), 99–100, 184–85, 250–57.

24. On the Gospels' lack of interest in narrative for the sake of narrative, see Campbell, *Preaching Jesus,* 54–56, 190–93.

25. The two major branches of narrative preaching have emphasized either storytelling (see, e.g., Richard Jensen, *Telling the Story: Variety and Imagination in Preaching* [Minneapolis: Augsburg, 1980]) or "plot" (Eugene Lowry, *The Homiletical Plot: The Sermon as Narrative Art Form* [Atlanta: John Knox, 1980]), both with an emphasis on form, rather than content.

terms, sermons shaped not simplistically by narrative forms, but by a deep narrative logic. Drawing on Hays's work, I want to suggest several characteristics of this logic in relation to preaching from Revelation.[26] First, "narrative logic" does not involve strict "logical necessities," but embodies the contingencies of narrative itself. Rather than moving inexorably from proposition to conclusion, narrative logic involves a kind of "fitness," like the fitness of the movement of a story. The movement is more like a jazz improvisation than a logical argument. Within a particular "story" or theme, which the jazz musician states at the beginning, the musician proceeds to improvise, restrained by the chords of the theme, but within that framework performing only one of many possible improvisations. No logical necessities are involved. Similarly, within the framework of a story, particularly a rich and metaphorical story like Revelation, numerous improvisations— numerous claims and arguments—will be possible, for narrative logic is not monolithic, but always polyvalent.

Second, and more specifically, in this kind of narrative preaching the story of Jesus provides the *warrant* for the claims that are made. In this sense, narrative preaching moves beyond the traditional categories of deductive and inductive. Such preaching does not begin with universal truths of reason and deduce particular propositions. Nor does such preaching begin with human experience and move logically to general conclusions. Rather, the preacher begins with the particulars of the story of Jesus and moves—again with a kind of improvisational "fitness" rather than logical necessity—toward specific claims.

Such narratively grounded warrants are particularly critical in preaching from Revelation. One simply cannot get to the claims of Revelation—for example, the reign of the slaughtered Lamb— from the truths of reason or general human experience. As apocalyptic resistance literature, Revelation draws on the story of Jesus to interrupt and subvert assumed rational or experiential truths, which are often simply the product of the myths of empire that have come to pass for common sense. Consequently, preaching from Revelation *must* be "narrative preaching," which grounds its

26. The characteristics of narrative logic are drawn from Richard Hays, *The Faith of Jesus Christ,* Society of Biblical Literature Dissertation Series 56 (Chico, Calif.: Scholars, 1983), esp. 7, 85, 196, 223–24, 235, 247, 257, 264–66. See also Campbell, *Preaching Jesus,* 208–10.

claims in the story of Jesus. Deductive and inductive approaches simply will not work.

Third, whatever specific form the sermon may take, preaching shaped by narrative logic will be rich with allusions to the story of Jesus. The movement, again, is much like a piece of jazz in which the musician repeatedly returns to the theme or basic story within which he or she improvises, often through brief allusions rather than exhaustive repetition. In Revelation, for example, John early on sets up the story of the slaughtered Lamb as the central, guiding story (chap. 5), then returns regularly to the image of the Lamb in the rest of his "oral performance." In these regular allusions to the Lamb, John reminds his hearers/readers of the story of Jesus' crucifixion, resurrection, and enthronement, which governs the entire work. Contemporary preachers will likewise use such repeated allusions to the story of Jesus when they preach from the Book of Revelation.

Finally, narrative logic remains open-ended and tensive. Its language is rich and polyvalent. Unlike univocal arguments, whether grounded in deductive or inductive logic, narrative preaching is rich with multiple meanings, inviting—indeed requiring—the active participation of the hearers. Such tensive language is particularly characteristic of the story of Jesus performed in the Book of Revelation. As Saunders notes, the particular telling of the story of Jesus in Revelation invites numerous interpretations; congregations necessarily engage the material in creative and imaginative ways. With each performance new insights and interpretations emerge. When, for example, the story of the "cosmic warrior" merges with the story of the slaughtered Lamb, the "logic" resists any rational closure and calls congregations to engage the narrative with both their minds and their lives. Such tensive, multivalent language characterizes the narrative logic that will shape preaching from the Book of Revelation.

Narrative preaching, as I have depicted it, is thus not confined merely to storytelling or homiletical plots. Rather, it is preaching grounded in the story of Jesus and shaped by a narrative logic. Although such narrative preaching may include stories and involve aspects of plot (disequilibrium, reversal, resolution), it is not limited to these formal characteristics, but rather embodies narrative—specifically the story of Jesus—at a deeper level of content and logic.

In the sermon that follows I hope to demonstrate these various claims, which may seem rather abstract at the moment. While the sermon may not at first glance appear to be a "narrative sermon" as traditionally defined, I have tried to work within the kind of narrative logic I have described, and I have sought to proclaim the story of Jesus as a counterstory to the myths of empire. At the same time, within the context of this story, I have tried to expose the powers of death, envision the new creation, and empower the congregation for resistance. This sermon was preached at Central Presbyterian Church in Atlanta, Georgia (the church I described earlier), on Christ the King Sunday, 2002. At that time the church was in a period of transition, beginning a search for a new senior pastor.

꙼

AUDACITY

Then I saw in the right hand of the one seated on the throne a scroll written on the inside and on the back, sealed with seven seals; and I saw a mighty angel proclaiming with a loud voice, "Who is worthy to open the scroll and break its seals?" And no one in heaven or on earth or under the earth was able to open the scroll or to look into it. And I began to weep bitterly because no one was found worthy to open the scroll or to look into it. Then one of the elders said to me, "Do not weep. See, the Lion of the tribe of Judah, the Root of David, has conquered, so that he can open the scroll and its seven seals." Then I saw between the throne and the four living creatures and among the elders a Lamb standing as if it had been slaughtered, having seven horns and seven eyes, which are the seven spirits of God sent out into all the earth. He went and took the scroll from the right hand of the one who was seated on the throne. When he had taken the scroll, the four living creatures and the twenty-four elders fell before the Lamb, each holding a harp and golden bowls full of incense, which are the prayers of the saints. They sing a new song: "You are worthy to take the scroll and to open its seals, for you were slaughtered and by your blood you ransomed for God saints from every tribe and language and people and nation; you have made them to be a kingdom and priests serving our God, and they will reign on earth." Then I looked, and I heard the voice of many angels surrounding the throne and the living creatures and the elders; they numbered myriads of myriads and thousands of thousands, singing with full voice, "Worthy is the Lamb that was slaughtered to receive power and wealth and wisdom and might and honor and glory and blessing!" Then I heard every creature in heaven and on earth and under the earth and in the sea, and all that is in them, singing, "To the one seated on the throne and to the Lamb be blessing and honor and glory and might forever and ever!" And the four living creatures said, "Amen!" And the elders fell down and worshiped. (Rev. 5:1–14)

Now that's a grand vision—even for Christ the King Sunday. And this vision of the heavenly worship becomes truly audacious when you think about the church that imagined it. At the time the Book of Revelation was written the church was miniscule, probably about one one-hundredth of 1 percent of the Roman Empire. That would be the equivalent of about four hundred Christians—not many more than those of us gathered here today—in all of metropolitan Atlanta. The church was tiny, and it was ostracized and persecuted. John, the writer of Revelation, was in exile in Patmos because of his faith. That was the situation of the church.

But this tiny church has a huge vision: myriads of myriads and thousands of thousands of angels singing praises with full voice. Every creature in heaven and on earth and under the earth and in the sea, and all that is in them—everyone and everything in all creation singing praises to God and to the Lamb. This little church has this enormous vision. It seems crazy, like a fantasy. At the very least, it is audacious.

And such a vision may create some problems for many of us reasonably realistic and practical people. It's just too big, too extravagant; it even seems a little triumphalistic. I know visions like this one are difficult for me. At times I even have trouble with much smaller visions.

Several years ago I attended a funeral at a very small church in rural Arkansas. The church sat out in the middle of nowhere; there wasn't even a small town nearby. As I sat down in my pew I noticed a sign at the front of the church where everyone could see it. It was one of those wooden signs with slots in it—the kind you can slide different numbers in from week to week. Like the signs churches use to post the hymns for the morning; you've seen them. Well, this particular sign had two sets of numbers on it. The top line read, "Attendance Goal: 75." Then the second line stated, "Last Sunday's Attendance: 12." I remember sitting in that church staring at that sign throughout the funeral thinking, "This is crazy!" Can you imagine sitting in that congregation week after week, looking at the sign: Attendance Goal: 75; Last Sunday's Attendance: 12 . . . 14 . . . 11. I mean, that church wasn't *ever* going to have 75 people—not on the best Easter imaginable. They were just setting themselves up for disappointment. It was crazy!

As I look back on that experience, however, I'm embarrassed. The little church in Revelation has this enormous vision of all creation worshiping God. But I couldn't even imagine seventy-five folks in that little country congregation. And maybe some of you reasonable, realistic folks can relate. Such visions come hard for us. It's crazy to hope for more than the possible; that's just to court disappointment.

And yet, as I have thought about it, this attitude seems a bit strange, even today. After all, grand visions are not really foreign in our world. Other folks don't seem nearly as hesitant about such visions as we Christians often appear to be. Right across the street, there's a museum that claims the whole world to be the "World of Coca-Cola." That's pretty grand! And just recently I was reading the new National Security Strategy developed by the Bush administration. You should read it. The document presents a grand global vision of American values and priorities spread to every nook and cranny of the earth. Some have said it is a vision of empire—*Pax Americana,* American Peace. While that may be debatable, it is at the very least a grand vision—an audacious vision.

It's odd, isn't it? We Christians say we worship the creator of heaven and earth—the Alpha and Omega—but often our visions are not even as big or bold as those of Coca-Cola. That grand vision in Revelation may come as a challenge to many of us, myself included.

And, I hate to tell you, it gets even tougher. For the vision in Revelation is audacious not simply because of its size and scope. It's also audacious because of its *content.* In this vision all creation worships the *slaughtered Lamb.* Even the Book of Revelation itself struggles with this vision at times; our text this morning wrestles with it for a moment. An angel proclaims in a loud voice: "Who is worthy to open the scroll in God's hand and break its seal?" That is, who can show us the meaning of history; who can show us the things that really last in the world? But no one can be found to open the scroll. So John begins to weep bitterly. But then one of the elders announces, "Don't weep! Someone has been found who can open the scroll. The Lion of the tribe of Judah has conquered; he can open the scroll." Yes, surely the Lion of Judah reveals the meaning of history. Surely the Lion King—a messianic military ruler—will come and open the scroll. That's what lasts: military might and power. Lion Kings.

But that's not who appears. The one who appears is the very opposite of a messianic military ruler. The one who appears is the slaughtered Lamb—the crucified Jesus. In the midst of the empire, that little, persecuted church proclaims that the slaughtered Lamb unveils the true meaning of history. Talk about audacity! Can you imagine the scorn of the empire for that vision? After all, the empire slaughtered the Lamb, crucified him. "Why, we've already dealt with him," the empire must have responded. "His power was nothing compared with our economic and military might. What a ridiculous vision. All creation worshiping the slaughtered Lamb. Absurd!"

I myself got a sense of this kind of response a couple of weeks ago. I was participating in the Peace March and Rally here in downtown Atlanta. Before the beginning of the march, I was standing with some others, holding a banner that read, "Christians for Peace." And I noticed a woman walking toward me. It was hard to miss her because she was dressed like the devil. Literally. She wore a red suit, had two horns on her head, and carried a pitchfork. She walked right up to me and looked me in the eye. And I'll never forget what she said in a voice dripping with sarcasm: "I saw your quaint little sign." It sounded to me like the voice of empire, with all of its military and economic power. "Christians for peace. What a quaint little vision." And it reminded me of the audacity of this vision from Revelation. The slaughtered Lamb opens the scroll and reveals the meaning of history. The slaughtered Lamb provides the key to the future. The slaughtered Lamb redeems the world. In the midst of empire, that is audacity!

And that vision is so audacious because we live even today in a world governed by what Walter Wink calls the myth of redemptive violence.[27] According to this myth, the way to bring order out of

27. Wink, *Engaging the Powers*, 13–31.

chaos is through violence. The way to make things "right" in the world, the way to deal with threats, is through violence. This myth permeates our culture, from the old Popeye cartoons—many of you remember those: Popeye eats his spinach, beats the fool out of Bluto, and order is restored and the world is at peace again— to Westerns to *Star Wars* to video games. Can you imagine Disney making a movie entitled, *The Slaughtered Lamb King*? Who would go? The myth of redemptive violence—it's everywhere: from the death penalty to terrorism to the war on terrorism to the threat- ened war on Iraq to those cannons on the lawn of the Capitol across the street, which are pointing *right at us*. And we're sur- prised when even little children at times turn to guns as the means of dealing with their enemies?

I remember the night after the shootings at Columbine High School. I was watching a "Special Report" about the tragedy on television. President Clinton made a passionate plea for all of us to teach our children nonviolent ways to deal with conflict. He de- clared that we must show our children that violence is not the way to solve their problems. It was a moving and important speech. Shortly after the president's address, however, the "Special Re- port" on Columbine was interrupted by another "Special Report" announcing that NATO's bombing of Belgrade had resumed.

The myth of redemptive violence. It's not a Democratic thing or a Republican thing. It's a human thing.

But the witness of the gospel—the vision of the slaughtered Lamb—offers an alternative to this myth. In his ministry Jesus challenges the "powers that be." He disturbs the established order. So, the powers crucify him—one more instance of the myth of redemptive violence. On the cross, however, the slaughtered Lamb draws this myth out into the open; he unveils it for what it is: not the way of God, but the way opposed to God—the way that kills the very Son of God. Jesus strips away the illusions and unveils the myth as the way of death, not life.

Martin Luther King Jr. did a similar thing in his marches: He drew racism out into the open so we could see it for what it is. And King knew exactly what he was doing; he understood the way of the slaughtered Lamb. "Let them get their dogs," he shouted, "and let them get the hose, and we will leave them standing be- fore their God and the world spattered with the blood and reek- ing with the stench of their Negro brothers." We must, he continued, "bring these issues to the surface, bring them out into the open where everybody can see them."[28] That's what the Lamb does, splattered with blood on the cross. He exposes the myth of redemptive violence; he helps us see that myth for what it really is: not the way of life, but the way of death. And in place of this myth, the Lamb embodies the story of redemptive love and sets us free for life in *that* story.

And here in the vision from Revelation, all creation worships the slaughtered Lamb. The way of the slaughtered Lamb ultimately overcomes the violent ways of the world. The story of redemptive love is the true story of creation, the story that lasts. Talk about audacity! I have trouble even imagining that. For a long time I thought, "Jesus' way is okay, but eventually God will have to come and whip things into shape using the world's means, which seem far more effective than Jesus'." And even the imagery of Revelation at times seems to point in this direction. But that's not the vision here in Revelation 5—the central vision of the book. Here the way of the slaughtered Lamb transforms creation. For you cannot get to the new creation on the path of redemptive violence. You can only get there on the way of redemptive love, the way of the slaughtered Lamb. And to be honest, I can't imagine how that will work. I can't imagine how long it will take. And I can't imagine how much trust in God it will require.

But the little church in Revelation imagined it. They trusted God could handle it. And that audacious vision and trust empowered them for a new way of life. For their vision was not just about some pie-in-the-sky future, much less about the triumph of Christianity. It was about a way of living now—a way that was the opposite of domination and triumphalism. That audacious vision empowered that fragile, little church to give a risky, subversive witness in the midst of the empire. It empowered that small, marginalized community of faith to embody an alternative to the ways and priorities of the "powers that be"—even at the cost of martyrdom. That audacious vision empowered that little church for audacious living.

And I often wonder today if the church hasn't grown so timid because our imagination has become so small. In the midst of our world today, I don't think we need a church that is simply reasonable and realistic. We need a church that will trust God and dare

28. Richard Lischer, *The Preacher King: Martin Luther King, Jr., and the Word That Moved America* (New York: Oxford University Press, 1995), 157.

audacious visions. I think it's time for the church, like the church in Revelation, to take up what someone has called the poetics of the impossible, rather than the prose of the probable.[29] Today what the church needs is a vision that is big enough and demanding enough and empowering enough to shape lives and communities worthy of our baptisms.

And here at Central, in this time of transition, I think God invites us to dare audacious visions and wild imaginations. Now is not the time for us to be timid and tentative, drawing up reasonable little plans and realistic little goals. Rather, it's a time to look ahead with visions that are big enough—and, yes, subversive enough—to build up a church as audacious as the gospel itself. It's time for audacious visions and wild imaginations.

And those visions begin here in worship—in Word and Sacrament and song. Those visions begin here in worship—in daring and bold worship that challenges the ways and myths of empire and takes up the story of the Lamb King. For here in worship God forms our vision. God builds us up as a people who together can risk far more than we ever could alone. In our worship and our life together, it is time for audacious visions.

For you never know what might happen if such a vision gets hold of us. A number of years ago, South African Christians, right in the midst of apartheid, confessed such an audacious, subversive vision and began to live into it. And we know what happened there. Their vision is in fact a lot like the one in Revelation 5. Maybe it's a vision for us. It goes like this:

> It is not true that this world and its inhabitants are doomed to die and be lost;
> This is true: For God so loved the world that [God] gave [the] only son so that everyone who believes in him shall not die but have everlasting life.
> It is not true that we must accept inhumanity and discrimination, hunger and poverty, death and destruction;
> This is true: I have come that they may have life, and have it abundantly.
> It is not true that violence and hatred shall have the last word, and that war and destruction have come to stay forever;
> This is true: To us a child is born, to us a son is given in whom authority will rest and whose name will be prince of peace.

29. Webb, "Hyperbolic Imagination," 67.

It is not true that we are simply victims of the powers of evil that
seek to rule the world;
This is true: To me is given all authority in heaven and on earth,
and lo, I am with you always to the end of the world. . . .
It is not true that our dreams for the liberation of humankind,
our dreams of justice, of human dignity, of peace, are not
meant for this earth and this history;
This is true: The hour comes, and it is now, that true worshipers
shall worship God in spirit and in truth.[30]

The hour is now. Let us worship God and the Lamb.

---

30. *The Iona Community Worship Book* (Glasgow: Wild Goose, 1997), 72.

8

Narrative Reading, Narrative Preaching: Inhabiting the Story

Michael Pasquarello III

The story of the sermon and the hymns and of the processions and of the sacramental acts and of the readings is to be God's story, the story of the Bible. Preachers are the greatest sinners here: the text already is and belongs to the one true story; it does not need to be helped out in this respect. What is said and enacted in the church must be with the greatest exactitude and faithfulness and exclusivity the story of creation and redemption by the God of Israel and Father of the Risen Christ. (Robert Jenson, "How the World Lost Its Story")

Students at the seminary where I teach tell me that, for them, the most important factor in preaching is the "authenticity" of the person speaking, a person who is "real" and not just another "talking head." When pressed for a definition of authentic or real, they typically say they are looking and listening for a preacher whose life is characterized by credibility; that he or she gives evidence of genuine and passionate commitment to the message preached; that the content, purpose, and style of the preacher's speech are appropriate to Scripture and aim to promote its faithful performance by the church. Although these concerns do not represent a new development in the preaching tradition, I believe my students are on to something very important. Their perceptions point to a growing need for a recovery and appropriation of the practice that has been presented in this book: narrative reading and preaching as a primary means by which the identity and mission of the church is created and sustained by God, whose speech authors its life and secures its future.

Throughout their history, Christians have generally read the narrative of Scripture to guide, correct, and edify their faith, worship, and practice as essential aspects of their ongoing struggle to live faithfully before the Triune God.[1] This chapter therefore discusses narrative reading and preaching as a theological and ecclesial practice, which embodies the wisdom classically associated with theology, a knowledge and love of God and its correlative way of life that is learned through inhabiting the world of Scripture.[2] As Joel Green has persuasively argued in his introductory chapter, if the primary task and witness of the church is to continue this particular narrative of God in its particular ways, then the source, means, and goal of our reading and preaching must be the immersion of ourselves in the biblical drama, so that our sense of past, present, and future as God's people is congruous with its story of the universe.

Has the Church Lost Its Story?

Robert Jenson has written about what every preacher knows; in our time we preach to people, within and without the church, who live in a world that has lost its story.[3] For the church to speak the gospel, says Jenson, is to speak a story with a God-given past and future; however, the postmodern world, having lost both memory and hope, and engulfed by innumerable competing stories, neither credits the promise nor claims its hope.

Until fairly recently, it was expected that people thought their lives were part of a story, and the church's business was to propose the gospel as the true and deep meaning of that story. Christian-

---

1. Stephen Fowl, introduction to *The Theological Interpretation of Scripture: Classic and Contemporary Readings*, ed. Stephen Fowl (Oxford: Oxford University Press, 1997), xiii.

2. Richard Lischer, *A Theology of Preaching: The Dynamics of the Gospel*, rev. ed. (Eugene, Oreg.: Wipf and Stock, 2001), i.

3. In this section I am indebted to the discussion in Robert W. Jenson, "How the World Lost Its Story," in *The New Religious Humanists*, ed. Gregory Wolfe (New York: Free Press, 1997), 135–49.

ity claimed to tell a universally encompassing story, and posited as a correlated notion the universal possibility of finding one's place in the narrative. As Jenson notes, modernity appropriated the church's claim and idea, hoping to maintain the form of the Christian story without telling it about the particular God of Israel and Jesus Christ and its peculiar way of life. This was the attempt to have a universal story without the universal storyteller, a role that was embraced with enthusiasm by enlightened humanity, presumably emancipated from the oppressive authority of its past. Thus, the story told by modernity was "that we should have no story except the story we chose when we had no story."[4]

It is a centuries-old commonplace of preachers that people love stories. For example, the preaching friars of the medieval period transformed the use of homiletic illustrations, fables, and *exempla* into an art form, which became, in its excessive use, a victim of its own success.[5] In the modern period we have witnessed a similar kind of homiletic success and self-victimization. While the homiletic use of story, illustration, vivid imagery, personal anecdote, and auto-biography abounds in the ears of listeners, the theological use of Scripture, which invites the church to imagine and indwell the world of the Bible to receive its life and destiny by means of the surprising drama of salvation unfolded in its hearing, is largely silent.[6]

Although preachers continue to visit the Bible to search for relevant and useful ideas, topics, and stories as resources for producing "meaning" or "understanding" and evoking "moving experiences" and "spirituality," too few speak the language of Christian Scripture with a homiletic wisdom capable of forming a people whose corporate life is identified by the story of the Triune God who creates and saves the world. Preachers have followed the "great reversal" of interpretive strategy that has dominated the modern period. Interpretation for preaching has become simply a matter of fitting the biblical story into another world, which is constituted by that range of experiences and understandings

4. Stanley Hauerwas, *Sanctify Them in the Truth: Holiness Exemplified* (Nashville: Abingdon, 1999), 237–38.

5. See the discussion in John O' Malley, "Medieval Preaching," in *De Ore Domini: Preacher and Word in the Middle Ages*, ed. Thomas L. Amos et al. (Kalamazoo, Mich.: Medieval Institute, 1989), 1–11.

6. See the discussion in Ann Monroe, *The Word: Imagining the Gospel in Modern America* (Louisville: Westminster/John Knox, 2000).

open to any human being, rather than incorporating that world into the story of God narrated by Scripture.[7]

In the self-assured world of modernity, which encouraged us to believe that each of us authors our own story, the primary task of preaching was to provide insight and inspiration to assist anxious, stressed, and bored church members and seekers to make sense of the Bible on terms compatible to their world. Adherents of this kind of preaching often point to numerical evidence that suggests its "effectiveness," but often neglect a much larger and enduring theological and pastoral task. This is to articulate the necessary wisdom to see, or to make sense of ourselves, as people created and destined to know, love, worship, and serve the Triune God.

We need an alternative to modernity's "great reversal." This will not come in the form of new styles of communication or homiletic theories, but rather by having our lives shaped by a wisdom necessary to recover the practice of reading and speaking Christian Scripture as a spiritual, communal, and interpretive art learned by inhabiting the story of God and the world, from its beginning to its ending. We must rediscover, from within our own tradition, habits of thinking and speaking that will enable us to construe the biblical narrative as the only true story of the world, all other stories being at best partial renditions of the world story disclosed in the Bible. Insofar as we allow God's story to become our home rather than a distant land, we no longer will approach the Bible as consumers of religion seeking quotations, illustrations, self-help tips, and practical applications; rather, we will reverently receive it as the living Word addressed to God's people, as the story which furnishes our vocabulary, shapes our imagination, and forms our life for the sake of the whole creation.[8]

Recovering the Church's Story

George Lindbeck observes that the early Christians derived their communal self-understanding from the story of Israel. They

---

7. See the excellent discussion in Charles L. Campbell, *Preaching Jesus: New Directions for Homiletics in Hans Frei's Postliberal Theology* (Grand Rapids: Eerdmans, 1997), 117–88.

8. Hauerwas, *Sanctify Them,* 235–41; Eugene H. Peterson with Marva Dawn, "Paul: Finishing Up in Rome," in *The Unnecessary Pastor: Rediscovering the Call,* ed. Peter Santuci (Grand Rapids: Eerdmans, 2000), 59–78.

were the people of God who were living between the times after the messianic era had begun but before the final coming of the kingdom. The church's identity was therefore narrative-shaped and characterized by its story; Israel's history was their history, as seen through the prism of Christ, and the Hebrew Scriptures formed their sole ecclesiological textbook. "Church," therefore, referred to concrete groups of people, a public, social reality that was constituted by actors and communities of actors inhabiting and performing the biblical narrative in continuity with the story of Israel. As Lindbeck asserts, "The Trinitarian calling, constituting, and empowering of God's people stands revealed. It is a new epoch of unheard-of possibilities and actualities—not a new Israel—which begins at Pentecost." Thus, the church's story, understood as continuous with Israel's, tells of God's doing in this time between the times what God has done before: choosing and guiding a people to be a sign and witness in all that it is and does, whether obediently or disobediently, to who and what God is.[9]

If we take the Bible as our script, authored by God and spoken in our own language and life, its story can be retold through our words and actions. This happens most readily when we do not approach the Bible as an alien document, the record of an ancient people, and try to make sense of it, but when we instead set ourselves to learn the sense it has and to become critical participants in the community whose life and witness is first recorded there.[10] Scripture, therefore, lives and has its churchly meaning within the church's pastoral and liturgical practice and its enactment in a common life of Christian discipleship. Sermons are preached from biblical texts. Real sermons do not expound an idea or theme chosen by the preacher or demanded by the people, nor do they tell any story other than the story embodied in or around the biblical text. Rather, all our pastoral discourse—homilies, sermons, devotions, and instruction—communicate the gospel as we try to say the same things that Scripture says. As Scripture guides and informs our homiletic discourse—its scope, substance, and

9. George Lindbeck, "The Church," in *Keeping the Faith,* ed. Geoffrey Wainwright (Philadelphia: Westminster; Allison Park, Pa.: Pickwick, 1988), 186, 181–85.

10. Charles M. Wood, *An Invitation to Theological Study* (Valley Forge, Pa.: Trinity, 1994), 107.

style—it identifies our lives as participants in the story of God and the world.[11]

Preaching in a "Tournament of Narratives"

The ancient church found itself engaged, just as we are, in a "tournament of narratives."[12] Irenaeus, second-century bishop of Lyon, sought to differentiate churchly reading and preaching from that of the Gnostics, whose scholarly interpretation pointed in directions alien to the purposes of the church and its faith. Gnostic teachers wreaked havoc in Christian congregations, luring the faithful with their creative and engaging exegetical expertise. According to Irenaeus, these heretics treated Scripture as a sort of mine from which to dig spiritual nuggets of wisdom. Jenson observes, "Their exegesis supposed that scripture is a congeries of sayings and stories and commands and so forth, and that each component bit is a lump of ore from which we may extract precious insight if only we know the technique." Gnostic exegesis regarded Scripture as a discrete set of opportunities to acquire or display religious and spiritual truth. Jenson likens this to the homiletic practice of many contemporary preachers who make occasional visits to the Bible in order to find stories, sayings, wisdom, and rules, one at a time, to be individually exploited by the discovery of whatever relevant idea, theme, or topic it inspires.[13]

Irenaeus's great work, *Against Heresies,* exposed and challenged this way of reading Scripture, since this method fails to discern the larger biblical framework, its story, and actors according to the witness of the prophets and apostles.

> Such then is their system, which the prophets did not announce, the Lord did not teach, and the Apostles did not hand down; but which they boastfully declare that they understand better than others. . . . They attempt to make ropes of sand in applying the parables of the Lord, or prophetic utterances, or Apostolic statements

11. Robert W. Jenson, "Hermeneutics and the Life of the Church," in *Reclaiming the Bible for the Church,* ed. Carl E. Bratten and Robert W. Jenson (Grand Rapids: Eerdmans, 1995), 92.

12. I have borrowed this term from Rodney Clapp, *A Peculiar People: The Church as Culture in a Post-Christian Society* (Downers Grove, Ill.: InterVarsity Press, 1996).

13. Jenson, "Hermeneutics and the Life of the Church," 95–96.

to their plausible scheme, in order that they may have foundation for it. But they alter the scriptural context and connection, and dismember the truth as much as they can. . . . It is just as if there were a beautiful representation of a king made by a skilled artist, and one altered the arrangement of the pieces of stone into the shape of a dog or a fox, and then should assert that this was the original representation of a king. In much the same manner, they stitch together old wives' tales, and wrestling sayings and parables, however they may, from the context, attempt to fit oracles of God into their myths.[14]

Irenaeus proposed a ruled way of reading Scripture, the *regula fidei*, which served the church's hope of articulating and authenticating a world-encompassing story or metanarrative of creation, incarnation, redemption, and consummation. His aim was to assist Christian communities that were striving to tell their stories of faith in the construction of a unifying worldview, an embracing, overarching narrative of salvation in Jesus Christ. As Paul Blowers asserts, "The challenge of Christian identity was to reconstruct the story of Jesus Christ in its dramatic fullness as both the cosmic story—a narrative comprehending the destiny of all creation and all peoples—and as the genuine 'final act' to the peculiar sacred story of Israel."[15]

The earliest exponents of a Christian rule regarded it as representing the kind of authority Scripture conveyed: It was essentially the authority of a story, or a divine gospel enshrined within a grand story, with God as the primary narrator. It was a drama gradually unfolded with a coherent plot, climaxing in the coming of Jesus, who held the secret to the story's ending. Although the denouement was certain due to the early plot of the story that pointed to it, enlisting the participation of living audiences in the drama was crucial, their own performance in the drama's last act.

Irenaeus, therefore, instructed preachers to read each text with the whole Bible in mind, to locate individual sermon texts within the whole canon. Christian Scripture is a whole because it is the whole narrative of the one Triune God, and in order to follow the whole story preachers must know the whole story's plot and its

14. Irenaeus *Against Heresies* I.8.1 (cited in Frances Young, *Virtuoso Theology: The Bible and Interpretation* [Cleveland: Pilgrim, 1990], 47).
15. Paul M. Blowers, "The Regula Fidei and the Narrative Character of Early Christian Faith," *Pro Ecclesia* 6 (1997): 203–4.

characters. The church, moreover, does know the plot and characters of the scriptural narrative. Since the church is a continuous community with the story's actors and narrators, it does not need to make the biblical story relevant for contemporary listeners; rather, it simply must see itself as one with God's people across the centuries, members of a single community.[16] The rule, therefore, provides a constant touchstone by which preacher and people can test their internal and external witness to Jesus Christ, sharpen their collective memory, and articulate their ongoing experience of life "in Christ" or "in the Spirit."[17]

Augustine: Inhabiting Scripture

The substantial wisdom, integrity, and flexibility of the rule is further evidenced in the spiritual and moral fidelity of those who received it and lived under it to carry on faithfully the Christian story in their own virtuous lives. Augustine of Hippo was arguably the most salutary exemplar of narrative reading and preaching during the early centuries of the Western church. As Hans Frei notes, "Long before a minor modern school of thought made the biblical 'history of salvation' a special spiritual and historical sequence for historiographical and theological inquiry, Christian preachers and theological commentators, Augustine the most notable among them, had envisioned the real world as formed by the sequence told by the biblical stories."[18] Augustine began with the scriptural word, with the particular story the Bible has to tell, through which the stories of Christian people and the peoples of the world are then told. Immersing himself in the world of Scripture, his imagination and life were so shaped by its grand narrative that he struggled to "insert everything from Platonism and the Pelagian problem to the Fall of Rome into the Bible."[19]

Uniting doctrinal and biblical exegesis, the life of the Christian community, and pastoral ministry, Augustine demonstrates a wisdom that speaks to both our desire for "real" and "authentic" preachers, and our search for a method or style that will close the

16. Jenson, "Hermeneutics and the Life of the Church," 98.

17. Ibid., 99.

18. Hans W. Frei, *The Eclipse of Biblical Narrative: A Study in Eighteenth and Nineteenth Century Hermeneutics* (New Haven: Yale University Press, 1974), 1.

19. George A. Lindbeck, *The Nature of Doctrine: Religion and Theology in a Postliberal Age* (Philadelphia: Westminster, 1984), 117.

gap between "text and sermon" for the task of praising God and edifying the church.[20] As bishop of Regius Hippo in northern Africa, Augustine (d. 430) was confronted by numerous challenges that accompanied the legalization of Christianity by the Roman Empire.[21] He thus worked during a time when the stability of neither Christianity nor the empire was secure, while the last twenty years of his life, beginning with the sack of Rome under Alaric in 410, saw the crumbling of the Western empire under barbarian invasions. His experience of the church, although officially post-Constantinian and with some benefit of government favor, was more that of the diaspora, because his world was still intellectually and religiously pluralistic.

Not unlike our contemporary situation, Augustine's ministry was not conducted within an environment of comfortably established catholic orthodoxy. Fierce competition for the loyalties of his people came from heretical groups who had provoked a bitter and violent schism within the church, and also from the surrounding pagan culture which, in addition to a variety of religions, philosophies, and folk superstitions, offered numerous enticements in the form of sensual pleasure and frivolous entertainment at the racetrack, theater, fights, and public baths.[22]

Moving in a direction that runs counter to modern homiletic sensibilities, Augustine perceived that his primary pastoral task was theological in nature: to wean his people from idolatry, to purify their desires, and to establish an alternative culture responsive to God. "For Augustine the performance of scripture in Church is intended by God and empowered by the Holy Spirit to build communal and personal virtue and to accomplish personal salvation. It moves the reader and hearer from idolatrous alienation into the direct presence of the Triune God."[23]

20. For a good introduction to patristic practice, see Christopher A. Hall, *Reading Scripture with the Fathers* (Downers Grove, Ill.: InterVarsity, 1998).

21. Here I follow Frederick Van der Meer, *Augustine the Bishop* (London: Sheed and Ward, 1961); Carol Harrison, *Augustine: Christian Truth and Fractured Humanity* (Oxford: Oxford University Press, 2000); Peter Iver Kaufman, *Church, Book, and Bishop: Conflict and Authority in Early Latin Christianity* (Boulder, Colo.: Westview, 1996), 75–102; Peter Brown, *Augustine of Hippo: A Biography* (Berkeley: University of California Press, 1969).

22. See Van der Meer, *Augustine the Bishop*, 29–45.

23. Telford Work, *Living and Active: Scripture in the Economy of Salvation* (Grand Rapids: Eerdmans, 2002), 307.

Augustine, moreover, was no stranger to the human struggle with disordered longings and desires. He learned through a long process of transformation that human loves can only be satisfied when rightly ordered through participation in the life of the Triune God; it was only after radical conversion from a world centered on himself to a world centered in God that he began to overcome the distance between the world he claimed as his own and the world received from God by indwelling the narrative of Scripture. Augustine thus discovered the drama of Scripture's revelatory narratives: that we find in them, not confirmation of ourselves, but the very constitution of a new self; that we do not place the actions of God within the horizon of our stories; rather, we place our stories within the action of God.[24]

Augustine's Christian identity was constituted by a new narrative: the story of Christ told in Scripture and enacted by the common life of the church. This was the new world he entered through conversion, and which enabled him to make sense of the gap he perceived as dividing the world of the Bible and the world of history, science, and culture. Not of Augustine's making, this was a world constructed on the basis of the Word made flesh and constituted by a particular way of rendering reality, namely, Scripture.[25]

Soon after his election to the office of bishop, Augustine began to write the church's first handbook for preachers, *De Doctrina Christiana* ("Teaching Christianity" [*DDC*]), to equip pastors to discover and communicate the divine wisdom disclosed in Scripture so as to enable their congregations to embody the pattern of faith and obedience given in the Word of God.[26] In book 4, at the conclusion of the work, Augustine summarizes his purpose,

> I, for my part, give thanks to our God that in these four books I have set out to the best of my poor ability, not what sort of pastor I am myself, lacking many of the necessary qualities as I do, but what sort the pastor should be who is eager to toil away, not only for his

24. Christopher J. Thompson, *Christian Doctrine, Christian Identity: Augustine and the Narratives of Character* (Lanham, Md.: University Press of America, 1999), 90–92.

25. William H. Willimon, *Pastor: The Theology and Practice of Ordained Ministry* (Nashville: Abingdon, 2002), 199–200.

26. Augustine, *De Doctrina Christiana*, in *The Works of Augustine: A Translation for the Twenty-first Century,* trans. John E. Rotelle, ed. Edmund Hill (Hyde Park, N.Y.: New City, 1996), I/II.

own sake but for others, in the teaching of sound Christian doctrine. (*DDC* 4.31.64)

The prologue of the work provides a clue for understanding what Augustine means by "what sort the pastor should be." He states that there are certain rules for dealing with Scripture that must be passed on to those who are willing and qualified to learn, since to read and preach in the church is to be situated within a tradition, the story of a community of interpreters and speakers. Individual inspiration, intelligence, creativity, or charisma do not rule out the need for preachers to acquire the wisdom of faithful exemplars. As the biblical narrative demonstrates, Paul was taught by God but sent to Ananias to receive the sacraments; the centurion was addressed by an angel but later turned over to Peter; Moses learned from his father-in-law how to govern; Philip explained Isaiah's mysteries in words to an Ethiopian eunuch (*DDC*, prologue).

Augustine's instruction for reading and preaching Scripture provides a framework, a grammar of the rules of Christian faith and conduct shaped around the Creed and embodied in the story of salvation: the doctrine of the Trinity; the mission of Christ; the meaning of Jesus' resurrection; the church in pilgrimage; the love of God and neighbor to which all Christians are summoned. The church's worship of the Triune God is the ground and enactment of the gift of divine love for the world; it unites God and his people in the enjoyment of the Father through Christ in the fellowship of the church, his body.

One, therefore, must come to a personal knowledge of and attachment to the subject matter of Scripture, the Triune God, in order to make sense of its words. Thus the task of pastoral exegesis requires learning to inhabit Scripture in a manner that transforms the preacher, fitting him or her into the inner life of God. One only comes to know the wisdom of Scripture, which is of God, through a willingness to be taught and shaped by that reality. Moreover, the particular source and goal of this training is the divine wisdom incarnate in Christ who graciously accommodated himself, reaching out and coming into the world to lead humanity on its homeward journey to God.

That is why, since we are meant to enjoy that truth which is unchangeably alive, and since it is in its light that God the Trinity, author and maker of the universe, provides for all the things he has

made, our minds have to be purified to enable them to perceive
that light, and to cling to it once perceived. We should think of this
purification process as being a kind of walk, a kind of voyage to our
home country. We do not draw near after all, by movement in
place to the One who is present everywhere, but by honest commitment and good behavior. (*DDC* 1.10.10)

Pastoral formation occurs by means of contemplation, knowing
and loving God with both the intellect and will. This knowledge,
however, cannot be acquired by approaching Scripture as strangers
or occasional visitors, but rather by immersing ourselves in its "storied" way of life. This sense of theology, *theologia,* is best defined as
a habit, *habitus,* a disposition which has the character of personal
knowledge of God and the things of God, a practical habit which
has the character of wisdom, *sapientia,* in relation to the mystery of
God.[27]

Augustine's discussion of Scripture is therefore conducted
within a theological "rule" or "grammar": Only the Triune God
and the revealed mysteries of faith are to be worshiped and en-
joyed for their own sake and not as commodities; everything else,
including the Bible, must be used wisely to acquire the gifts of
faith, hope, and love, thereby promoting a truly Christian way of
life in relation to God and others.

> Scripture, though, commands nothing but charity or love, and cen-
> sures nothing but cupidity, or greed, and that is why it gives shape
> to human morals. . . . The only thing, though, it ever asserts is
> catholic faith, with reference to things past and in the future and
> in the present. It tells the story of things past, foretells things fu-
> ture, points out things present; but all these things are of value for
> nourishing and fortifying charity or love, and overcoming and ex-
> tinguishing cupidity or greed. (*DDC* 3.10.5)

Augustine does not assume that the teaching of Scripture is self-
evident. Christian doctrine, a grasp of the whole economy of creation and redemption, frames the context within which Scripture
should be read and preached. "So when, on closer inspection, you
see that it is still uncertain how something is to be punctuated or
pronounced, you should refer it to the rule of faith, which you
have received from the plainer passages and the authority of the

---

27. Edward Farley, *Theologia: The Fragmentation and Unity of Theological Education* (Philadelphia: Westminster, 1983), 34–35.

church" (*DDC* 2.2.2). Moreover, this kind of reading and preaching requires the formation of certain moral dispositions within us, including reverence, humility, and love before God, especially when Scripture rebukes us for our vices, lest we think we know better than its author. Because of our complicity in sin and our captivity to destructive patterns of living, we must submit ourselves to a continual process of conversion. Christian knowledge and speech that is of God, therefore, occurs only as we are personally situated within the reforming and reorienting drama of salvation.

> Furthermore, we are still on our way, a way however not from place to place, but one traveled by the affections. And it was being blocked, as by a barricade of thorn bushes, by the malice of our past sins. So what greater generosity and compassion could he show, after deliberately making himself the pavement under our feet along which we could return home, than to forgive us all our sins once we had turned back to him, and by being crucified for us to root out the ban blocking our return that had been so firmly fixed in place? (*DDC* 1.17.16)

According to Augustine, this is not optional for preachers, since directing God's people in the performance of Scripture requires a form of wisdom that transcends technique or information; it requires a sense of both knowing what and how to speak in rendering faithful and fitting improvisations of the biblical story for particular times, places, and situations. In the end, says Augustine, the preacher must be a person of learning, devotion, and prayer, assimilated to Christ so as to become an "eloquent sermon" (*DDC* 4.27.59). As he advises,

> They should familiarize themselves with the kinds of expression in the Holy Scriptures and be on alert to observe how things are commonly said in them, and to commit them to memory. But much more important than that, and supremely necessary is that they should pray for understanding. After all, in this very literature, which they are eager to study, they read that the Lord gives wisdom and from his face comes knowledge and understanding. (*DDC* 3.37.56)

Performing Scripture

In his preaching, Augustine attributed special status to Christian revelation, including Scripture and its oral expression, *verbum*

Dei and *sermo Dei,* for mediating God's truth to the understanding, the heart, and the will.[28] He thus preached to instruct, to delight, and to change lives, trusting the language of Scripture and the work of the Holy Spirit to empower his speech and engage his listeners. When he preached, "its drama was salvation, its script was the Scriptures, and its actors included everyone."[29]

Peter Brown has written of the manner in which bishops like Augustine presented Christianity to the ancient world, offering a universal way of salvation that was gathering all nations and all classes into its bosom, *populari sinu.* The Bible itself, with its layers of meaning, was a microcosm, a textual world, of the social and intellectual diversity to be found in Christian churches, so that the humblest of the earth should be drawn, moved, and at home in them. As Augustine acknowledged in the *Confessions,*

> I now began to believe that you would never have conferred such preeminent authority on the scripture, now diffused through all lands, unless you had willed that it would be a means of coming to faith in you, and a means of seeking to know you. . . . The authority of the Bible seemed the more venerated and more worthy of a holy faith on the ground that it was open to everyone to read. . . . The Bible offered itself to all in very accessible words and the most humble style of diction. . . . It welcomes all people to its generous embrace, and also brings a few to you through narrow openings. Though the latter are few, they are much more numerous than would be the case if the Bible did not stand out by its high authority and if it had not drawn crowds to the bosom of its holy humility. (*Confessions* 6.6.8)[30]

The language and style of Scripture, and its embodiment by preachers, formed the basis of a Christian populism, *sermo humilis,* humble speech endowed with divine authority to address both the "high and low" of the empire. The diversity of Christian congregations, the simplicity of Christian Scriptures, the lack of culture

28. See the discussion of Augustine's preaching in Carol Harrison, "The Rhetoric of Scripture and Preaching: Classical Decadence or Christian Aesthetic?" in *Augustine and His Critics: Essays in Honour of Gerald Bonner,* ed. Robert Dodaro and George Lawless (New York: Routledge, 2000), 214–30.

29. William Harmless, *Augustine and the Catechumenate* (Collegeville, Minn.: Liturgical, 1995), 235; see also Van der Meer, *Augustine the Bishop,* 405–12.

30. See the discussion in Peter Brown, *Power and Persuasion in Late Antiquity* (Madison: University of Wisconsin Press, 1988), 74–75.

of many Christian heroes, the Christian care of the poor—all lent a sense of concreteness to the grand outlines within the Christian imagination that articulated a vision of a church empowered by God's providence, a narrative capable of absorbing all levels of Roman society.

Brown argues that Christian gestures of compassion to the poor emphasized a basic level of human solidarity, just as God, in the person of Christ, freely identified himself with human flesh, becoming a fellow son of the earth, a kinsman of the human race.[31] The appeal of Christianity still lay in its radical sense of community; it absorbed people because the individual could drop from a wide impersonal world into a miniature community, whose demands and relations were explicit.[32] As Averil Cameron observes, "Out of the framework of Judaism, and living as they did in the Roman Empire and in the context of Greek philosophy, pagan practice, and contemporary social ideas, Christians built themselves a new world."[33]

Conclusion: On Continuing the Story

Robert Jenson has proposed that our task in a postmodern world is similar to the mission that was undertaken by Augustine's church within the fragmented, dying world of late antiquity: "The obvious answer is that if the church does not find her hearers antecedently inhabiting a narratable world, then the church must herself be that world."[34] Our theological and pastoral task is to continue a narrative that possesses dramatic coherence; a story of humankind called from nowhere, *ex nihilo*, toward its proper place, a promised *polis*, the new Jerusalem.[35]

Augustine's grand narration of the Christian story, the *City of God*, depicted the church's identity as a pilgrim people ruled by

31. See ibid., 76, 153; Peter Brown, *Authority and the Sacred: Aspects of the Christianization of the Roman World* (Cambridge: Cambridge University Press, 1995), 10–11.

32. Peter Brown, *The World of Late Antiquity* (London: Thames and Hudson, 1971), 76.

33. Averil Cameron, *Christianity and the Rhetoric of Empire* (Berkeley: University of California Press, 1991), 21.

34. Jenson, "How the World Lost Its Story," 142–43.

35. Nicholas Lash, *The Beginning and the End of Religion* (Cambridge: Cambridge University Press, 1996), 233–34.

Christ and devoted to the Triune God, resident aliens on a journey, a "theo-drama" through time toward its destiny in the heavenly city.[36] By way of contrast, Augustine depicted the earthly city as a community constituted by self-love to the point of contempt for God; it glories in itself, its wisdom, and its strength. By his "reading" of the world through the lens of the biblical story, Augustine came to understand history as an open-ended narrative involving two cities and their opposing ways of life based on a love for God or a love for domination. The church in history, however, remains a thoroughly mixed body, ever engaging in a dramatic struggle with questions regarding who we are and whose we are until attaining the eschatological peace of the heavenly city.[37] As Augustine advised, "The Church proceeds on its pilgrim way in this world, in these evil days. Its troubled course began . . . with Abel himself . . . and the pilgrimage goes on right up to the end of history" (*City of God* 18.52). Thus, in a world of competing and violent interests, the most faithful service the church can render is to embody the weakness and humility of its crucified Lord, thereby disclosing a fundamental truth about human beings and society: Without true worship and love for God there can be no human fulfillment, happiness, or genuine communal life; that we are made in the image of God, and are restless until we find our rest in God.[38]

> Justice is found where God . . . rules an obedient city to his grace . . . so that just as the individual righteous man lives on the basis of faith which is active in love, so the association, or people, of righteous men lives on the same basis of faith, active in love, the love with which a man loves God as God ought to be loved, and loves his neighbor as himself. But where this justice does not exist, there is certainly no "association of men united by a common sense of right and by a community of interest." (*City of God* 9.890)

36. Augustine, *City of God*, ed. David Knowles, trans. Henry Bettenson (New York: Pelican, 1972).

37. See the discussion of Augustine's ecclesiology in Nicholas M. Healy, *Church, World, and the Christian Life: Practical-Prophetic Life* (Cambridge: Cambridge University Press, 2000), 54–56.

38. Robert Wilken, *Remembering the Christian Past* (Grand Rapids: Eerdmans, 1995), 60–61; idem, "Augustine's City of God Today," in *The Two Cities of God: The Church's Responsibility for the Earthly City*, ed. Carl E. Braaten and Robert W. Jenson (Grand Rapids: Eerdmans, 1997), 28–31.

In a postmodern world, the formation of ecclesial identity as God's pilgrim people requires that our liturgical gatherings be characterized by attentive, reverent reception and enactment of the biblical script, a communal sacrifice of praise to the Triune God whose love creates, redeems, and perfects all that is. As Jenson notes,

> The church must her self be a communal world in which promises are made and kept. . . . It is the whole vision of an *eschaton* that is now missing outside the church. The assembly of believers must therefore itself be the event in which we may behold what is to come. . . . If, in the post-modern world, a congregation or whatever wants to be "relevant" its assemblies must be unabashedly events of shared apocalyptic vision. "Going to church" must be a journey to the place where we will behold our destiny, where we will see what is to become of us.[39]

We are the stories we inhabit, tell, perform, and celebrate. The purpose of our narrative reading and preaching is the formation of Christian identity and mission, of a people who indwell a real, substantial, living world in accordance with the scope and sense of Scripture's commands and promises, its will and wisdom. God is making a world of peace; for love of God and love of others the sense of which past, present, and future is congruous with the story of the universe told by Scripture.

39. Jenson, "How the World Lost Its Story," 147.

Index

Abraham tradition, 51
Acts 2, 56–57
Acts of the Apostles, 38, 51
    economic sharing and, 60–65
    summaries in, 57–58
Against Heresies (Irenaeus), 182
Alaric, 185
Apocalypse of John. *See* Revelation,
    Book of
Augustine of Hippo, 37
    conversion of, 186
    exegetical guidelines, 188–89
    ministry of, 185
    on pastoral formation, 186–88
    view of history, 192

Babylon, 119, 138
Barr, David, 120, 165
beast, the (Book of Revelation),
    119, 154
Bede the Venerable, 40
biblical spirituality, 26
biblical text
    church's use of, 178–80
    communal identity and,
        180–82
    history and, 19–20,
        21–22
    interpretations of, 33–36
    "location" of, 19
    open-endedness of, 32–33
    as Scripture, 22–28
biography, as genre, 43

Blowers, Paul, 183
Boring, M. Eugene, 120, 148
"breaking bread," 62
Brown, Peter, 190, 191
Brueggemann, Walter, 163
Bultmann, Rudolf, 83–84
Bush, George W., 111, 113
Buttrick, David, 81, 107

Caesar Augustus, 133–34
Callahan, Allen Dwight, 123, 131
Calvin, John, 40
Cameron, Averil, 191
Celsus, 39–40
Central Presbyterian Church (At-
    lanta), 168
Certeau, Michel de, 118, 129
City of God (Augustine), 191–92
Clement of Alexandria, 39
Clinton, Bill, 172
Clinton, George, 123
Collins, Adela Yarbro, 128
Columbine High School, 172
Confessions (Augustine), 190
Corinthians, as community, 87–88

Daniel 7, 138
"day of the Lord," 90
De Doctrina Christiana (Augustine),
    186–89
dianoia, 85
Diatessaron (Tatian), 40
"discourse," meaning of, 28–29

dislocation, as resistance practice, 135–36
Domitian, 126

ecclesiology, emergence of, 69
Ephesus, 126
epistles, New Testament. *See* letters, New Testament
Essenes, 60
Exodus, Book of, 49–50

Fitzmyer, Joseph, 40–41
France, R. T., 49
Frei, Hans, 184
friendship, Greco-Roman world and, 60
Friesen, Steven J., 136, 137

Gadamer, Hans-Georg, 17
genre criticism, 42–43
Georgia State Capitol, 155
global capitalism, 160
Gnostic exegesis, 182
God
    as focus of Scripture, 31–32
    grand narrative of, 55, 86–87, 100, 183
Goldingay, John, 13
"Gospel harmony," 39–40
Gospels
    beginnings in, 50–51
    Israel and, 52
Greco-Roman biography, 43
Green, Garrett, 14, 35
Greider, William, 159–60
Guelich, Robert, 48–49

Hauerwas, Stanley, 158
Hays, Richard, 165–66
Hebrews, Book of, 82
Hegel, G. W. F., 14
"hidden transcript" (Scott), 135
Hirsch, E. D., 84
historical-critical method, 82, 83, 108

historiography
    ancient forms of, 45–46
    as genre, 43
Holy Spirit, 56
Homiletic (Buttrick), 81
homiletical theory, 18–22, 81–82
hospitality, as biblical quality, 26
"hyperbolic imagination" (Webb), 161, 163

"idiolect" (Book of Revelation), 131
interpretation
    Scripture and, 16–17
Irenaeus of Lyons, 24, 39, 182–84
Isaiah 40–66, 49, 101
Israel
    Book of Exodus and, 49–50
    narrative story of, 86–87, 101
    Paul's experience and, 89

Jenson, Robert, 178–79, 182, 191, 193
Jerusalem, 136, 138, 147, 164
Jesus Christ
    biblical interpretation and, 34
    in Book of Revelation, 119–21, 165–67
    crucifixion story, 54–55
    death of, 148
    New Exodus and, 52
    table fellowship and, 62
    as Word of God, 152
John, Gospel of, 51
John the Baptist, 58
John the Seer, 156
Judaism, practices of, 63–64

King, Martin Luther, Jr., 172–73
koinonia, 59, 61

Lamb, the (Book of Revelation), 138–39, 147–50, 161
letters, New Testament
    characteristics of genre, 84–85
    logical sequence in, 87

narratives in, 85–87
preaching on, 82–84
as Scripture, 83
Lindbeck, George, 180–81
Linton, Gregory, 127
Lion of Judah (Rev. 5:5), 146, 148
Lowry, Eugene, 17
Luke–Acts narrative, 51
Luke, Gospel of, 38, 40–41

"maps" and "itineraries" (Certeau),
    129
Mark, Gospel of, 37–38, 48–49
Matthew, Gospel of, 50–51
meal-sharing, Gospels and, 63
Murdoch, Iris, 158
myth, 132
mythos, 85

narrative
    aims of, 31–32
    biblical text and, 28–36
    church and, 38–41
    compared with letters, 84–85
    as discourse, 29
    forms of, 29–30
    structure of, 44
"narrative logic," 166–67
narrative of resistance, 118
narrative preaching
    Augustine and, 184–90
    Book of Revelation and,165–68
    motivations for, 70
    New Testament and, 53–56
    strategies for, 17–18
"narrative world," 86
natural religion, 14–15
Nero, 126
New Exodus, 50
new Jerusalem, 164
New Testament
    modes of discourse, 10
    relationship to Old Testament,
        24
Niebuhr, H. R., 68

O'Connor, Flannery, 159
Old Testament, witness of, 52
One World, Ready or Not (Greider),
    159
oral cultures, 123–24

Passover, festival of, 49, 147
Patmos, island of, 119, 125, 129,
    151
Paul
    conversion of, 93
    Corinthians and, 87–88
    defense of ministry, 95–96
    identification with Jesus, 93–94,
        99
    narrative technique, 85–87
    new-covenant expectation and,
        92–93
    perceptions of, 82
    personal details, 86, 109
    suffering servant and, 97
    "third parties" and, 88
    See also individual letters
Pauline eschatology, 84
Pentecost, 56, 71
Pergamon, 125
"pericope," meaning of, 42
Peterson, Eugene, 122
polysemy, of biblical text, 27
Popeye cartoons, 172
positive religion, 14–15
Powell, Mark Allan, 119

Qumran, 60

reconciliation, in Pauline writings,
    102–3
redaction criticism, 40–41
redemptive violence, myth of,
    138–39, 155, 171
regula fidei. See "rule of faith"
Revelation 21, 162–64
Revelation 4–5
    imagery in, 143–45
    narrative in, 142–43

Revelation 4–5 (*continued*)
    throne scene, 143–45
    worship in, 140–41
Revelation, Book of, 82
    christological images, 147
    combat myth in, 132–33, 138
    conceptions of time in, 136–38
    genre of, 127–28, 164
    images of worship in, 139–40
    metaphorical visions, 158–61
    narrative characteristics, 119–22
    new creation in, 161–64
    Old Testament and, 121, 139
    as oral performance, 122–25
    practices of resistance and, 124,
        126–27, 130–31, 135–38,
        139–40, 151–53
    preaching from, 153–54
    principalities and powers in,
        154–57
    reactions to, 117–18
    Roman world and, 118
    social location of, 125–27
    "solecisms" in, 130
    structure of, 128–29
    use of dialect, 130
    use of Greek, 130
Roman Empire, 125–26
Roman imperial cult and myth,
    132–34
Rome, 134, 136, 138
Root of David (Rev. 5:5), 146–47,
    148
"rule of faith," 25, 35, 39, 183–84
"rules of truth" (Irenaeus), 25, 35,
    39

Satan, 154
Schüssler Fiorenza, Elisabeth, 123,
    131

Scott, James C., 118, 130, 134
Second Corinthians
    epistemological change in, 100
    fool's speech in, 90
    Old Testament echoes in, 89,
        92–93
    Pauline autobiography and, 89
    propositio of, 90
    as rhetorical unit, 91
    use of "commend," 96
Seducer, the (Book of Revelation),
    154
servant figure of Isaiah, 103–4
"Servant Songs" (Isaiah), 147
Smyrna, 126
Song of Moses (Exodus 15), 50
Sternberg, Robert J., 12, 13
"story," meaning of, 28–29

table fellowship, 59. *See also* Jesus
    Christ, table fellowship and
Tatian, 40
Tertullian, 39
text-based cultures, 123
Thompson, Leonard L., 139
throne of God, 136
throne scenes, Old Testament, 144
Titus, 88
Torah, 49
"tournament of narratives," 182

Virgil, 133

Webb, Stephen, 161–62
Wink, Walter, 171
"World of Coca-Cola" (Atlanta),
    156, 170